CURRENT TECHNOLOGIES IN THE LIBRARY

AN INFORMAL OVERVIEW

CURRENT TECHNOLOGIES IN THE LIBRARY

AN INFORMAL OVERVIEW

WALT CRAWFORD

G. K. HALL & CO.
BOSTON

CURRENT TECHNOLOGIES IN THE LIBRARY:
AN INFORMAL OVERVIEW

WALT CRAWFORD

Library of Congress Cataloging-in-Publication Data

Crawford, Walt.
    Current technologies in the library.

    (Professional librarian series)
    Includes index.
    1. Libraries--Automation. 2. Information
technology. 3. Library science--Technological innovations.
I. Title. II. Series.
Z678.9.c7 1988   025.3'0285   88-21226
ISBN 0-8161-1886-8
ISBN 0-8161-1888-4 (pbk.)

Contents

List of Tables

List of Acronyms

ACM   Association for Computing Machinery

ALA   American Library Association

CLR   Council on Library Resources

ERIC   Educational Resources Information Center

ILL   Interlibrary loan

LITA   Library and Information Technology Association

MARC   Machine-readable cataloging

OCLC   Online Computer Library Center

RLG   Research Libraries Group

RLIN   Research Libraries Information Network

WLN   Western Library Network

Acknowledgments

My debt to the many authors cited at the ends of chapters is obvious and extends to hundreds of authors *not* cited. To the extent that I understand the technologies discussed here, that understanding comes from years of reading as well as, in some cases, practical experience. In the areas of publishing media and computer-related technologies, much of that reading has been for pleasure and general interest. I thank the writers who kept me interested far beyond the limits of directly applicable information.

My wife, Linda Driver, encouraged me in this project and commented on portions of the manuscript. Carol Chin, editor of the Professional Librarian Series at G.K. Hall, provided thoughtful guidance and specific editorial suggestions throughout the project; others at G.K. Hall also contributed their time and expertise. Lennie Stovel, Kathleen Bales, and C. James Schmidt, all of the Research Libraries Group, and Martha Schmidt of the San Jose Public Library reviewed the manuscript and provided useful comments.

I relied heavily on the Engineering Library of the Stanford University Libraries and the Green Library at Stanford; the Mathematics/Computer Science Library and Education Library at Stanford also proved to be valuable resources. In addition, Palo Alto City Library served as an important source of materials.

Finally, the usual disclaimer. Opinions in this manuscript are mine. While I have endeavored to substantiate the factual information, I have deliberately avoided footnotes and must be held responsible for any errors. Given the techniques used to produce this book, typographical errors are almost certainly my own responsibility. Corrections are always appreciated.

Introduction

Every library depends on technology, and every librarian is a technologist. Books are unnatural objects--that is to say, nature does not produce books. Books represent triumphs of technology--using applied science and engineering to spread dreams, ideas and observations beyond a person's immediate circle and to retain those dreams, ideas, and observations for the enrichment of later generations.

A library uses many aspects of technology, some of them more obvious than others. Libraries frequently adopt new information technologies before most other segments of society, and they sometimes retain vanishing technologies longer than might be expected. As repositories of recorded knowledge, libraries contribute to the emergence of new technology to a greater extent than we sometimes recognize.

We all work with a changing mix of technologies; new technologies emerge, old technologies change and vanish. We become sensitive to aspects of technology as they cause us difficulty or as we specialize in their application. Each of us specializes in one or more aspects of technology, and few if any of us are comfortable with all aspects of technology relating to libraries and librarianship.

We all need to broaden our personal and professional horizons. One way to sample unfamiliar aspects of current technology is to read an article or attend a program. Unfortunately for librarians wishing to sample new areas, most articles and programs assume some basic understanding of the subject. Without that assumption, every article and program would be nothing more than a basic introduction, leaving no room to advance the topic.

That's true in every area of librarianship, not just in obviously technological areas. You can't hold a coherent program on special problems in retrospective conversion of serial records if you need to explain to the audience the concept of seriality and all the concepts that underlie retrospective conversion. Every writer and speaker makes some assumptions about the background of the readers or audience.

This book provides some background for many areas of current technology. It won't make you an expert in any area, but will introduce you to some of the terminology, some of the basic concepts, and some specific ways in which the technology may affect libraries now or in the near future. It will also offer suggestions for further reading, should you wish to delve more deeply into a particular field.

You should be able to read this book from beginning to end, gaining some basic insight into several aspects of current technology. You should also be able to refer directly to a particular chapter to renew your understanding of one particular subject.

SCOPE AND TREATMENT

This book is concerned with tools, techniques, and media rather than systems, solutions, and messages. This is a sampler, not an encyclopedia; it does not attempt to cover every possible aspect of technology. The contents page shows the range of topics included; the choice of subjects is not wholly arbitrary but follows some deliberate guidelines.

The following categories may help explain the basis for this book:

1. *Invisible and underlying technology.* We depend on technologies that support all contemporary life, such as electronics, the electrical transmission system, heating and cooling systems, materials testing, and fabrication techniques. These technologies affect libraries no more and no less than any other institution. They are not covered in this book.

2. *Media and carriers.* Each method of storing and transmitting information represents complex technology. Carriers and media are of special interest to libraries, either to store and circulate information for direct use by patrons or to store and

transmit information on behalf of the library. Most of this book deals with media and carriers.

3. *Tools and techniques.* The remainder of the book examines some tools and techniques of special interest to libraries. Many areas, such as programming languages, are omitted, as are most techniques that are *exclusively* part of librarianship, with no other applications.

4. *Systems.* This book does *not* deal with library automation systems as such. Online catalogs, circulation systems, serial check-in systems, and other library automation systems are beyond the scope of this book.

Current Technology

Current technology may be recent or may be old, but for our purposes must have some established use and some vitality. Books represent current technology, as do compact discs. It is a contemporary fashion, particularly among some computerists, to think of all established technology as passé and essentially obsolete. In this view, any area of technology is either emerging or receding. From that perspective, this book is mostly about boring old stuff, "obsolescent" and "obsolete" technology. Some observers seriously say, and apparently believe, that anything you can buy is already obsolete. That is a curious meaning for the word "obsolete" and one that should not concern libraries.

Emerging technologies generally complement active and mature technologies rather than replace the older technologies; rarely does an old technology vanish overnight. New technology sometimes replaces old technology, but the process is almost always a gradual one. Peculiarities of the marketplace and of journalism may make it seem that an existing technology has vanished overnight, but this is rarely the case.

I consider almost every aspect of technology in this book to be current as of 1988--either emerging with the likelihood of success, active, or mature. Most topics covered here should still be current in another decade, though some will have passed into obscurity and a few may prove largely evanescent. New technology may appear at a rate that seems phenomenal (although much of this is marketing rather than reality), but active technology does not die easily.

Treatment

This book includes twenty-one chapters dealing with aspects of current technology and is divided into two parts:

1. Publishing media: the items that libraries do or could circulate. This part includes firmly established media, some that have never become as firmly established, some new possibilities, and a chapter on preserving media.

2. Computers and communications: the devices that form the basis of all automation, library and otherwise, and some aspects of telecommunications-related technologies.

Each chapter is an informal discussion of one or more current technologies. The discussion may include a brief history, an informal explanation of the technology, notes on the current impact of the technology on libraries, or key points and cautions for considering the technology. Most chapters end with a few sources for further reading. In most cases, sources include articles in the library press and books (mostly outside of the library press).

A glossary at the back of the book includes all terms introduced in each chapter and a variety of other terms commonly used within the current technologies covered. While the glossary can't substitute for contemporary technical dictionaries in each of the fields covered, it does provide a single compact source for the range of technologies included in this book.

This book is intended to be readable and informative, not scholarly. Most facts are stated without specific citation to a source, and sources used are included in the reading lists. Opinions are my own, based either on experience or on reading and analysis, and my intention is neither to be controversial nor to avoid controversy.

PARTICIPANTS IN THE GROWTH OF INFORMATION TECHNOLOGY

As you read the historical notes in many of these chapters, certain companies turn up time after time. Inventions may still come from the lone genius, but the developmental work required to turn an invention into a practical technology normally requires corporate backing. And some companies innovate more often and more successfully than others.

Within the information technologies, several companies have historically favored innovation, devoting significant resources to research that may have no immediate payoff. American Telephone and Telegraph may be the oldest example of such a company; Bell Labs has always been a source of innovation, both at the fundamental level and at the developmental level. Much of the history of sound is attributable to the work of Bell Labs; its scientists invented the transistor, and the list goes on. More recently IBM has combined its considerable talent for marketing with an ongoing commitment to research and development. IBM developed most of the basic disk storage technologies and probably knows more about keyboard design than any other company--whether it applies its knowledge or not.

Innovation is not unique to the United States. Despite the claims of some protectionists, Japan's successes in the field of technology have not strictly been the result of stealing or even licensing technology from the United States. The first patent for AC bias in magnetic recording, one key to good fidelity, was apparently issued to a Japanese scientist. Sony (to name the most obvious example) has consistently *developed* new ideas, not simply copied the work of others. In consumer electronics, another consistent source of innovation is Philips of the Netherlands. Other companies in other countries also add to the pace of technological innovation. While American companies and scientists have certainly accounted for many key developments, innovation does not reside in any single company or country.

The Ingenuity of Small Developments

Most of the technologies discussed in this book are Big Deals: technological developments that have made a major impact. In preparing the book, I began to be aware of the hundreds of Little Deals that make everything else work more smoothly. If you were able to step back into the office or library of a decade ago, two decades ago, or six decades ago, you could predict some of the things that now make work easier and more effective, but would probably overlook others.

Consider the Post-It note, a recent example of the ingenuity of 3M and of the impact of a seemingly peculiar idea (an adhesive that doesn't adhere very well). 3M had some initial difficulty marketing these little wonders, but once people tried them there was no turning back. A longer-term history of improvements, some subtle and some dramatic, has resulted in the huge variety of ball-point pens available today. From the original ball-point, introduced a mere four decades ago, we have seen continuing improvements in inks, plastic, material for the ball and the reservoir, and all other aspects of pens.

We accept small improvements as part of everyday life, which is probably the right attitude. It is unfortunate but true that we are usually more aware of technological failings than successes; in bemoaning the lack of perfection, however, we should not ignore the remarkable improvements technology has made in our work and home lives.

TERMINOLOGY

One key purpose of this book is to provide a quick reference to the basic terminology or jargon of each technology discussed. Unfortunately, anyone familiar with a field adopts some or all of its terminology as his or her own, and becomes unaware that the words represent specific terminology. Librarians are notorious for this habit (e.g., do you recognize *heading, imprint* and *see reference* as library jargon?). Fortunately I come to most of the technologies in this book as a relative outsider, and may be able to recognize the jargon involved. If not, and if terms that you consider specialized do not appear in the glossary, my apologies, and my invitation to report those terms to me.

Part 1

Publishing Media

The largest part of this book concerns those technologies most fundamentally important for libraries: publishing media, the forms in which information, entertainment, and ideas are packaged and made available for use and circulation.

A small library can still survive quite nicely in 1988 with no computers or computer peripherals and with no communications technologies more advanced than the telephone. Except for very specialized libraries, no library can serve its patrons without publishing media. Books and other media represent the heart of almost every library.

Publishing media no longer represent the only ways that libraries can make information available to patrons. Some theoreticians posit a day in which published media will be less significant to libraries than electronic access to information. If that day ever does arrive, it will not be in the immediate future. For now and for the next several years, publishing will be far more important for libraries than electronic access.

A view of libraries as nothing more than purveyors of information is too limiting and certainly does not reflect actual uses for public libraries. A library offers access to dreams, ideas, and entertainment in the form of fiction, philosophy, music, and many creations beyond simple facts and information. Those dreams, ideas, and entertainment are available through published media.

The 10 chapters that follow deal with several of the more prominent publishing media and with issues of preserving published items. Beginning with print, the earliest current technology and still the most important technology for libraries, the section goes on to deal with alternative forms for storing print; sound recordings in

9

older and newer forms; visual recordings; the most recent publishing media using optical technology to store text, graphics, and data; and software as a library medium. The last chapter in the section considers some preservation issues.

LIBRARY CONSERVATISM IN MEDIA USE

Some observers regard libraries as overly conservative in adopting new media. The term *printist* has been used as a derogatory description of librarians who prefer to spend money on books and serials rather than on nonprint media. Those who wish to promote new publishing media and other new technologies will decry the reluctance of librarians to jump on their particular bandwagon.

To some extent, charges of excessive conservatism may be justified. To a great extent, however, it's a bum rap. Enthusiasts for new media frequently, and not surprisingly, denigrate print in order to build up the alternatives. Most new media have special areas in which they offer special value, and librarians do well to seek out those special areas. But new media do not automatically deserve *greater* consideration than older media; a library that substantially decreases its book budget in order to acquire large quantities of videocassettes or CD-ROM services may be damaging itself and its users.

Librarians who view new media with some caution may also be aware of history. As later chapters in this section illustrate, not every new medium achieves success. Publishing specifically aimed at libraries has not always yielded lasting innovations, to which libraries with collections of microprint materials can testify. Commercial media do not always succeed either. The history of different video playback systems is full of failures and minimal successes. Will newer media succeed with more predictability and uniformity than those that have failed in the last few decades?

Libraries have good reason to be conservative in adopting new publishing media. The older media continue to be most important in providing information and entertainment in inexpensive and easy-to-use form. Public libraries can also legitimately take the view that they should not be far ahead of their users in adopting new media, particularly since almost every new publishing media requires special equipment for use. When a library reduces its purchase of books to increase purchase of a medium that can only be used by one out of a hundred readers, is the library fulfilling its duty?

These chapters describe some of the important technologies underlying publishing media, some of the problems in dealing with media, and some of the background of various media. Libraries should recognize the special virtues of different forms of publication, while continuing to recognize the primary role of print. This part should provide some information on how various media work and their special roles in libraries.

1

The Printed Page

The most important current technology for libraries is the printed page. Ink, paper, and (sometimes) binding: these three elements come together as books and serials. Books have been the most important factor in libraries since the development of printing, and will continue in that role for the indefinite future.

A THUMBNAIL HISTORY

Every library professional should be familiar with the history of the printed page and how books are made. While bound books go back to at least the fourth century A.D., printed books from movable alphabetic type date back only a little more than five centuries, to around 1456. Publishing spread rapidly: by 1500, some 30,000 different titles had been published in Europe.

For the first three centuries, printing was almost entirely manual labor. Even so, some books were published in large editions. For example, 10,000 copies of a pirated book were printed in 1585 and up to 30,000 copies of almanacs were printed in the 1660s. Periodicals (as opposed to serially published books) first appeared in the 1650s, with magazines appearing in the eighteenth century.

Machine presses, emerging in the nineteenth century, made much larger editions and cheap mass-produced reprints feasible, further spreading the printed page in its many forms. Paperbacks predate the twentieth century, but the establishment of Penguin Books in 1935 may be considered the beginning of quality mass-market paperback publishing. In a very real sense, mass market paperbacks and large-circulation periodicals represent a twentieth century revolution, making knowledge and literature universally available in reasonably durable form for a modest price.

Varieties of Printing

Most books have four things in common: some form of press, that may or may not involve mechanical pressure, is used to transfer some form of ink, that may or may not be liquid, onto some form of paper or other flat, thin surface, following some intentional pattern that can be replicated many times.

Beyond that basic description, technologies used in printing have varied quite extensively throughout the history of the book, and show greater variation today than ever before. New printing techniques, new inks, and new methods of creating printing masters supplement older methods but almost never completely replace them. The range of printing technologies is too broad to mention fully here, but a few high points should be noted.

Cold Type and Letterpress

Perhaps the most enchanting form of printing is the earliest form involving movable type. Hand-cut steel forms are used to make copper or brass matrices or "mats" (solid metal bars containing negative impressions of characters). Individual type is cast from mats using molten lead combined with antimony and tin. The type is stored in printers' cases--capital letters in the upper case, small letters in the lower case (hence the usual terms for capital and small letters).

Text is composed by selecting individual letters and spaces, one at a time, and placing them in a "stick." The compositor transfers lines of composed type to a galley, a long steel tray. When the tray is full, galley proofs (to check for accuracy) can be taken by spreading ink over the type and pressing a long sheet of paper over it.

From galleys, the type goes to page forms mounted on the bed of a press. Printing consists of inking the type, setting paper on top, closing the press and applying pressure, then opening the press and removing the paper. (This is a simplified version.)

That simple process can be modified by adding power to the press itself, providing automatic paper feeding and removal, and speeding up the process in other ways. But the fundamental process continues to produce some of the highest-quality printing available-- metal letters inked and pressed directly against paper. The present tense is used in this description because handset type and letterpress printing continues to play a role in publishing, if usually for very small runs of books produced by small, special presses.

Intaglio and Lithography

Letterpress printing or relief printing involves the application of ink to a raised surface, which is then applied to paper, pressing the ink onto and into the paper. Relief presses can work with relatively low pressure.

Intaglio printing, which began in the sixteenth century, works in an opposite manner. The material to be printed--text or illus- trations--is engraved into a printing plate. Ink is forced into the en- graving, the surface is wiped clean, and a rolling press forces paper into the engraved lines to take the ink. This technology requires higher pressure and stiffer ink.

The third technology for transferring ink to paper was dis- covered in 1796 and became workable in 1798, when Aloys Sene- felder of Bavaria developed lithography. This technique treats a flat surface--originally a stone--in such a way that some areas will reject ink and others will attract it. The inked stone and paper are pressed together, using even higher pressure than intaglio, transferring ink to the paper. Offset lithography, a form of lithography using metal plates and rubber intermediate cylinders, began in 1904 and spread widely.

Beyond Cold Type: Other Typesetting Technologies

By the end of the eighteenth century, printers had begun to ex- periment with stereotyping, the process of pressing a sheet of ab- sorbent material over a made-up form of type, letting the material harden, then casting single metal forms from the hardened material. Apart from the wonderful word "flong" (alternate layers of blotting paper and tissue, the earliest stereotyping material), stereotypes allow printers to preserve the original type from the wear of printing and to print much larger editions by casting multiple forms. A later technique uses a wax "negative," graphite, and electroplating to create printing forms.

Stereotypes permitted almost infinitely long press runs, but did not speed up the actual typesetting. To aid in this process, Ottmar Mergenthaler developed the Linotype in 1886 and Tolbert Lanson developed the Monotype in 1893. Both systems used keyboards and permitted faster typesetting and a broader range of typefaces, by casting type from molten metal as it was needed and melting it down after it was used. The age of hot type had begun. Mechanical typesetting largely supplanted (but never entirely replaced) handset type during the first half of the twentieth century.

In the 1920s the first composition systems eliminating metal type altogether appeared. Photocomposition systems, preparing photographic images of letters, did not come into widespread use until the 1940s. Photocomposition may work by projecting images of letters onto a photosensitive surface or by building an image on that surface from individual points of light. Since World War II photocomposition has had much the same effect on mechanical typesetting as the Linotype and Monotype did on handset type: it has replaced it in many applications, but mechanical typesetting continues to be widely used.

Many photocomposition systems are now computer-driven, eliminating the keyboarding role of the typesetter altogether. In an increasing number of cases, a writer's keystrokes when first composing a piece represent the only time the characters are keyed. (That is true of this book, for example.) By avoiding rekeying, publishers can simplify proofreading and save time and money.

The computer can replace the compositor, but well-designed books still require designers to select suitable combinations of typefaces and fonts and to instruct the computer to build attractive, legible pages.

This brief tour of composition and printing techniques omits many important aspects, including most aspects of illustration and the different uses of different forms of paper.

THE CONTINUING DOMINANCE OF THE PRINTED PAGE

Printed books and serials will continue to be the media of choice, for most people, for most applications in which text is involved. New techniques to store and communicate textual information have emerged, and these techniques will affect libraries; later chapters discuss some of these. But none of the new techniques seems likely to replace the printed page as the primary carrier of knowledge and literate entertainment, at least not within the next few decades. New techniques may substantially reduce the use of printed books for large and specialized reference works, but that seems to be the only area where the printed page is in serious jeopardy.

Books will continue to dominate partly because they are familiar--not a trivial factor, but also not the only factor. When librarians worry about the future of the book, it may be worthwhile to consider a few of the virtues of books--virtues not readily replaceable with other media or techniques.

Portability

Books offer better portability than any other text medium. A traveler can, for example, add a 300-page guidebook, five full-length novels, and two science-fiction magazines to his luggage. The reading material will add less than three pounds of weight and take up very little space. The traveler does not need any special equipment for his books, or even electricity, if the sun is out.

Portability counts at home as well as on the road. Books need no equipment. A book can be read in any position, in any location, at any time, as long as some light is available. A reader may be in a dozen different locations in the course of reading a single book: at the breakfast table, in an easy chair, in the bath, in bed, in a hammock in the backyard. In each case, all the reader needs to do is find some light and be able to lift half a pound or find a surface to set it down. No other text medium currently offers that flexibility or seems likely to in the near future.

Readability

Print on paper is easier and more pleasant to read than text in any current electronic medium. Some of the problems inherent in reading text in electronic form can be overcome now or in the near future, but some may take decades to overcome, if they can be conquered at all.

Proportionally spaced text is generally easier to read than monospaced text, since letters in proportional text blend more readily into words and words into phrases. Almost all books use proportional text; few electronic media do so. Some newer electronic media do offer proportional fonts, but these are less successful than print on paper, for reasons discussed in the following paragraphs.

	Character	Screen	Ratio
Screen	128	166,000	1
Laser printer	1,070	1,500,000	9
Photocomposition	68,000	96,000,000	578

Table 1.1: Element Density of Display and Print

Print on paper offers much more clearly defined characters than most electronic media. Table 1.1 may make the point clear. This table compares high-quality text on a computer screen, the output of a normal desktop laser printer, and output from a high-quality photocomposition system. The screen, in this case, is 20 lines of 65 characters each--about the most that can fit on a screen and maintain good continuous readability. That's about half a page of this book. The numbers in Table 1.1 show the number of "picture elements," dots or lines making up a single character (left column) and all of the characters on the screen or half-page (right column). That is, a single character on a screen may be composed of 128 picture elements, while the full screen may contain 166,000 picture elements--but a single character of high-quality photocomposition may be composed of 68,000 picture elements.

Note the ratios: the laser printer uses about nine times as many elements to form a letter as the display screen. High-quality photocomposition (2,400 lines per inch) uses 64 times as many elements as the laser printer. (Lower-quality photocomposition systems use 1,200 lines per inch, 16 times the density of a laser printer.)

Good printing has much better definition than good-quality text on a screen. The difference between photocomposition and laser printer output is subtle but quite real and can be seen by almost any observer comparing the two carefully. The difference between laser printer quality and on-screen definition is obvious and makes a substantial difference in long-term readability.

Print on nongloss paper also offers almost total freedom from glare and reflection and is "easy on the eyes"; people can and do read for hours on end without headaches or eyestrain. Books can be set at any desired angle to the eyes and at any desired distance, with the angle and distance changing from minute to minute at the whim of the reader. No other medium offers such flexibility.

Ease of Use

People certainly need training to use books, but that training is necessary to deal with any written text. Once a person learns to read, no further training is required. Books work well for quick lookup (if they contain tables of contents or indexes) and for sequential reading at any appropriate speed. Readers can pick up a book, set it aside (easily marking their spot), and come back to it with no startup time.

No other medium requires so little preparation and offers such easy access and use. Even the most user-friendly computer or online database requires some training to use the keyboard, locate material, and read through it; other nonprint media also require some instruction. More significant, nonprint media rarely offer the ease of browsing, casual reading, and place-marking that make print so convenient.

Aesthetics and Economics

Books give pleasure to the eye as well as to the mind. The intelligent use of space, typefaces, and other elements of typography can be aesthetically satisfying. Many magazines and some books offer color photographs and graphics with a resolution and range of color not possible in any other publishing medium, combined with text in informative and pleasing combinations.

Print can offer economic advantages difficult to duplicate in other media. The best examples may be daily newspapers and large-circulation, special-interest magazines, where advertising pays much more of the production cost than do the readers. Daily newspaper advertisers know that people will see an ad while scanning adjacent news and features. Advertisers in some magazines can assume that readers will use ads as sources of additional information.

The role of advertising in alternative text media is unclear, but one thing is certain: random-access media will lead to much less awareness of advertising. Readers who pay for information "by the minute" or "by the character" will not spend much time on ads.

To date no other medium offers the combined virtues of print for most textual applications. Books have never been the best medium to store large quantities of raw data, and most raw data will never appear in print. Other media may well gain dominance in certain areas such as large or specialized reference works, where other virtues outweigh the virtues of print. But for literature, articles with broad audiences and monographs with a coherent organization--intended for reading, not simply lookup--books seem likely to maintain their primary role.

There is little point in discussing the current and potential use of books within libraries. The main business of most libraries is, and will continue to be, the acquisition, control, and circulation of printed, published material.

THE PROBLEM WITH PAPER

The most serious technological problem relating to print media is endurance. Books should last, not simply for years but for decades and centuries. Too often, they do not. Books fail to survive for two reasons: because bindings fail and because paper fails. This section does not take up bindings, but does consider the problem of acid paper.

Paper is primarily cellulose, ribbonlike molecules made up of glucose, a common sugar. Cellulose molecules bond together into sheets and layers through hydrogen bonds and electrostatic forces. Those sheets and layers make up microfibrils, submicroscopic bundles with strong internal bonding. Microfibrils further bond to make up bundles, which bond to make up fibers. These larger and larger clusters have weaker and weaker bonds, since the forces that maintain the bonds weaken over distance. Paper consists of cellulose fibers mixed with water, beaten and spread, pressed and dried into sheets using forms that establish a directional grain. (Several other processes may also be applied to make paper more suitable for special uses; examples include coating, sizing and calendering.)

That brief description is an ideal. Pure cellulose fibers and water, with no contaminants, will yield paper with a long life expectancy. Until 1849 almost all books were printed on pure rag papers, made from linen and other rags. Such papers, essentially free from impurity, can be expected to last for centuries (and have done so). Unfortunately, linen and similar fibers are expensive to obtain and nearly impossible to grow and process in the quantities needed by an explosively expanding publishing industry.

Papermakers began to use wood pulp around 1850, grinding it finely, using chemicals to digest it into pulp or using some combination of the two processes. By 1870 papers consisting partly or entirely of fibers derived from wood had replaced pure rag paper in most American publishing. Unfortunately such paper requires chemical treatment and the finished product tends to contain chemicals and other impurities.

These impurities can create acidic conditions in paper, or allow paper to become acidic. Acids can break the bonds between glucose units within cellulose molecules creating shorter, weaker molecules. As this process continues, the paper becomes weaker and weaker until it simply crumbles into dust.

The curious result is that, while books published before 1850 (and some published since) can be expected to last indefinitely (at least when protected from environmental hazards), many of the books and serials published since 1850 are destroying themselves.

There is no single solution to the threatened loss of a century's literature. Several different tactics are being pursued to preserve some of the literature; some of these are discussed in chapter 10. Meanwhile, the problem continues, and most paper currently used for books is likely to deteriorate badly within a few decades.

Permanent Paper

The library and publishing fields, acting through the National Information Standards Organization, NISO, have established a standard for uncoated papers that can be expected to last several hundred years under normal library use and storage conditions. The standard, Z39.48-1984, *American National Standard for Information Sciences--Permanence of Paper for Printed Library Materials*, is intended for use by publishers and paper producers and to serve as a buying tool.

The standards establish minimum requirements for "permanent" paper, which are moderate alkalinity, a level of resistance to folding and tearing, and the absence of unbleached pulp or groundwood. Each requirement is stated so as to be testable and verifiable. The standard also establishes a symbol to be used in books and serials published on permanent paper: the infinity symbol within a circle. When books are published on permanent paper, the information should also appear within the Cataloging in Publication information as a qualifier to the ISBN, usually stated as "(alk. paper)."

Some publishers already used alkaline papers designed for permanence before Z39.48 was approved. Since its approval, more books and periodicals use such paper and show the explicit symbol. While such use grows slowly, it does result in larger markets for alkaline paper. Larger markets encourage more papermakers to produce more permanent paper, thus reducing the premium required to use the paper. With contemporary methods, permanent paper does not cost significantly more to produce than acid paper; permanent paper costs more because the current demand for it is smaller. That demand should grow, with more books appearing on permanent paper--books that can be expected to survive.

SUMMARY

Print on paper will survive and prosper as the primary medium for literature and for many forms of information and knowledge. As libraries take advantage of newer media, they must not lose sight of the importance of print. Libraries should encourage efforts to see that the paper itself survives, so that the published record may be maintained and serve future generations.

SELECTED READING

Many good books deal with the history of print and publishing. The sources given here are those specifically used to prepare this chapter.

Gaskell, Philip. *A New Introduction to Bibliography.* New York: Oxford University Press, 1972. 438 pp. (A thorough treatment of the processes of book production. Source of most information used in this chapter on the growth of printing and changes in paper manufacture.)

Hollinger, William K., Jr. "The Chemical Structure and Acid Deterioration of Paper." *Library Hi Tech* 1, no.4 (Spring 1984):51-57. (Why acid conditions cause some paper to break down. The description in this chapter is based partly on the Hollinger article.)

2

Microform

Microform is the Rodney Dangerfield of information media: it doesn't get any respect. Libraries need microfilm and microfiche, but users will accept them only when no other medium is available. There are good reasons for the almost universal disdain and avoidance of microform materials. There are also good reasons why microforms will be with us for some time to come, and represent an essential technology for certain library applications. This chapter deals with all varieties of microform, that is, all methods for printing or reproducing text and related material at a greatly reduced size.

HOW IT WORKS

Microform technology is neither mysterious nor arcane. Microfilm is high-resolution, high-contrast film; microfilm production is simply another form of photography. If you take a picture of a landscape using a 35-millimeter camera and print the results on paper, with the print size larger than the photographic image, you're engaged in photography. If you take a picture of a book or magazine page using a 35-millimeter camera (probably with different film, probably with a specialized camera) and copy the results to another piece of film, with the copy size equal to the photographic image, you're creating a microform.

The preceding paragraph tells you almost everything you need to know about 35-millimeter reel microfilm, but there are many other varieties of microform. One example is microprinting: printing a small, high-resolution image on an opaque material rather than copying it to film, retaining the small image size or shrinking it further. Another example is ultrafiche: shrinking the original image to less than one percent of its original size in each dimension, compared with the four percent that is typical for most photographically created microfilm. Other varieties of microform, such as computer output microform (COM), use computers to create images by generating images of letters directly onto the film, so that the film is an original, not a copy. Some varieties involve the use of color film or faithful reproduction of shades of gray. But all microforms begin with photographic images, and almost all use materials and techniques developed for photography.

Brief History

Microforms go back more than a century. J. B. Dancer produced microphotographs in 1839; microfilm was suggested as a publication medium for scholarly material in 1853; pigeons flew microfilmed news dispatches into besieged Paris in 1871. An 1896 proposal set forth the basics of the current design and format for microfiche.

Commercial microphotography dates back to 1928; the first planned use was to photograph canceled checks as a deterrent to fraud. Kodak formed the Recordak Corporation, which perfected the 35-millimeter microfilm camera by 1935. Recordak issued a file of the *New York Times* on microfilm in the 1930s. Other companies entered the field shortly thereafter and some libraries began their own microfilming projects. University Microfilms was founded in 1938, the same year that Harvard began the Foreign Newspaper Microfilm Project.

Writers proposed microform publication as a replacement for book publication as early as 1944, at least for library storage. In recent decades, vendors and librarians have considered microform publication for an extremely wide variety of uses, including use as replacements for card catalogs. During one period, some felt that microforms could even become significant circulating media, with large numbers of library patrons owning their own readers or borrowing the readers along with the publications.

In 1950 Readex Microprint Corporation began to publish research materials as opaque microprints. Other microforms emerged during the 1960s and since. The contemporary standard size and format for microfiche stabilized around 1960. Ultra-high-reduction fiche involves processes first developed in 1960; the first commercial uses of such fiche began about 1970.

The 1960s and 1970s may have been the "glory years" for microform, with no competitors for low-cost, small-run publishing and compact storage of information. The last few years show microform settling into a different role, as a mature technology that continues to be important for a narrower range of uses than originally envisioned. The glamour is gone, as are predictions that microforms could replace books, but many uses will continue. For preservation of textual information, short-run publication of computer-generated union lists, indexes and other reference tools, and other uses, no other medium can currently replace microform.

The Need for a Reader

You can't read microfilm or microfiche without a reader. Microforms are the oldest text media that require special equipment. That need for a reader has been one of the longstanding problems with acceptance of microforms, and may foreshadow problems with widespread use of other information media such as CD-ROM. Even though microforms are much lighter and more compact than books and magazines, the total package is almost always heavier, bulkier, and tied to electrical outlets.

The need for a reader does not pose a serious problem for most business uses of microform media, but substantially reduces the usefulness of microform for readers and scholars. Modest microfiche readers cost less than most compact disc players, but few individual readers see them as desirable purchases. Despite some early predictions, no significant home market for microform ever developed. Mass-market microform does not exist, never has, and probably never will.

VARIETIES OF MEDIA AND READERS

The term *microform* covers dozens of media, most of them requiring their own special readers. Many vendors have offered microfilm, microfiche, and microprint or micro-opaque media in a variety of sizes, formats, and reductions. The examples that follow do not represent a comprehensive survey, but do include major varieties currently produced for the library market.

Photographic Processes

Most contemporary microforms are transparent, either positive or negative polarity, and use one of three types of film. Most computer output microfilm (COM) is negative (light characters on a dark background), as are many other microforms. Positive microforms offer the only plausible full-color microform images and the best images for pictorial microforms.

Archival microfilm uses silver halide emulsion, a traditional photographic process that turns silver grains dark on exposure to light and chemical development. Silver halide film should, when stored properly, last as long as permanent paper. Silver halide film is generally black, dull on one side, and shiny on the other.

Diazo film, frequently used for copies of COM fiche and other copy uses, suspends diazonium salts in a film emulsion, exposed by ultraviolet light and developed using ammonia compounds. Diazo film can fade in strong light and will fade over time. The film is glossy on both sides; while dark blue diazo film may be most familiar, it is also produced in black.

Vesicular film suspends diazonium salts in a plastic layer; exposed salts deform the plastic and, when heated, form permanent bubbles or vesicles. Vesicular film does not fade under light but can be damaged by heat and pressure; some microfilm readers run hot enough to damage vesicular film.

Closed Systems

A closed system combines film and reader in a single unit; the reader becomes part of the publication. Current examples include *Newspaper Index* and *Magazine Index*. A good closed system offers high capacity, easier use than most other microform media, relatively fast access (the readers are usually motorized), and relatively good physical security. The readers take up quite a bit of space, but for certain offerings the combination makes sense.

Closed systems marketed to libraries may be on the decline, although closed systems and computer-based systems are marketed to business and industry. Most closed systems are based on COM; vendors can use the same information to create CD-ROM or videodisc publications instead of COM. CD-ROM offers much faster and more sophisticated access, easier use and, at least theoretically, lower production costs. Further, there is no good reason why a single microcomputer and CD-ROM player cannot use many different CD-ROM services, reducing a library's overall space requirements and costs.

Roll Microfilm

Thirty-five-millimeter roll microfilm offers a combination of clarity and capacity that seems to suit many library needs. Roll microfilm is a nuisance to use and store, but libraries can produce such microfilm in-house. One small reel holds 1,200 to 1,500 pages, the equivalent of three good-sized books or a stack of newspapers, with little danger of pages or portions of pages being torn out.

Microfilm need not be 35-millimeter; 8-millimeter, 16-millimeter, 70-millimeter, and 105-millimeter microfilm also exist, but 35-millimeter is the most popular for library purposes. It does not require the more exacting photography and reader quality of 8-millimeter and 16-millimeter, but does provide high capacity.

Microfiche is actually 105-millimeter film, and such film has been used as "roll fiche," filmed at a high reduction (or using computer-generated images) and storing several pages in a vertical column as with fiche. A 100 foot roll of "roll fiche" has the capacity of 200 individual fiche: up to 19,600 pages at 24x photographic reduction or up to 54,000 frames of COM. A single roll of 105-millimeter roll fiche could have a greater capacity than a single CD-ROM disc, but with much slower access.

The dominance of 35-millimeter roll film for open library systems is probably due to the low reduction ratio and, as a result, relatively easy maintenance. Readers for 35-millimeter film can be and usually are reasonably priced and use simple optics. Small scratches and dusty lenses will not obscure the information to the extent that they would with higher reduction ratios. Additionally, 35-millimeter reels are a "comfortable" size: about the same thickness as a 500-page book, they are a bit too large for easy theft and large enough so that fumble-fingered patrons and librarians can handle them.

Microfiche

Several sizes of microfiche have been produced, but one standard size dominates current American use: 4 by 6 inches or 105 millimeters by 148 millimeters. Service bureaus create COM fiche by the tens of thousands each day for business and other uses, including a fair number of fiche for use in libraries. COM fiche generally use 48x "reduction" (a misnomer, since in fact the fiche is the original publication) and store 269 frames on each fiche, in addition to index frames. Since a COM frame can be 60 (or more) lines of 132 characters, a single fiche can store an impressive amount of information.

Most photographic fiche use 24x reduction and store 98 frames per fiche, or 20x reduction storing 60 frames per fiche. Some moderately priced fiche readers have two lenses on a turret, offering both 24x blowup and 42x or 48x reproduction.

Fiche offer several advantages over roll microfilm. Access can be fast: each fiche contains an eye-readable heading and, normally, an index frame, and standard grids make it easy to move to a given frame. Readers can be quite inexpensive. Fiche are compact, can be directly reproduced at low cost, can be mailed in regular envelopes, and are generally easy to handle.

On the other hand, fiche are equally easy to misplace. If a union catalog consisting of 90 fiche is stored in a box rather than in a series of slotted pages, the chances of the fiche being in correct order are good only if the catalog is never used. Fiche can "walk away" accidentally, and a 200-fiche set with a single missing fiche may be useless.

Microfiche work particularly well for technical reports and other brief documents such as technical standards. Fiche also serves well for lengthy computer-generated publications used for brief lookup and requiring a small number of copies, anywhere from two or three to a thousand or more.

COM production can be remarkably inexpensive once the information is generated, and fiche copies are almost always cheap. For example, one university's arrangement with a commercial COM vendor in 1988 specifies a charge of $2.10 for each master fiche (269 frames) and 10 cents per copy. Such prices are available only when an institution generates large quantities of fiche, but suggest the low underlying production costs of fiche.

Given that price, a union list 2,600 pages long and requiring 10 copies would cost a total of $31 to produce, and each copy could be mailed out with a covering letter in a standard letter envelope for 50 cents in postage (1988 prices). The total "printing" and mailing cost would be $3.60 per copy. This figure ignores the major cost, that of generating the print tape from which the COM is produced, but does illustrate the extremely low costs of short-run COM publishing.

Other Microforms

Publishers have introduced many microforms, but few have achieved wide success. Microfiche can be as small as three by five inches or as large as six by eight inches. Single frames of 35-millimeter or 70-millimeter microfilm can be mounted in standard Hollerith tab cards, creating "aperture cards." Several different ultrafiche projects were announced in the 1970s, with reductions ranging from 90x to 200x. At 90x, an ultrafiche would store 1,000 book pages on a 3-by-5 inch fiche; at 150x, a 4-by-6 inch fiche could store the full text of 7 to 10 books. Finally, several different versions of micro-opaques have appeared, ranging from 3 by 5 inches to 6.5 by 8.5 or 6 by 9 inches.

Some libraries have publications in several of these formats, but no other formats have achieved the ongoing success of standard fiche and 35-millimeter roll film. Ultrafiche are problematic, since the extremely small images are quite susceptible to damage and require perfectly maintained precision readers. Aperture cards do not provide the dense document storage useful for libraries, and make less sense with the decline of punched-card processing. Micro-opaques require more complex readers than microfilm and microfiche and have a number of other problems for use. They have all the handling problems of microfiche (being small, thin, easy to lose and misplace) but require large editions to be economical. They do not offer the low production cost of fiche or the high capacity of COM.

Startling new developments in open microform systems seem unlikely for two reasons. First, vendors find a larger market in industrial applications, where they can sell hundreds of readers and closed systems to a single customer. Second, microform technology is mature; the excitement centers around CD-ROM and other digital media.

MICROFORM IN LIBRARIES

Libraries use microform to acquire materials and to provide information not otherwise available, to build compact files of journals and newspapers, and to preserve deteriorating materials. Some large libraries have millions of items in microform, huge collections that could neither be acquired nor housed in paper form.

Research Collections

Many microform projects, commercial and otherwise, yield compilations of research materials that would not otherwise be available to libraries. Some compilations reproduce rare or out-of-print books; others offer government reports, nongovernment technical reports, theses, and other materials that are never published in book form. Still others are concerned with manuscripts or collections of archival materials. A single microform publication may be a single technical report or may include thousands of books and pamphlets.

Published microform collections cover a wide range of topics and historical periods, such as University Microfilm's project to film books in the Pollard and Redgrave *Short Title Catalog*, several collections in black studies, sets of religious writings, English literary periodicals of the seventeenth and nineteenth centuries, Russian historical sources, and others.

Information Sources

Libraries can offer information on microfilm or microfiche that is not available in paper form, or that is too bulky or expensive to maintain in paper form. Examples include statewide and regional union lists of serials or monographs; research reports through ERIC (Educational Resources Information Center); complete sets of technical standards; and many others.

Journal and Newspaper Backfiles

One important use for microform is back volumes of newspapers and journals. Many contemporary journals are available on microfilm or microfiche to libraries who also subscribe to the printed form. The microform copies allow the libraries to discard back issues after their period of heaviest use, but still make the information available to the few who need earlier volumes. Back issues of periodicals require binding and shelf space, and can become an enormous problem in almost any library.

Newspapers take up even more space than journals, so much more space that retention in print form is nearly impossible. Newsprint also deteriorates so rapidly, except in tightly controlled conditions, that backfiles of newspapers become useless. Finally, newspapers are so voluminous that a researcher would find it cumbersome to deal with backfiles in print form. A scholar may get headaches from hours spent at a microfilm reader, but there are no reasonable alternatives for access to extensive newspaper backfiles.

Preservation

Chapter 10 discusses a few aspects of preservation. Libraries face a massive national crisis as books published during the last century become brittle and unreadable. While microfilm does not preserve the book as an object, it does preserve the information within the book and some sense of the pages as images.

Libraries are engaged in large-scale microfilming projects to try to preserve materials. Perhaps not surprisingly, the catalogs that inform libraries about other microfilmed materials (e.g., the *National*

Register of Microform Masters and the *Research Libraries Group Preservation Union List*) are themselves issued in microform.

PROBLEMS WITH MICROFORM

Most microforms are difficult to handle and painful to read. They require special equipment, frequently lack proper bibliographic access, may be difficult to store, and are frequently a literal pain in the neck. People don't like to use microform media.

There is little point in describing the problems in detail. If you have used roll microfilm or microfiche for a full day of research in a typical library setting and found the experience enjoyable, you are a rare reader indeed. Even an hour's use is enough to drive most users to other sources of information, if any such sources are available.

This is not to say that people will not use microform or even that people cannot be convinced of the need for microform publications. But it is fair to say that, given reasonable alternatives, most users will avoid microforms--experienced users perhaps somewhat more so than others. Guidelines such as those in *Microforms in Libraries* (cited at the end of this chapter) can help libraries to make microform use as pleasant as possible. Since microforms serve a growing and unique function in preserving print, improvements in ease of use will come as a relief to current and future scholars.

Replacing Microform

A single CD-ROM disc can contain as much information as 100 or more sheets of COM fiche, with room to index every word of that information for very fast access. If the market for the information is large enough and the information is in machine-readable form, CD-ROM offers a much better medium than microform. Cheaper computers and storage devices may make online access a practical substitute for microform in some other cases.

But CD-ROM will not replace all microform, any more than microform or CD-ROM will replace books. Preservation microfilming preserves the image and the text, something possible only at great expense using current digital media. Backsets of journals and newspapers seem unlikely to migrate from microfilm to CD-ROM. Many COM products serve a small group of users, too small to justify CD-ROM production.

SUMMARY

Microform may not be exciting or pleasurable but fiche and film will continue to serve libraries well. Since microforms won't simply go away, libraries should make them as useful and accessible as possible. Many standards and guidelines for microform media, production, readers, and use have been published. Libraries using microform media should be aware of these standards; libraries planning to produce microform media should pay particular attention to the standards and guidelines. The sources that follow include some standards and can lead to others; the standards and guidelines are too voluminous and (in some cases), arcane, to discuss or summarize here.

SELECTED READING

Diaz, Albert James, ed. *Microforms in Libraries: A Reader.* Weston, Conn.: Microform Review, 1975. 428 pp. (Wide variety of articles on various aspects of microforms. Includes some realistic assessment of user reactions.)

Spreitzer, Francis, ed. *Microforms in Libraries: A Manual for Evaluation and Management.* Chicago: American Library Association, 1985. 63 pp. Glossary, bibliography, index. (Very good discussion of library issues for microform management.)

3

Analog Audio

Most libraries maintain and circulate collections of sound recordings. This chapter and the next consider the media used in such collections. Until the last five years, all audio collections used analog media, primarily discs and audiocassettes. Analog media store physical patterns or patterns of magnetic particles that represent a direct analogy to the pressure waves that constitute sound.

Historically, the most important analog sound medium has been the disc sound recording, currently represented by vinyl discs. Vinyl discs appear to be giving way to digital competition in the form of compact discs. In the market vinyl discs have already yielded to audiocassettes as the most popular medium for sound recordings.

VINYL DISCS

The vinyl disc is the final chapter in a century-long history of development, presenting the sounds of life in mechanical analog. Most public libraries probably circulate more stereophonic discs than any other nonprint medium, and those that do circulate discs probably find them troublesome. Vinyl discs (vinyl for short) also represent a mature technology changing to a receding technology. After 111 years of progress, the storage of sound patterns in physical analogs seems destined to fade away, rapidly or slowly, replaced by magnetic and digital storage.

While the future of vinyl as a publishing or circulating medium is dim, vinyl and its predecessors play an important role in the libraries of today and the archives of recent history. The technology of mechanical sound recordings is almost a miracle of triumph against the odds; the history of sound recording is interesting and important. The transition from vinyl disc to compact disc is the latest in a series of dramatic changes that have occurred over the past century. From the library perspective, the latest change is almost certainly a change for the better.

How They Work

Vinyl discs result from mass production to exacting standards. A sound recording begins when a cutting stylus carves a path in a lacquer disc. The cutting stylus is driven by an amplifier that may have as its source a tape recording (analog or digital) or microphones picking up sound directly. In either case, the stylus translates sound waves into physical traces within the disc. That disc is sprayed with silver nitrate and covered with silver. A plating bath fuses copper to the silver; the copper-silver shell, stripped from the lacquer, becomes the master--a negative image of the lacquer.

The master is plated again to produce positive metal "mothers." Those are plated to produce "stampers," which are coated with copper and chromium to make them hard and durable. Stampers, like masters, are negative images of the recording. Two stampers, one for each side of an album, are mounted in a press. A chunk of vinyl compounded with plasticizers, with paper labels for each side, is placed between the stampers and the press is closed. Heat and pressure force the vinyl to take on the images of the stampers, making a record.

A 12-inch disc may contain slightly more than 30 minutes of music on each side: 36 million complex "squiggles" in the walls of a groove almost half a mile long. In the inner grooves of a long classical recording, undulations may be as little as $^{7}/_{10,000}$-inch (0.7 mil) apart to carry a 20 kiloHertz signal, the upper limit of human hearing. The squiggles are not just side to side, but up and down as well. A diamond stylus possibly smaller than 0.2 mil by 0.7 mil at its tip must trace a complex three-dimensional path in order to play back the recording accurately.

The two channels of a stereophonic recording actually appear as physical impressions on the diagonal, at 45 degree angles from the vertical. Each channel becomes squiggles on one wall of the V-shaped groove.

The Problems with Vinyl

Vinyl discs can carry extremely accurate reproduction and last for decades, but are subject to a great many perils. The technology of disc manufacture and playback includes several weaknesses and dangers, any or all of which can make the reproduction less accurate and eventually make the disc useless. Following are a few of the perils:

1. Recycled vinyl, the wrong mix of additives, too little vinyl, worn stampers or incorrectly mounted stampers may result in discs that are noisy or defective before they leave the factory.

2. Vinyl warps easily when exposed to heat (including sunlight) or uneven pressure (improper shrinkwrapping, improper storage), resulting in physical aberrations that may make the record difficult or impossible to play.

3. The grooves of a vinyl disc are fragile. Sloppy handling can damage them, and the stylus exerts enough pressure to grind dust or dirt permanently into the grooves. Chemicals, including the oil from fingers, may leach the plasticizers from vinyl, making it brittle and easy to damage.

4. A worn or chipped stylus will carve its own path in the vinyl. Various forms of maltreatment may cause the stylus to chip pieces of vinyl from the record. If the tracking force is too heavy or too light, even a new stylus may damage grooves.

5. While the downward force on the stylus may be a gram or so in a high-quality cartridge, that force is concentrated to create substantial pressure on the tiny area where the stylus contacts the sides of the groove. Even the highest-quality cartridge temporarily deforms the groove. Playing a record over again without giving the vinyl enough time to recover will permanently deform the groove.

Libraries and library patrons deal with the cumulative results of those and other perils every day. It is rare for a disc to survive even a few circulations without significant damage. Most audiophiles will not consider borrowing discs from libraries; not only do they sound even worse on a high-quality system, but a damaged disc can destroy an expensive stylus.

Given the mechanical tolerances involved in a modern recording and the many sources of damage, it is somewhat remarkable that vinyl discs work at all, and particularly remarkable that they work as well as they do. A properly handled disc will last for decades and survive hundreds of playings with little change in reproduction quality. While audiocassettes represent a more durable medium for most playback purposes, vinyl is a much better archival medium if properly handled and stored.

A Brief History of Recording

Thomas Alva Edison developed the first phonograph in 1877, and coined the term "phonograph." The first unit--built by John Kreusi, one of his aides--used a brass cylinder engraved in a continuous spiral groove, with a thin sheet of tinfoil wrapped around the cylinder. A diaphragm of mica vibrated a metal stylus up and down, indenting the tinfoil, as the operator cranked a handle to spin the cylinder and move it laterally. On playback, a different stylus rode the indentations, vibrating a diaphragm with an amplifying horn attached.

Edison built a few hundred phonographs. Alexander Graham Bell and the Bell Labs took the invention several steps further in 1886. The Bell "graphophone" used a loosely mounted stylus, which cut a smoother hill-and-dale (vertical) groove in a wax-coated cardboard roll slipped onto a metal cylinder. The recording was higher in quality but lower in volume: listeners needed ear tubes to hear the recording.

Edison improved the Bell model still further, moving to a solid wax cylinder, a sapphire stylus, and a groove only one mil deep. Edison saw the unit as a dictation machine; the solid wax cylinder could be shaved and reused several times. Two companies with similar products engaged in various legal battles and sold small numbers of graphophones and phonographs to offices and other customers.

The first coin-operated phonograph appeared in 1889, beginning the use of phonographs as personal entertainment devices. Columbia began to produce cylinders in 1891. Two-minute cylinders with poor sound were popular and increasingly successful. Already, however, an alternative method had been demonstrated: Emile Berliner exhibited a disc "gramophone" in 1888. He used lateral cutting (side to side) rather than vertical cutting, and established a disc production method that raised playback volume again, eliminating the need for ear tubes.

First Revolution: Discs

Commercial disc production began in 1893; meanwhile, commercial and legal battles between graphophone and phonograph companies continued. The year 1901 saw the founding of the Victor Talking Machine Company, direct forerunner of RCA Victor. Columbia added disc players and discs in 1902. The two most important competitors in American recording history were in place.

The first Victrola, with its horn hidden inside the cabinet, appeared in 1906. From then on, it was all downhill for cylinders, although Edison continued to manufacture cylinders until 1929. The first dramatic change in sound recordings was complete. Cylinders held the stage for 16 years and competed for another 19, but discs won out. Discs had several advantages over cylinders: they were easier to produce in quantity, easier to store and more durable. Cylinders provided the first form of home recording, but the ability to record did not keep cylinders active for home use (although they continued to be used for dictation for some years).

In 1912 discs could be lateral or hill-and-dale, but they were all produced acoustically, with performers singing and playing into a horn that focused sound onto a diaphragm, causing a stylus to cut into a wax recording blank.

Second Revolution: Electrical Recording

Microphones entered the entertainment field in 1919, when radio station KDKA began broadcasting. Bell Labs started experimenting with microphones and electrical recording in that same year. Victor and Columbia both began to make electrical recordings in 1925. Until this time all recordings were still "direct-to-disc" (i.e., the master disc was cut as the musicians played and sang). The second revolution was much faster than the first: after only 13 years in which all commercial recordings were acoustical discs, electrical recording took over rapidly.

The first attempt at an electrical "long-playing" record came in 1931. RCA Victor announced a 33 1/3 revolutions per minute (rpm) record (made of plastic rather than shellac), more than doubling the playing time of 78 rpm records. The attempt was not a success because the heavy tone arms then in use wore out the softer discs rapidly. After a year, RCA gave up. True long-playing records did not emerge for another 17 years.

Third Revolution: The LP

The third revolution in sound recordings was far more dramatic than the first two. The material of recordings, the way they were made, and the length of a single recording all changed dramatically. The revolution was the result of five elements coming together in 1948:

1. High-quality tape recorders made it possible to record complete orchestral pieces without interruption. Producers could edit recordings, correcting errors without redoing the complete recording session. Direct-to-disc was no longer the only way to make a record.

2. Much narrower recording grooves, 300 per inch instead of 85 per inch, made it possible to put much more on a single disc. Columbia/CBS, which developed the technique, called them "microgrooves."

3. The narrower grooves were on a slower-moving disc, running at the same 33 1/3 rpm that RCA had abandoned 17 years before, further increasing recording time to more than 20 minutes per side.

4. Vinyl plastic could take an accurate impression of the much more detailed recording, but was much softer than shellac.

5. A lightweight cartridge designed by Philco could track the vinyl without destroying the grooves; the eight-gram tracking force is heavy by current standards but was a breakthrough for 1948.

Despite RCA's attempt to establish 7-inch 45 rpm microgroove records as the standard, the 12-inch LP was the major winner. By 1950 the third revolution was complete. Electrical direct-to-disc recordings at 78 rpm dominated the recording field for a quarter century. Some 78 rpm recordings were made from tape recordings, and some LPs are still recorded direct-to-disc, although never acoustically.

Fourth Revolution: Stereo

The fourth revolution was less dramatic and much faster. Stereo records came only eight years later, in 1958, and became dominant by the early 1960s.

The first stereophonic recordings were made early in the century at Bell Labs, using acoustic techniques. The first *electrical* stereo recordings were made in 1931. Prerecorded stereo tapes were available in the early 1950s, but the tape market was never a large one. Several different techniques for recording stereo on a disc were attempted but the 45 degree, single-groove technique triumphed, largely because the discs were compatible with monophonic record players.

The Revolution that Failed

A fifth revolution never happened. Quadraphonic sound ("quad"), introduced commercially in the late 1960s, essentially disappeared in the middle 1970s. The reasons are unclear, but several possibilities come to mind:

1. Quadraphonic recording required two more speakers and another stereo amplifier: a large capital investment, and the difficult task of placing speakers so that they sounded right but did not dominate the listening room.

2. Three different quad recording systems competed for the dollars of the few who were willing to buy the equipment. Nei-

ther Columbia's "SQ" nor the Japanese "QS" offered perfect separation. RCA's "CD-4," which did offer perfect separation under ideal conditions, required nearly perfect recordings and sophisticated playback equipment in order to function at all.

3. Most early quadraphonic recordings were unnatural. Those that were natural did not show enough apparent improvement for most people to justify the massive expenditures needed.

That brings us to today, when a fifth revolution is succeeding. Chapter 4 discusses the revolution of compact disc, an entirely different technology for sound recording. This revolution is not occurring as rapidly as the change to stereo or the change to electrical recording, and vinyl discs should be with us for several years to come.

Libraries and Vinyl Discs

Vinyl discs will be useful as archival material well past the turn of the next century, just as earlier discs are still useful today. However, vinyl discs as circulating media have never been ideal, and will decline gradually. Although vinyl as a medium is receding in importance, vinyl records continue to be produced in great numbers and manufacturers continue to improve turntable and cartridge design.

Libraries can take steps to help vinyl discs survive. Records need to be kept clean and protected from heat and uneven pressures. Cleaning must be done carefully; improper cleaning will damage records. Specially designed protective fluids can help records to last longer, but nothing can protect records from the casual abuse and poorly maintained playback systems that doom most circulating records to early destruction.

AUDIOCASSETTES

Philips developed the compact cassette in the late 1950s, not as a high-fidelity medium but as a convenient tool for dictation and other low-fidelity uses. Magnetic tape began much earlier (as discussed in chapter 15), but reel-to-reel tape recording never became a mass medium. Most people did not want to deal with threading tape through heads, and few people saw any need to record sound. Reel-to-reel tape recording continues to be at the heart of professional recording, but most companies have stopped making reel-to-reel recorders for home use.

The compact cassette is compact and self-contained. It does not require threading or much thought on the part of the user: drop it in the recorder, close the top, and press a button. Philips was not the only company to recognize the need for simpler tape recording, but its design was straightforward, sensible, and had promise for future development.

Philips fully intended to license its patents to other companies for a modest continuing royalty such as 2 cents per cassette. Around 1960 Sony convinced Philips to make the license royalty-free and offered in exchange a patented automatic recording level system that would make cassette recorders much more useful for casual recording. The Sony-Philips cross-licensing marked the beginning of many agreements between these two companies that would influence non-print media, and helped to make the compact cassette a worldwide standard.

From Voice to High Fidelity

High fidelity tape recording was possible in 1960, but not on an audiocassette. The audiocassette gains its compactness through two means. First, the recording tracks are much narrower than on reel-to-reel tape recorders--one-half the width of home recorders; one-quarter or one-eighth the width of professional recorders. Second, the tape moves much more slowly--one-quarter as fast as the lowest speed ever used widely for high-fidelity recording. That combination means that the recording head on a cassette recorder has only (at most) one-eighth as much magnetic material to work with over a given period, resulting in poorer frequency response, more noise relative to signal, and more difficulty with speed variations because of the lower speed.

But audiocassettes worked. They became increasingly popular, and had obvious consumer appeal. Audio companies saw the need to improve the fidelity of cassette recordings, since even at low fidelity they were being used for music. Four forces came together to turn audiocassettes into a valid medium for high fidelity:

1. Ray Dolby developed a noise-reduction system, "Dolby B," that could reduce the audible noise enough to make the wide dynamic range of music work. The Dolby process compresses the dynamic range of high-frequency signals during recording, making softer signals louder. On playback, the process expands the dynamic range, reducing the level of the signals that were increased during recording. As these sounds become softer, so does tape hiss and noise, making the background noise substantially less audible. The process is sometimes called "companding" or "compansion." Dolby Labs later introduced Dolby C, with more dramatic results. Dolby A was and is used in professional recording systems to reduce tape noise in the original recording process.

2. Tape manufacturers such as 3M, BASF, and a number of Japanese firms improved the magnetic formulations used in tape to make better recordings possible and improved the backing materials to make thinner, longer-playing tapes more durable. BASF introduced chromium dioxide as an alternative to the ferric oxide (rust) used for most tape. These manufacturers and others also improved cassette shell designs to reduce friction and improve durability.

3. Manufacturers improved the design of cassette recorders, making them more durable but also reducing speed variation and improving the accuracy of tape handling.

4. Continued improvements in electronics made better recordings possible on a given tape formulation and kept pace with improved tape.

A three-country combination of talent and ingenuity came together when the relatively unknown Japanese firm Nakamichi combined the Dutch invention of the compact cassette, the American developments of Dolby noise reduction and the high-quality Wollensak deck (produced by 3M), international developments in tape, and their own electronics to produce the first high-fidelity cassette deck in the late 1960s.

Cassette tape and cassette recorders have continued to improve throughout the relatively long history of the medium. Philips's strict licensing agreement assures total compatibility; with very few exceptions, any cassette can be played on any cassette recorder. That leaves companies free to compete on incremental improvements: better sound, better features, better prices. The results can be seen in today's inexpensive portable cassette players and tape decks, featuring better sound than would have been possible at any price when the medium was introduced.

Cassettes in the Marketplace

Cassettes started out slowly as a medium for prerecorded sound. Eight-track cartridges had become popular in automobiles and, at the beginning, offered better quality sound. Very few eight-track units offered recording capabilities. Recording companies saw this as an advantage; some record and motion picture companies have always been suspicious of media that permit recording. But eight-track cartridges wear themselves out, are much bulkier than cassettes, and require more complex playback mechanisms. While some eight-track players are still in use, cassettes came to dominate the tape market as sound quality improved.

The advent of Sony's Walkman marked the real turning point. Now, it would seem, everybody has at least one cassette player. Prerecorded cassettes passed vinyl discs in total sales a few years ago. In 1987 cassette sales were as much as twice those of discs. While most prerecorded cassettes do not offer the sound quality of the best vinyl discs, they do offer more convenience and greater freedom from casual wear. Prerecorded cassettes now offer material not available on vinyl, including recordings of books and stories, old radio broadcasts, and other special material. The true mass analog medium of 1987 is not the vinyl disc but the prerecorded cassette.

Cassettes in the Library

Librarians who circulate cassettes know the good and bad points of the medium. Cassettes cost no more than vinyl discs, require less shelving space, and generally suffer less during normal circulation. Since cassette cases offer better protection for cassettes than regular disc jackets do for discs, libraries have less need for special cases. (Libraries do need a supply of empty cassette cases, since the cases themselves break fairly easily.)

On the other hand, cassettes are easy to steal and hard to catalog. Publishers seem to provide less information with cassettes than with discs, and the information can be less consistent. The security problem has three facets: several cassettes will fit in a coat pocket; placement of security devices may be difficult given the small available surface of a cassette; and some "discharging" devices can damage cassette recordings.

Finally, cassettes are not archival. The thin tape snarls, breaks, and stretches easily and will not retain a recording forever. Any ill-intentioned user can erase a prerecorded cassette or record something else on top of it. When this happens, the damage is intentional, as every compact cassette has a mechanism to prevent accidental recording.

Cassettes make sense as circulating media, but not nearly as much sense as compact discs. But cassettes have such a huge market and are so cheap and convenient that they should last for years to come. Cassettes may eventually be replaced by digital audiotape--discussed briefly in the next chapter--but only at the right price. Despite generally inferior sound quality, prerecorded cassettes outsell vinyl discs substantially, indicating that most purchasers regard convenience as more important than the ultimate in sound quality. Unless digital audiotape can provide equal convenience at a comparable price, audiocassettes may continue as a major medium indefinitely.

SUMMARY

The ingenuity of Edison began a century-long series of advances in techniques and technology, all working toward more perfect ways to represent sound in mechanical form. The pioneers would no doubt be astounded to hear the quality of contemporary recordings, even those made as early as 1958.

The technology of analog recording made it possible to preserve the speeches of politicians and the songs of performers for later generations, and has made it possible for people around the world to hear the music they want to hear, when they want to hear it. Analog audio has done for sound what books do for text: preserve it and make it widely available over a long time span.

SELECTED READING

The written history of sound recordings is a rich, vivid one. A few examples appear here.

Berger, Ivan, and Hans Fantel. *The New Sound of Stereo.* New York: New American Library, 1986. 265 pp. Index. (Broad introduction to high fidelity. Good contemporary information.)

Lyons, Nick. *The Sony Vision.* New York: Crown, 1976. 235 pp. (An earlier view of Sony, as of the introduction of Betamax [and before the introduction of VHS]. Noteworthy on the role of Sony in spreading audiocassettes.)

Morita, Akio. *Made in Japan: Akio Morita and Sony.* New York: Dutton, 1986. 309 pp. (Excellent background for understanding Sony's role in consumer technology.)

Read, Oliver, and Walter L. Welch. *From Tin Foil To Stereo: Evolution of the Phonograph.* 2nd ed. Indianapolis: Howard W. Sams, 1976. 550 pp. (An earlier history of the recording industry, particularly strong on very early history.)

Schicke, Charles A. *Revolution in Sound: A Biography of the Recording Industry.* Boston: Little, Brown, 1974. 246 pp. (Very readable history of the recording industry [primarily cylinders and discs] through 1974, with a section on the current nature of the industry. Lacks any bibliography or identification of sources.)

4

Digital Audio

Sound recordings began with cylinders and went through four revolutions in the last century: disc recording, electrical recording, the long-playing record with tape recording as an intermediate step, and stereophonic recording. The fifth revolution in sound recordings features 12 centimeter plastic-and-metal discs, low-power and low-priced lasers, and low-cost application of extremely sophisticated electronics.

Compact disc players and CDs reached the Japanese market in 1982, and Europe and America in 1983, in small quantities and at high prices. Soon quantities rose and prices fell; within three years, CD became the most successful new consumer product in recent history.

CDs solve many longstanding problems in sound reproduction such as surface noise, fragility, and inevitable deterioration through heavy use. They also solve some severe problems for libraries wishing to circulate sound recordings, while possibly causing others. Although compact discs generate ongoing controversy among some "golden-ear" audiophiles, their future is assured.

The Nature of Digital Audio

Sound consists of vibrations in the air. A single vibration (a pure tone) has a pitch and an amplitude. Pitch is described in terms of frequencies, the number of vibrations per second, and is usually called Hertz in honor of the German physicist Heinrich R. Hertz, who established the electromagnetic nature of light. People with excellent hearing can hear frequencies between 20 Hertz (or 20 cycles per second) and 20,000 Hertz. Amplitude or volume is normally specified in decibels, fractions of the larger unit Bel named for Alexander Graham Bell.

Music never consists of a single vibration; even a single note played on a flute generates several overtones at reduced volumes. The sound of an orchestra may be made up of dozens of tones and hundreds of overtones. All of those frequencies combine to make music. Those frequencies and amplitudes don't follow independent paths through the air, but combine to form complex waveforms. An LP groove consists of two such complex waveforms expressed as physical undulations in vinyl, one for each stereo channel.

Mathematical analysis shows that you can describe music up to a certain frequency by describing the amplitude twice as often as that frequency. In theory, if you take samples of a performance 40,000 times per second and store the volume at each sample, you can use those samples to reconstruct the performance within the limits of human hearing. That's what digital audio does: it records the volume of each channel at least 40,000 times per second and stores each sample volume in digital form--as a binary number.

Digital audio can be described in terms of its sampling rate and the precision with which it can store the volume. The latter factor depends on the length of each binary number. CD recordings use 44,100 samples per second, stored as 16-bit numbers, sufficient to describe volumes over a range from 1 (the softest) to 65,535 (the loudest). That translates to a range of more than 95 decibels.

The Significance of Digital Audio

Why turn music into a series of numbers? Because we know how to store, manipulate, and retrieve binary numbers accurately. Every physical medium has imperfections. Sound recorded on magnetic tape in analog form cannot be played back exactly as it was recorded because the tape itself will add something to the original sound. Each generation of recording adds distortion and subtracts from the original information, and analog playback cannot completely separate the original information from the contributions of the medium, since the physical vibrations or waves of magnetic orientation must be taken as a whole.

Numbers can be stored as a series of on and off, yes and no decisions. When the only possibilities are yes or no, a one percent error in the recording medium makes no difference: one percent is "off" as much as zero percent, and 99 percent is "on" as much as 100 percent. More significant, binary numbers can be transformed to add sophisticated error detection and correction capabilities. As a result, the 100th copy of a digital recording should be *identical* to the original.

Digital Audio Before Compact Discs

What do Jean-Pierre Rampal playing Telemann and Ry Cooder playing contemporary music have in common? Both represent early uses of digital audio in their respective areas. Odyssey Y33200, Telemann: "Twelve Fantasias for Flute," was originally produced in Japan by Nippon Columbia, Ltd. The recording dates from 1973, and was produced using a Pulse Code Modulation recording system developed by Nippon Columbia with the cooperation of the NHK Technical Research Laboratories. It was one of the first digitally produced recordings to reach the United States.

Six years later, Warner Brothers released Ry Cooder's "Bop Till You Drop," recorded on 3M multitrack digital equipment and probably the first American popular recording entirely recorded and mastered using digital techniques. The total absence of tape hiss on Rampal's solo flute performance was startling; in some ways, the crystalline clarity of Cooder's guitar was even more amazing.

During the late 1970s and the early 1980s, more and more recording companies switched to digital tape systems for classical recording. Digital recording for rock, jazz, country, folk, and other forms also increased, though far more slowly.

Historical Notes

NHK Technical Research Institute developed the first practical digital recorder, demonstrating a prototype in May 1967. The recorder was based on a one-inch videotape recorder, and was only a promise of future possibilities. (See chapter 5 for a discussion of video recorders and helical scanning.) With 30 kiloHertz sampling (limiting high frequencies to 15 kiloHertz, as good as FM radio but not up to the best analog recordings) and 12-bit recording, the quality was passable but not first-rate.

By 1969 Nippon Columbia had a 13-bit recorder sampling at 47.25 kiloHertz, a high enough rate to include the entire audible spectrum. Several companies in Japan (such as Sony and JVC), Europe (primarily Philips), and the United States (3M and Soundstream) further developed and improved digital recording techniques. Digital recorders entered recording studios in the early 1970s while research and development continued.

Sony introduced a digital audio processor based on a videotape recorder in 1977. In May 1978, the Electronics Industry of Japan established a standard for digital audio processors using standard videotape recorders; since then, several Japanese companies have introduced professional or audiophile digital processors. Record producers on a budget and audiophiles who make live recordings have for some years been able to purchase PCM (pulse code modulation) processors that work with VCRs. The combination of a PCM processor and a VCR makes it possible for any producer with taste, intelligence, and a few thousand dollars to achieve sound quality as good as, or better than, that of the largest recording companies.

By 1982 there were hundreds or thousands of digital audio recorders in use, and thousands of vinyl disc releases originated from digitally recorded masters. Dozens of manufacturers had been working on digital audiodiscs for some years. The first demonstrations of digital audiodiscs took place in September 1977. Development continued, and companies involved in the field began to discuss possible standards.

In June 1980 Sony and Philips announced a joint product based on Philips laser optical systems and Sony error-detection and correction techniques: the compact disc. Philips and Sony took advantage of their earlier experience--Philips in freely licensing compact cassettes and Sony in failing to sign up licensees for Betamax at an early stage. The new product was widely licensed and, in effect, precluded any other developmental system. Like audiocassettes, digital audiodiscs reached the market in a single, universally compatible form.

COMPACT DISC: THE NEW PLAYBACK STANDARD

The little shiny disc is replacing the big black disc, surely and not very slowly. In its first four years, CD grew from an expensive curiosity to a mass-market success that has already overtaken vinyl discs in total dollar sales. In the next four years, CD will become the primary playback-only mechanism, with analog discs holding a shrinking share of the market.

From a contemporary viewpoint, CD makes simple good sense. By comparison, vinyl discs represent a miracle of sorts: that they work at all, and that they work as well as they do. Digital audio has a different set of problems, but is in some ways a simpler way of handling sound. All the recording medium must do is record on and off, yes and no. In contrast, analog audio must represent a continually varying pattern, one that is *inherently* error-prone and easy to damage.

The simplicity of digital audio reflects decades of sophisticated development in electronics. Digital audio does simple things, but at incredibly high rates of speed: a compact disc player reads on-off decisions and acts on them from 4 to 16 *million* times per second.

The Technology

A compact disc stores 19 billion pieces of information in a 2-mile spiral track covering an area equivalent to a square 10 centimeters on a side. A plastic disc carries pits 0.6 microns (millionths of a meter) wide and from less than 1 to less than 4 microns long, arranged in a spiral containing as many as 20,000 adjacent tracks. That disc can be expected to provide perfect reproduction of up to 75 minutes of music for an indefinite number of playings, over a life of at least 10 to 25 years.

The physical characteristics of compact discs and players are impressive, but are not the most significant factors in the success of compact discs. The keys to their success are error detection, error correction, and a worldwide technical standard adopted before any marketing began.

Physical Characteristics

A CD master begins as an optically flat glass disc coated with adhesive and a photo resistive substance. A high-powered laser driven by a master tape burns patterns into the coating which are then eaten away chemically. The result is a pitted track.

As with vinyl discs, the master disc presses a negative father or submaster; the submaster presses multiple positive "mother" discs; those, in turn, press multiple negative stampers. Injection molding or other techniques replicate the original pits in polycarbonate plastic, similar to Plexiglass. A thin layer of metal (typically aluminum) coats the pits; lacquer coats the metal. The pits and unpitted areas represent bits, binary digits. Pits and unpitted areas or "lands" always represent binary zeros and ones are represented by the transitions between pits and lands.

During recording and playback, a CD does not spin at a constant speed. The speed is constantly changing, varying from around 430 rpm near the center and beginning of the disc to roughly 200 rpm at the outer edge. The constantly changing rotational speed provides constant *linear* velocity or CLV: at any point on the disc, the same *length* of recorded track passes under the laser during each second. The speed of a CD is 1.25 meters per second; 1.25 meters takes up more than twice as many turns of the spiral at the center of the disk than at the outer edge.

By comparison, a phonograph stylus reads the outermost band of a vinyl recording of "Carmina Burana" at a rate of roughly 0.5 meters per second while the innermost band moves at a rate of roughly 0.2 meters per second. In both cases, however, the relevant factor is the constant *angular* velocity (*CAV*) of 33 rpm. A CD player uses a portion of the information on the disc itself, called the synchronization pattern, to control the speed of the turntable motor.

Error Detection and Correction

Simple multiplication shows that 74 minutes of music, sampled 44,100 times a second and stored as one 16-bit number for each channel, requires a little more than 6 billion bits of information. Yet a 74-minute compact disc contains a little more than 19 billion bits of information. Where do the other 13 billion bits go? Table 4.1 shows the components that make up CD information.

Factor	Change	Bits
One sample, one channel		16
Twelve samples per group	* 12	192
CIRC encoding	* 1.33	256
Subcode information	+ 8	264
EFM encoding	* 2.125	561
Synchronization pattern	+ 27	588
Total for one group of twelve samples		**588**
Groups per second (stereo)	* 7,350	4,321,800
Seconds in 74.5 minutes	* 4,470	19.3 G
Total disc		**19,318,446,000**

Table 4.1: Information Usage on Full-Length CD

The Philips-Sony CD standard combines 12 samples into a group. The first expansion of data is to add information so that a player can detect and, in most cases, correct errors in the pressing. A scheme called a cross-interleaved Reed-Solomon code (CIRC), named for the two MIT professors who first developed the theory, makes it possible for a CD player to correct 99 percent of all errors and to detect virtually all uncorrectable errors. The scheme adds roughly 33 percent more data.

One character (eight bits) of subcode information is added to each group, to tell the player where it is on the disc and to provide track and timing information for display. Then the group with subcode information added is transformed by a method called eight-to-fourteen modulation (EFM), which assures that "one" bits (transitions between pits and lands) will always be separated by at least two zero bits, making the disc manufacturing process slightly less demanding. Three "merging bits" are added to each fourteen-bit result. Finally, a synchronization pattern of 27 bits added to each group assures that the player will maintain proper speed. Thus, each 192-bit group actually reaches the disc as 588 bits.

Error detection and correction make the other advantages of digital audio work within a mass medium. While compact discs are produced under more exacting conditions than most vinyl discs, they are still mass-produced items and can be expected to have defects. No home is free of dust, and no CD will stay perfect even if it began that way. It is fair to assume that a CD player is interpolating at some points, which means it is dealing with an uncorrectable error by taking the average of the sample before and after it, on the assumption that music doesn't change amplitude or frequency suddenly. The audible result of all this overhead and computation is that CD provides the most trouble-free, defect-free audio medium ever developed. Since no physical contact with the playing surface occurs during playback, it should also be the most durable medium (in terms of heavy use, although possibly not in terms of archival longevity).

Standardization

Twelve different digital audiodisc systems were announced in 1977 and 1978 by different Japanese companies and by Philips. For-tunately, the companies were sensible enough to see the need for a common standard. In September 1978 35 Japanese companies studying digital audio formed the DAD (Digital Audio Disc) Convention, aimed at reaching a single standard for such discs before bringing them to market. Thus, when Sony and Philips proposed a fully-worked-out system, other companies chose to adopt it rather than bring out rival systems.

The advantages of mass production, competitive production, and marketing from many firms brought fast acceptance and a rapid drop in prices. Digital audio might have succeeded without standardization; videocassette recorders have become enormously successful. But the road to success for VCRs was much slower and rockier than for compact discs, and the failure to adopt a single standard was surely part of the problem.

Advantages

Even casual audiophiles build rituals around playing phonograph records: Discwasher, stylus brush, antistatic gun, possibly record preservative, and a motorized record cleaner. These rituals, and the attendant panic if records lean at an angle or are touched on the grooves, are part of a futile effort to avoid damaging the discs.

CDs require no such ritual. Under normal conditions, CDs will sound as good on the 500th playing as on the first, even when used casually or on cheap equipment, thus making them ideal for library circulation. If a borrower with an inexpensive CD player plays a CD 10 times over, the disc will sound as though it were new to the next borrower with a $3,000 high-end player.

The music on a new compact disc will have much less noise and distortion than the music on a brand-new vinyl disc. CDs offer other advantages for listeners including easy access to any track, the ability to program a series of selections and the order in which they should be played, and the ability to repeat a selection immediately and with no risk of damage. Most of these advantages are less significant for libraries; more important is that CDs require little care and will retain superb sound for hundreds of playings.

Problems

Nothing is perfect. CDs, like audiocassettes, can walk out of libraries rather easily. CDs have a metallic coating that may interfere with some library security systems although, unlike audiocassettes, they cannot be damaged by ordinary magnetic fields. CDs are also expensive, currently almost twice as much as vinyl or cassette recordings. While the cost per circulation may turn out to be lower than for other media, the cost of building a collection and replacing stolen items is relatively high.

CDs can cause cataloging and storage problems, similar to those created by cassettes. Like cassette cases, CD "jewel boxes" are relatively fragile and libraries may need supplies of empty jewel boxes. Record companies have generally done a better job of including liner notes and other information in booklets with CDs than with cassettes, but the type in such booklets is generally small and may be almost unreadable for some library patrons. From an aesthetic viewpoint, although CDs themselves are attractive, their smaller size reduces the impact of cover art when compared to 12-inch vinyl discs. While CDs are extremely durable for heavy circulation, nobody yet knows the anticipated life span in years; so far, predictions range from 10 to 25 years, less than ideal as an archival medium and a shorter life span than vinyl stored under archival conditions.

Finally, some audiophiles proclaim that compact discs ruin music, since the sampling loses nuances of the music and performance. That is a hard charge to answer because serious audiophiles know what they hear, and it would be wrong to dismiss their claims out of hand. Fortunately, libraries need not be too concerned with this question. The nuances lost in the first few circulations of a vinyl disc far outweigh any conceivable loss through digital sampling.

Compact Discs and Analog Audio

CD sales had already passed vinyl disc sales in dollar volume by the end of 1987, making CDs the second largest audio medium (far behind cassette sales). The trend is clear, and is most apparent in classical music sections of record stores: CDs displace vinyl, and vinyl releases become harder to obtain.

CDs serve most audiophiles better than vinyl because they offer better quality and longer life. Compact discs serve casual listeners better than vinyl because they are more durable, more compact, more convenient, and generally easier to use. They can even be used in some car players and a growing number of portable players, only twice the size of cassette players.

The advantages of compact discs over vinyl discs suggest a general replacement of analog discs with digital. Early projections of a decade-long transition may have been too conservative. The Fall 1987 *Audio Magazine* directory of forthcoming classical releases no longer lists CD releases separately. For 1988 most labels will release everything on CD, and quite a few will *not* release everything on LP. Several smaller classical labels have already stopped producing vinyl, and labels as large as Angel Records now regard CD as their primary medium.

As of January 1988 CD is already the dominant disc medium for classical music. Popular music will move toward CD more slowly, with jazz and specialized areas moving slowest of all. Some companies will produce vinyl for years to come, and a fair sampling of vinyl discs should still be available in another five years. It would be ridiculous to make such a claim for a decade from now, for it seems certain that many record stores will stock only cassettes and CDs.

Analog cassettes should survive longer than vinyl, although digital audiotape could eventually supplant them. They are more convenient to carry than CDs and they are also much cheaper. But they are less convenient to use, in some ways. Getting directly to a given song takes longer on tape than with vinyl, and longer with vinyl than with CDs. But cassettes serve a large buying public, and seem likely to survive the digital onslaught for some time to come.

DIGITAL AUDIOTAPE: TOMORROW'S CASSETTE?

Digital audiotape (DAT) has the potential to provide relatively inexpensive high-quality recording and playback. Japanese manufacturers have adopted a single design standard for digital audiotape, DAT. It uses a small tape cassette and helical heads similar to those in VCRs (see chapter 5). DAT should provide the same sound quality as CD and add the ability to record. DAT recorders reached the Japanese market in 1986, but had not been marketed in the United States as of early 1988.

Producers kept DAT from the market well after its development to give time for CD to become solidly established. The continuing delay in U.S. marketing stems the from ongoing paranoia of the recording industry about illegal copies of recordings. The recording industry raises this cry from time to time. For example, it claims that it loses billions in revenue to audiocassettes, yet recording industry revenues are at an all-time high thanks to revenues from prerecorded cassettes.

The entertainment industry raised the same cry when video-cassette recorders came to market (see chapter 5). Disney and MCA sued Sony on the basis that VCRs were basically intended to steal movies and other restricted visual materials. Those same companies now gain major portions of their revenues from video-cassette sales and rentals--but some of them would still like to make it impossible for people to record on VCRs. Every home recording medium has raised the same claims, never backed by any definite statistical evidence, just as every successful home recording medium has improved the revenues of the entertainment industry.

The argument over DAT is another round of the same old story, this time enhanced by the fact that all DAT producers are Japanese: the entertainment industry can appeal to jingoism to support its own paranoia. The recent purchase of CBS Records (one of the major factors in anti-DAT lobbying) by Sony (one of the major DAT developers and producers) may help settle this political squabble.

When they do reach the market, DAT recorders will not be able to make direct digital copies of compact discs. DAT recorders are designed to use a different sampling rate than CDs in order to avoid the possibility of perfect digital copies. They will be able to make nearly perfect recordings, but the sound will still need to go through two conversions between digital and analog, inevitably losing some quality along the way.

DAT will cause more problems for libraries than CD. DAT is thin plastic tape with the same vulnerability as audiocassettes. Worse yet, DAT recorders use rotating heads, which will cause wear on the tape. Just as with videocassettes, DATs will not withstand in-definitely large numbers of playings. Finally, DAT lacks the fast random access and programmability of CDs, and while recording is a major advantage for some consumers, it can cause problems for libraries.

It is too early to predict the success or failure of DATs. Unless prerecorded DATs are close to the price of audiocassettes and players or recorders come down to the price of cassette players, DATs may appeal only to those who wish to make their own live recordings. For most others, regular cassettes may suffice.

SUMMARY

Digital audio marries the computer and the recording studio. Without advances in electronics, manufacturing techniques, and low-cost lasers, the high bandwidth needed for digital audio would prevent its use in the real world. With those advances and a single standard disc format, compact discs have started to displace vinyl discs.

Libraries can finally circulate serious music to serious music lovers and popular music to all varieties of music lovers, without endangering the equipment of the music lovers and without the expectation that most records will be ruined after a handful of circulations. The initial cost of CDs may be higher, but their useful lifetime should result in lower cost and better service to the listening patrons of libraries.

SELECTED READING

Brewer, Bryan, and Edd Key. *The Compact Disc Book: A Complete Guide to the Digital Sound of the Future.* San Diego: Harcourt Brace Jovanovich, 1987. 181 pp. Glossary; brief bibliography; no index. (A popular treatment that offers fairly thorough and consistently nontechnical coverage. Little or no consideration of supposed problems with digital sound.)

Connolly, Bruce. "The Compact Disc: Library Application of an Audio Revolution." *Information Technology and Libraries* 2, no. 3 (September 1983):279-85. (Very early commentary, much of which still applies. The early claims of player and disc invulnerability were exaggerated, but not the potential of CDs for library service.)

Hendley, Tony. *Videodiscs, Compact Discs and Digital Optical Disk Systems.* Hatfield, Eng.: Cimtech, February 1985. 208 pp. (Good overview of the systems, some of their applications, and some library-specific notes.)

Nakajima, H. et al. *Digital Audio Technology.* Blue Ridge Summit, Penn: TAB Books, 1983. 312 pp. (English translation of *Dijitaro odio gijutsu nyumon.*) Chapter bibliographies; index. (Four Sony engineers discuss principles and applications of digital audio in great detail. Includes more about error correction and actual design questions than most readers will wish to absorb.)

5

Videocassettes

Books carry text; several popular and standardized media carry sound, as discussed in the preceding chapters. Until recently, libraries found it far more difficult to provide media combining moving images with sound.

Before there were videocassettes, some libraries and library systems circulated motion pictures in 16-millimeter form, usually charging a rental fee, and frequently renting projectors together with the films. While 16-millimeter sound projectors became standard fixtures in schools, the expensive, bulky units were never seriously marketed for home use. The films are too expensive to duplicate, the projectors are expensive, and the process of setting up projector, speaker, and screen is clumsy and slow.

Many manufacturers worked on home playback systems for motion pictures for many years, seeing a huge potential market in renting movies and specialized programs. The next chapter takes up some of these efforts, including the one effort that has survived to the present day. As the history that follows notes, a number of different home videotape units were introduced before Sony finally produced a successful system in 1974. That introduction led to more than a decade of growth: tens of millions of American homes now use at least one videocassette recorder, and thousands of libraries use video in some capacity.

Libraries began to circulate audiocassettes shortly after they achieved commercial prominence; many added compact discs even more rapidly. Since relatively few libraries added video to their circulating collections until the last few years, the lag has been greater than that for other media.

There are several valid reasons for such conservatism, some of which are discussed later in this chapter. One important reason is a critical difference between the field of home video and the fields of audiocassettes and compact discs. Both of the latter entered the marketplace with a single universal licensed standard. By contrast, there have been several different videocassette formats. The current home marketplace includes five different standards in three incompatible families.

The growth of videocassettes and library acceptance of the medium have been slowed by incompatible competing standards, although the quality of videocassettes has been improved by the competition. Since most libraries waited until recently to circulate video, most circulating collections are likely to be mostly or entirely VHS, the dominant form. That decision fails to serve some portion of a library's patrons, but is quite defensible. The history of videocassettes, given later in this chapter, may help to show why multiple incompatible formats exist.

THE TECHNOLOGY

Audiocassette recorders use two or three fixed heads: an erase head, a record head, and a playback head or a combined record/playback head; the heads stay in one position as the magnetic tape moves past. But high-quality video recording requires a signal extending to 3 or 4 megaHertz, 150 to 200 times the bandwidth of audio. In order to achieve such bandwidth, magnetic particles must move past the recording head at a much faster rate.

One solution is to move the tape faster, which is what RCA tried in the early 1950s. The results are predictable: too much tape is required, and it must move too rapidly. Instead, a videocassette recorder (VCR) uses a spinning drum containing multiple recording and playback heads to record video and the recording heads move at an angle to the recording tape. The path of recording is helical; the recording is a series of diagonal strips along the tape. Recording heads are arranged in pairs, so that one will always be in contact with the tape as the drum is spinning. By combining the motion of the heads with the motion of the tape, VCRs achieve effective tape speeds in the low hundreds of inches per second, even though the tape actually moves at less than one inch per second.

Except for helical scanning, VCRs work in roughly the same way as audiocassette recorders. Electrical signals orient magnetic particles to create an analog of the original visual image and sound. Color video uses two frequency bands, one for brightness and one for color. Low-fidelity audio in VHS and Beta VCRs is recorded using a separate fixed head and a narrow track at the edge of the tape. High-fidelity audio uses different mechanisms in each variety of VCR, but always involves adding audio recording heads to the spinning drum.

The physical and electrical details of current VCR formats differ, but all use helical recording and low-speed cassettes. Beta and VHS recorders use half-inch-wide tape, twice as wide as audiocassette tape; eight millimeter recorders use tape that is eight millimeters wide, just a bit more than a quarter-inch. The U-Matic system used by some libraries for video production uses tape that is three-quarters of an inch wide, and professional videotape recorders typically use one-inch or two-inch tape.

Tape for video continues to improve, as it does for audiocassettes. Good videotape is similar to good audiotape, and may in some cases be identical. Eight millimeter and Beta ED (extended definition) formats require pure-metal tapes, while Super VHS uses extremely high-quality oxide tape. All legitimate videocassettes are produced to standards under license, as are all videorecorders. Videocassettes and VCRs require exacting precision: the recording track on a Beta cassette is only 60 microns wide--60 *millionths* of a meter, or roughly $^2/_{1000}$ of an inch.

A BRIEF HISTORY

Two decades of hard work, false starts, and high hopes resulted in the Betamax. Sony developed and marketed this innovative format, and a consortium of larger companies outmarketed Sony with cheaper recorders, longer recording, and lower quality. That sums up a long, complicated history with many interesting twists.

Table 5.1 and the following paragraphs summarize that history; anyone interested in the politics and other aspects of technology and mass marketing should read more of the history. The history of videocassettes more than justifies library conservatism in purchasing the new media, for many more formats failed than succeeded even temporarily.

Development (Successes in Bold)	Year
Toshiba: Helical scanning process	1953
Ampex: Working videotape recorder (VTR)	**1956**
Sony: first transistorized VTR	1961
Sony: first helical-scanning VTR	1961
Ampex: $30,000 "consumer VTR"	1963
Sony: first "home videocorder," CV2000	1965
Ampex: first practical color VTR	**1968**
Sony: U-Matic system (prototype 1969)	**1971**
Matsushita: half-inch videocassette (VCR)	1971
Philips: one-hour recording VCR	1972
Cartrivision VCR system marketed	1972
RCA: SelectaVision MagTape announced	1973
Toshiba, Sanyo: V-Cord VCR system	1974
Sony: Betamax (prototype 1974)	**1975**
JVC: Video Home System (VHS)	**1976**
VHS passes Betamax in sales	1978
Sony: HandyCam, first 8mm VCR	1985
Sony: Beta Hi-Fi	1985
JVC: VHS Hi-Fi	**1986**
JVC: Super VHS	**1987**
Sony: Extended Definition Beta	1988

Table 5.1: Some Highlights of Video Recording

Table 5.1 ignores some lesser developments and a number of failed VCR formats. It should be clear, however, that most attempts to market videotape recorders have been failures, either immediately or after several years. Ampex had the first clear success in videotape recorders, and Sony's U-Matic was the first VCR to achieve any lasting use.

The war between Beta and VHS has always been one-sided in the American marketplace, thanks largely to RCA's adoption of VHS. From 1978 to 1987 it was consistently true that Beta outperformed VHS but that VHS outsold Beta. By 1987 the sales margin was nine VHS recorders for every Beta recorder. The ongoing competition improved video for consumers, since JVC and Sony were always working to improve their formats under competitive pressure.

Initially only Beta had good slow-motion and stop-action. VHS overcame that disadvantage through sophisticated engineering. Later Sony developed SuperBeta to improve an already superior picture; VHS countered with HQ. Sony developed Beta Hi-Fi, bringing true high fidelity to video sound; VHS later developed VHS Hi-Fi. Then in early 1987 JVC went ahead for the first time with Super VHS, the first VCR with better quality than broadcast television. Sony has countered with Extended Definition Beta (even higher quality), but has essentially conceded the battle: ED Beta will be marketed for video professionals and semiprofessional use, not as a mass-market system.

The Beta-VHS war is largely over and VHS has won; even Sony introduced a VHS recorder in 1988. There are still seven million Beta recorders in the United States, however, so the format should continue to be useful for years to come. The battle of the formats also continues as Sony and several other manufacturers push eight millimeter video as the best medium for home videocameras. That means there are currently five active formats on the market: Beta, VHS, ED Beta, Super VHS, and eight millimeter. ED Beta recorders will play Beta tapes, and Super VHS recorders will play VHS tapes, but otherwise the five formats are all incompatible.

VIDEOCASSETTES IN LIBRARIES

Libraries can now produce videocassettes relatively cheaply, and inexpensive VCRs and camcorders should encourage wider use of video within libraries. Of course, inexpensive equipment does not lessen the need for careful planning and production in order to make videos worth watching. Good video production will always require time, experience, skill, and taste.

Some libraries already produce videorecordings for internal use, public relations, and public education. Some libraries also produce video for local cable channels or for local television. Every year, the Library & Information Technology Association's Video & Cable Communications Interest Group puts on a "Video Showcase" at the American Library Association Annual Conference, showing some of the recent library-generated videotapes. These tapes apparently range from amateurish productions to first-rate, broadcast-quality videos.

With the deregulation of cable television libraries may have fewer "broadcast" outlets for their video productions in the future, but that need not cause a decline in library uses for video. Video production no longer requires a studio or a large investment, although the entry cost to edit and produce broadcast-quality video is still high. With inexpensive VCRs and camcorders, libraries can and should consider video as a working tool. Medium-sized and larger libraries can easily afford the equipment needed to prepare training tapes, tape talks by celebrities, and storytelling sessions, and can use video in other ways to improve library operations and patron services.

Circulating Collections

It makes sense for libraries to circulate informational videocassettes that patrons would not otherwise be able to borrow or rent. Videocassettes for entertainment have as much place in libraries as genre novels--given demand and funds, they are perfectly appropriate. If libraries have been slow to develop circulating video collections, it may reflect not only the high cost of video (until recently), but also a realistic conservatism. Eighty-dollar movies are expensive compared to $15 novels, and, if a library needs to buy both VHS and Beta versions, the comparison is particularly unfavorable.

But many libraries have taken the plunge, and videocassettes circulate heavily at libraries that make them available. Those libraries with the space and money should seriously consider the special role of the library to offer videocassettes that would not be readily available elsewhere. There are thousands of instructional and special-interest videocassettes, many of them priced as low as $15 to $20; a collection of such videocassettes strengthens a library's role as an information center. There is nothing wrong with circulating today's "hottest" videos, but a library should go beyond bestselling videocassettes just as any responsible library goes beyond bestselling books.

Problems

Videocassettes need special care, but can work well in a typical library. Libraries face a few problems in dealing with videocassettes, but some of the problems can be solved or avoided and some are less serious than might be supposed.

Which Format?

Larger libraries should offer some special-interest cassettes in both Beta and VHS format, but libraries can reasonably concentrate on VHS. An average library can no more stock all videos in all formats than it can provide complete collections of literature in every language. But a library serving a population that is 10 percent Spanish-speaking should be expected to have some books in Spanish--not as many as in English, but a reasonable collection.

One would expect the same consideration for owners of Betamax recorders, since they are likely to represent at least 10 percent of a library's VCR-owning patrons. Yet many libraries with video collections buy only VHS. A curious form of favoritism is at work here, one that libraries should reconsider. While the analogy with Spanish-speaking patrons may not be perfect, it is valid. Of course, a library is under no obligation to provide materials for any VCR owners, but when a library holds hundreds of VHS cassettes and no Beta cassettes, Beta-owning patrons are being ignored by the library.

Eight millimeter cassettes do not yet represent a similar factor; very few prerecorded eight millimeter cassettes are available. To date the format is used primarily for home recording, and it seems likely that most eight millimeter owners also own either Beta or VHS decks. That may not always be the case, and libraries should keep that in mind.

Wear and Cost

Does your library rent videocassettes or circulate them freely? If the library charges a rental fee, what is the basis for such a fee?

A natural argument is that cassettes wear out rapidly, with all that friction between tape and head. Thus, a rental fee builds a replacement fund so that worn-out cassettes can be replaced and new cassettes can be purchased. Another natural argument is that cassettes are much more expensive than books and patrons should be expected to pay part of the cost.

Both arguments have some validity, but less than might first appear. Many videocassettes are becoming available at prices from $15 to $25, about the same as a typical hardbound book. And while cassettes do indeed wear out, some libraries find that they get more than 100 circulations from a single cassette. In that case the cost per circulation is likely to be no higher than for a hardbound book--after all, how many modern books survive 100 circulations intact?

Charges for patron services always raise difficult questions for libraries. The nominal charges likely to be assessed for videocassettes will not prevent patrons from using them. Anybody who can afford $300 for a VCR can afford 25 cents or even $1 for a cassette. I can't argue that libraries should *not* charge for cassette use, but the case for such charging is not clear-cut.

Erasure

One special problem affects audiocassettes and videocassettes alike, albeit with higher stakes for videocassettes: since both are magnetic recordings, both can be re-recorded. A patron can borrow a videocassette and bring back a tape that has nothing on it or some entirely different recording. The library's prized recording of *Citizen*

Kane could come back as two hours of Monday Night Football or, worse yet, the copy of *Snow White* could come back as *The Devil in Miss Jones*.

Any such change reflects malice, not clumsiness. A patron must deliberately override the record-protect device (an open hole on the case) on a videocassette or audiocassette in order to record over it. A patron can reasonably be held liable for such destruction, particularly since it cannot be accidental. Unfortunately, unless a library regularly plays back videocassettes when they are returned (an almost impossible task), the problem will not be discovered until the next patron has borrowed the cassette. At that point, the library should have separated the identity of the previous patron from the borrowing record, if the library wishes to respect the privacy of patrons. Since there have been no reports of widespread malicious re-recording of videocassettes circulated by libraries, it is fair to assume that the danger to privacy outweighs the small potential for damage to the library.

Performance and Copyright

Libraries should be cautious in using videocassettes for groups or allowing such use within the library. Motion picture producers feel strongly about performance rights. Libraries have as much right to circulate videocassettes as rental stores have to rent them, but libraries do not necessarily have the right to show videocassettes to groups: that may constitute public performance and infringe on copyright. Libraries concerned with this issue should refer to the excellent article by Debra J. Stanek cited at the end of this chapter.

SUMMARY

A large percentage of American homes now include at least one VCR. Video has as natural a place in public and some other libraries as sound recordings: to complement print and offer new services to the library patron. Videocassettes provide easy access to thousands of motion pictures and thousands of specialized programs; while video will never replace books, sound and motion offer a different form of information and entertainment that is also valuable.

Libraries can now use video cheaply, and should consider its possible value for training and other internal needs. Libraries need to consider how to circulate videocassettes, what mix of formats to offer, and whether or not to charge. Libraries also must have some sensitivity to issues of copyright, but those issues should not affect normal lending.

SELECTED READING

Bensinger, Charles. *The Video Guide*. 3d ed. Santa Fe: Video-Info, 1982. 254 pp. Glossary; index. (Covers an enormous amount of practical material in a somewhat erratic manner. Heavily illustrated.)

Lardner, James. *Fast Forward: Hollywood, the Japanese, and the Onslaught of the VCR*. New York: Norton, 1987. 344 pp. (Thorough treatment of the introduction and growth of consumer VCRs in the United States, with special emphasis on copyright, lawsuits, and the attitudes of the motion picture industry.)

Stanek, Debra J. "Videotapes, Computer Programs, and the Library." *Information Technology and Libraries* 5, no. 1 (March 1986):42-54. (Careful consideration of copyright issues relating to use and lending of videotapes and computer software.)

6

Videodiscs

During the late 1960s and throughout the 1970s, a number of companies worked to design video playback systems for the mass consumer market. Each company anticipated billions of dollars in revenues in an explosive market. Billions were never made, but hundreds of millions were lost as technology after technology disappeared into laboratory dead-ends or marketing fiascoes.

In the midst of this string of failures, one technology succeeded --not as a mass-market consumer product, but as a successful product for business, education, and industry with some consumer use. That technology, reflective optical videodisc or LaserVision, now sees growing acceptance as a consumer product thanks to its links to compact disc and compact disc-video. The only remaining videodisc system on the market may soon become sufficiently popular to warrant library support as a source of information and entertainment.

Several industries use industrial videodiscs for training and other purposes. Videodiscs find significant use as sales tools and in information centers; for example, Disney's EPCOT uses almost 300 players as part of a visitor information system. Museums, universities, and others produce videodiscs filled with photographs, paintings, film clips from space missions, and other combinations of sight, sound, and motion. In addition to school library use of instructional interactive videodiscs, some libraries have prepared videodiscs for instruction and preservation, and a number of libraries have used InfoTrac, a magazine index on videodisc. Videodiscs are coming back, although they never really went away.

LASERVISION TECHNOLOGY

Three different videodisc systems made it to market, either in the United States or in Japan: CED, LaserVision, and VHD. The only optical videodisc and the only one to use lasers is also the only one still on the market--LaserVision (LV), the Philips reflective optical videodisc system.

Disc Production

Videodiscs store analog signals; in the United States, videodiscs store NTSC (National Television Systems Committee) video signals. An LV disc the size of an LP can store 108,000 photographs or two hours of broadcast-quality video with CD-quality sound.

The Philips mastering process begins with a glass disc coated with a layer of light-sensitive material. This disc spins beneath a laser, which exposes spots that turn into pits in the coating. This is the same process used for compact discs, but the pits and lands have different meaning: the length and spacing of pits reflect the peaks and valleys of a television signal, a direct analog to the videotape used to prepare the disc.

LV discs typically have recordings on both sides; two surfaces are bonded together to make a finished disc. In the early years of LaserVision, the bonding process and other aspects of production yielded many defective discs, one of many factors that discouraged wide acceptance of the medium. Those problems have apparently been solved and industry use of LV continues to grow, with more than 2,000 consumer LV discs available in mid-1987. Since LV and CD discs require similar production facilities, some pressing plants produce both.

Playback and Control

All compact discs use constant linear velocity (CLV) recording--as do all videocassettes and audiocassettes. All vinyl discs use constant angular velocity (CAV). LaserVision supports both techniques.

Most home LV discs contain motion pictures, operas, rock concerts and the like; producers expect viewers to watch part or all of a program. Capacity counts for more than flexibility, since casual viewers don't want their movies interrupted every half hour. CLV videodiscs store one hour per side, or 108,000 video frames (30 frames per second, 36,000 seconds per hour). The player spins at a constantly changing speed when playing a CLV disc, from 600 rpm when playing near the outer edge of the disk to 1,800 rpm when playing near the center. CLV discs provide better quality video than videocassettes (except Super VHS and ED Beta) and high-quality stereo sound, sometimes CD-quality. But such discs are essentially a high-quality alternative to videocassettes.

Every LV player also plays CAV discs, with a much wider range of capabilities. A CAV disc always spins at 1,800 rpm. Each rotation covers exactly one frame, since there are 30 frames per second and 60 seconds per minute. Because the rotation speed is constant, a single frame can be located rapidly and played indefinitely as a still image. Control information (carried in the "vertical blanking interval," the portion of a video signal that is not visible on the screen) is always in the same place on each track, and can be read without delay.

CAV discs provide perfect stop-action or freeze-frame and can store photographs or encoded text as readily as moving images. A given frame can be reached directly, relatively quickly. The price for this speed and flexibility is capacity: a CAV disc contains 54,000 tracks per side and can, therefore, store only 30 minutes of video on each side.

For students of cinema, CAV versions can be enormously revealing. At least one company, Criterion, releases classic films such as *Citizen Kane* on sets of CAV discs; a student can study each frame or step through a sequence in variable slow motion. The producers can include commentary on a second soundtrack and, since most films are less than two hours long, can fill extra space with background material on the film. More recent films such as *Help!* and *Indiana Jones and the Temple of Doom* also appear on CAV discs. In 1988 Pioneer introduced an LV player with enough memory to store a complete frame, making perfect still frames from CLV discs possible; that technology does not, however, provide the fast access and flexibility of CAV.

Interactive Possibilities

One-half hour of video may not seem impressive, but 54,000 color images constitute a great deal of visual material. If a computer program can make use of those images as part of a game, a course of study, or a visual reference system, the single disc side becomes a uniquely valuable resource. Those 30 minutes of video can also be 180 10-second sequences or a mix of sequences and still images.

Most home LV players can support what is called "level one" interactivity. Users can get to any specific frame or to a marked chapter on the disc, and can use freeze-frame and slow motion. Murder mysteries, the National Gallery of Art "walking tour" (accompanied by more than 1,500 pictures of artworks), and a number of other interactive videodiscs have reached the consumer market.

More advanced players, largely for industrial use, can support "level two" or "level three" interactive programs. Level two systems contain their own microprocessors and can make use of digital information stored within frames to carry out a number of functions. (When digital information is stored on videodiscs, it is translated into a video signal, stored in analog form, then translated back into digital form on playback.) Level three systems work with separate computers and represent the most sophisticated uses of videodisc technology. The videodisc becomes a source of information for the computer and user, offering text, software, sound, still images, and moving segments to support a specific application. The book by McQueen and Boss and citations from *Information Technology and Libraries* and *Library Hi Tech* at the end of this chapter provide further information on interactive videodiscs.

SOME HISTORICAL NOTES ON VIDEO PLAYERS

Table 6.1 shows some significant points in the history of playback-only video development. Many systems were announced, a few made it to market, but only one survived.

Event (path to present in bold)	Year
Phonovision: first videodisc	1928
CBS announces EVR film-cassette player	1967
RCA announces Selectavision Holotape	1969
CBS brings EVR to market	1970
Telefunken/Decca announce videodisc	1970
CBS abandons EVR	1971
Telefunken/Decca demonstrate TelDec player	1971
RCA abandons Selectavision Holotape	1972
MCA demonstrates optical disc system	1972
Philips demonstrates optical disc system	**1972**
TelDec reaches market	1975
Philips and MCA: public demonstration	**1975**
RCA announces CED, a cheaper/simpler system	1975
Telefunken/Decca abandon TelDec	1976
Philips and Pioneer market LaserVision	**1978**
RCA brings CED to market	1981
RCA abandons CED system	1984

Table 6.1: Partial History of Video Playback Systems

J. L. Baird developed the first videodisc in 1928, recording 30 scan lines (an extremely crude image). In 1959 RCA began to investigate video playback systems, and Philips began work on optical disc technology in the 1960s.

The CBS Electronic Videorecorder (EVR) first appeared in August 1967 after five years of development. The system used film images rather than magnetic tape because Dr. Peter Goldmark, one of the developers of the LP record and head of CBS Labs, thought magnetic tape was too expensive. The 1967 announcement predicted $200 players and $7 film cassettes. CBS worked with Motorola (to manufacture players) and Twentieth Century-Fox (licensing films) to market the system in 1970. Unfortunately, the technology made no commercial sense. An electronic beam recorder was required to produce films, with expensive, erratic results, and copies had to be produced in real time (that is, it took an hour to make a copy of an hour-long film) using expensive equipment. The system could not survive the transition from laboratory to production line, and CBS shut it down in August 1971.

RCA pursued many paths toward a video player, always aiming for cheap players at the expense of quality and flexibility. The company announced Selectavision Holotape in September 1969, using holograms recorded on cheap plastic tape and reproduced with lasers. The demonstration showed poor pictures with interference patterns, barely detectable color, and sound supplied from a separate recording; the project was terminated in June 1972. Several other systems were attempted, culminating in CED (noted later).

Telefunken and Decca combined as TelDec to develop a videodisc system using flexible plastic foil discs, with relatively cheap players and discs with very short playback time (5 to 10 minutes). The system was marketed for one year before disappearing.

Philips demonstrated an optical disc system as early as 1972, using a laser and a disc able to play for 35 to 45 minutes. A public demonstration came in March 1975, at which point RCA proclaimed that its unfinished CED system was simpler to build and handle, thus superior for consumers. Philips made it clear that it was less interested in the mass market than in the medium itself, but the press had turned the situation into a "war of the videodisc formats."

At the end of 1978 a joint Philips/MCA system was finally marketed through Magnavox, a subsidiary of Philips, as LaserVision. Pioneer also introduced LaserVision players. Marketing was cautious, and consumer marketing never did succeed completely, but the system never left the consumer market. MCA eventually left the partnership and Philips temporarily withdrew from the American consumer market, but Pioneer kept the format alive. The format established itself in business, education, and industry with systems from Sony, Pioneer, Philips, and others, and has been successful in that marketplace.

RCA finally marketed its CED (capacitance electronic data) or SelectaVision VideoDisc system in February 1981, with assurances that it was in it for the long run. The RCA videodisc used a grooved disc and a stylus; it had none of the virtues of CAV LaserVision, and lower picture and sound quality than any LaserVision, but it was cheaper. The long run, in this case, proved to be 38 months: in April 1984 RCA discontinued videodisc player production. Even then, the company assured the half million who had purchased players that there would always be discs for them. "Always" turned out to be about two years and, by mid-1986, CED disc production had essentially ceased.

The most sophisticated videodisc system finally emerged as the only videodisc system, largely because educational and industrial use kept it alive. The future belongs to LaserVision if it belongs to any videodisc system; several companies have joined Pioneer in the consumer LV market beginning in 1987.

VIDEODISCS IN LIBRARIES

Videodiscs have unique value to store motion picture and visual information in a durable, readily accessible format. The Library of Congress and National Agricultural Library have both tested videodisc as a publishing and preservation medium, and to make archival materials available for research. The latter role is particularly interesting. Fifty-four thousand photographs or posters represent an enormous bulk of fragile material that could not be made readily available in the original. A disc version is not only readily available, but can be published for use in any number of libraries. The Avery Art & Architecture Library of Columbia University is carrying out a similar project to store architectural drawings on videodisc, with access through Research Libraries Information Network (RLIN) records. Bibliographic records can be used to call up drawings directly, providing a powerful tool for the study of architecture.

Should public and other libraries establish LaserVision videodisc collections? Fewer than one million LV players were in homes as of early 1988, but sales have risen sharply over the last year or two. Although the number of possible home users is still small, libraries can provide information on LV discs that would be impractical in any other medium. The Space Archives series from VideoVision Associates is an excellent example, containing discs of video clips, LandSat images, and other images based on NASA sources, providing a unique treasury of information at very reasonable prices. The National Air and Space Museum produces inexpensive LV discs containing huge quantities of aviation photographs: 100,000 on each disc costing $30 in 1988, supplied with index.

LaserVision may become more solidly established as a consumer medium. If there are five million players, some libraries will surely find that a significant percentage of their patrons have such players. Even now, libraries should consider the possibility of providing LaserVision players and discs for in-library use. The NASA and Air and Space videodiscs, together with collections of art, training discs, and other special sources, can provide a new dimension to library service for a modest investment. In early 1988 a player costs $500 or less, and discs run as low as $20 to $30.

Interactive videodiscs hold real promise as educational tools, and are already being used in some school libraries. Unfortunately such discs usually require not only the player but an accompanying computer and computer software. Public libraries may wish to consider interactive video systems when the systems become affordable and provide important services to public library users.

Advantages and Disadvantages

The advantages of videodiscs are clear: they provide a durable form of storage and high-quality reproduction of sight and sound. Since, like CDs, the laser never touches the disc during playback, videodiscs should survive heavy use quite well, much better than videocassettes. They are also typically cheaper than videocassettes, offer much higher picture quality than any prerecorded videocassettes on the market in early 1988, and offer fast random access to tens of thousands of still photographs, something videocassettes cannot do.

Historically, the greatest problem with videodiscs has been that too many versions were introduced, none of them successful in the mass market. Libraries did well to steer clear of the RCA disaster, and could reasonably avoid LV discs on the same basis. Videodiscs may have the same security problems as CDs, but are too large to fit into a normal pocket. At present, they also have the "advantage" that relatively few patrons would wish to steal them, since there are relatively few players.

Videodiscs cannot be erased, but can be damaged, and damage is almost always intentional. LV discs are quite durable but may be less durable than CDs (because they are laminated and more complex physically). The chief disadvantage at this point is that a library must provide player as well as disc if it is to serve its patrons.

SUMMARY

Libraries that specialize in visual areas should consider acquiring videodisc players and videodiscs. The players are inexpensive, as are the discs, and no other medium provides so much visual storage in so little space (or at such low cost). Videodiscs of photographs and artwork cannot provide the clarity and detail of art books, but a single videodisc can store as many photographs as 50 thick books. Few libraries could afford to buy a set of NASA photographic archives, even if any publisher could afford to publish them. But at $30 to $40 a disc (1988 prices), the videodisc series of NASA pictures, video clips, and satellite images can provide an impressive special resource.

SELECTED READING

Many articles on videodiscs have appeared recently and will appear in the future. This brief list includes two worthwhile monographs and two relatively early articles.

Graham, Margaret B. W. *RCA and the VideoDisc: The Business of Research.* Cambridge: Cambridge University Press, 1986. 258 pp. Index. (Fascinating history of RCA's long-term journey toward disaster in the field of proprietary video players. Based on information from within RCA and elsewhere, the history is actually too friendly to RCA in some details but well worth reading.)

Hessler, David W. "Interactive Optical Disc Systems: Part 1: Analog Storage." *Library Hi Tech* 2, no. 4 (Winter 1984):25-32. (Description of analog optical storage and its uses for information retrieval.)

McQueen, Judy, and Richard W. Boss. *Videodisc and Optical Digital Disk Technologies and Their Applications in Libraries, 1986 Update*. Chicago: American Library Association, 1986. 155 pp. (This study contains good detail on various disc storage systems with particular emphasis on their use in libraries.)

Sinnett, Dennis, and Sheila Edwards. "Authoring Systems: The Key to Widespread Use of Interactive Videodisc Technology." *Library Hi Tech* 2, no. 4 (Winter 1984):39-50. (Description of a commercial system for interactive videodisc. Posits videodisc as an alternative to books, which seems excessively optimistic.)

7

CD-ROM

Compact disc-read only memory (CD-ROM) is a new publishing medium with some unusual strengths and some important weaknesses. CD-ROM publishing can produce very large quantities of textual information at relatively low cost, and can potentially mix graphics, sound, computer software, and other nontextual items with text. A single CD-ROM can contain the textual equivalent of 1,000 books. That makes CD-ROM a powerful medium for certain uses, but does not make it a general replacement for books.

The first commercial CD-ROM product was marketed only to libraries, and the library field continues to have more *real* CD-ROM products (as opposed to announcements and prototypes) than any other field, at least as of this writing.

If audio compact discs represent the most successful new consumer product in decades, CD-ROM may represent the most oversold, excessively hyped new technology in many years. Underneath the hype, CD-ROM has real potential for libraries and special fields, but probably not the mass potential that some would predict. Librarians should understand CD-ROM because they have a great deal to say about the future of the field.

A BRIEF HISTORY

Philips and Sony, the patent holders for basic compact disc technology, established the precise specifications for compact discs in a published set of technical standards usually called the *Red Book*. Compact discs follow licensed standards established and maintained by Philips and Sony, assuring that all CDs and all CD players are compatible.

CD-ROM builds on the success of CD, using the same discs and essentially the same technology. A huge investment in research, development, manufacture, and marketing has made CD a success and brought the price down to modest levels. CD-ROM takes advantage of all that investment, particularly the cost of setting up pressing plants, to support a much different medium with, thus far, much more limited markets.

Event	Date
Philips/Sony: *Yellow Book* standards	1983
Exhibition of CD-ROM players, COMDEX	Nov. 1984
Library Corporation: *BiblioFile*	1984
Academic American Encyclopedia on CD-ROM	1985
First Microsoft Conference on CD-ROM	Mar. 1986
Microsoft *Bookshelf* issued on CD-ROM	1987

Table 7.1: Significant Events in CD-ROM History

Table 7.1 shows some significant events in the brief history of CD-ROM. Philips and Sony are both experienced at exploiting technology (i.e., putting techniques to work for as many markets and purposes as possible). With CD on its way to the marketplace, the two companies looked for other applications. A year after CD was first introduced, Philips and Sony produced the *Yellow Book*, a set of licensed standards for CD-ROM. Like the *Red Book*, the 1983 *Yellow Book* (available only to licensees) prescribes the precise physical characteristics of discs and playing requirements so that any CD-ROM is *physically* playable on any CD-ROM player, even if the computer is unable to make sense of the information.

The two companies first exhibited CD-ROM players at COMDEX, the Computer Dealers Exposition, in November 1984, and have since licensed the technology to more than 100 firms. The Library Corporation's *BiblioFile* (Library of Congress MARC data) was also introduced in 1984; similar data is now available on several other CD-ROM products from several suppliers.

The first consumer-oriented CD-ROM publication was a version of Grolier's *Academic American Encyclopedia*, the first consumer-oriented CD-ROM. Microsoft proclaimed the importance of the new medium in 1985 and sponsored the Microsoft First International Conference on CD-ROM in March 1986 in Seattle, Washington. Coincident with that conference, Microsoft Press published *CD ROM: The New Papyrus*. The conference and the book were both commercially successful and added to the hype surrounding CD-ROM. Other than a prototype CD-ROM issued at that conference, Microsoft's first real CD-ROM product, *Bookshelf*, was announced in early 1987 and came to market later that year.

The history of CD-ROM is just beginning. It is still an emerging technology in many respects, but some patterns may be clear. As the hype and oversell begin to die down, useful products for certain markets are emerging, even if none yet has the potential of a true best-seller.

THE NATURE OF CD-ROM

If a picture is worth a thousand words, an hour of music is equivalent to 90 million words. Like a CD (described in chapter 4), a CD-ROM carries a single spiral track as long as three miles. The three-mile spiral is one of those "gee whiz" facts that sounds more impressive than it really is. This book contains roughly one mile of text, if all printed lines are set end to end. *Webster's Ninth New Collegiate Dictionary* contains 12 to 14 miles of text. What is impressive is the *density* of information within the three-mile spiral. Three miles of 10-point type contains roughly 2 million characters; the CD-ROM spiral of pits can store some 275 times as much text per inch as the printed line.

CD-ROM is so closely based on CD that blocks of information are actually referenced by minute, second, and block: there are 75 blocks per "second," each block containing 2,048 characters or character-equivalents. Chapter 4 describes the makeup of CDs in more detail; while some details of groups and error-correction systems may not be identical for CD-ROM, most of the information in that chapter applies equally well here.

Since CD-ROM is read with a light beam, no physical damage should result from constant or continuous use. Like CDs, CD-ROM discs are not easily damaged. The life span of a CD is currently expected to be 10 to 25 years: not nearly enough to replace books, but certainly enough for a useful life. CD-ROM is designed for reasonably fast access to any point on the disc--no more than one second to any given block of 2,048 characters. That speed is possible only because each block is self-identifying, and can only be achieved once the CD-ROM player knows which block is wanted.

APPLICATIONS IN LIBRARIES AND PUBLISHING

CD-ROM is a publishing medium that requires an initial investment on the part of users. When publishers recognize the uses and limitations of CD-ROM and build appropriate markets, CD-ROM can succeed. If publishers fail to recognize CD-ROM limitations or identify appropriate markets, CD-ROM will fail.

Marketers must ask themselves: what information do people need and want in 500 million-character chunks? People don't buy books by the thousand, and would have no way to use them if they did; active readers may not have 1,000 books in their entire home library. A typical consumer has relatively little need for large-scale reference data. A good desk dictionary meets the everyday needs of most people. So why do they want a disc with 50 or 100 times the content of that dictionary?

Most likely, the answer is that they don't--particularly not with the following strings attached:

1. A consumer must purchase a CD-ROM player ($650 in early 1988 and unlikely to fall below $300 to $400 in the near future) to use the disc.

2. A consumer must have a personal computer (likely to be $1,000 or so in 1988) to use the CD-ROM player.

3. All reading must be done on the screen, with the computer and CD-ROM player turned on.

4. Currently, you can't assume that different CD-ROM discs can be used with the same retrieval software.

CD-ROM marketers are not asking people to spend $10, $20, or even $200 for this marvelous new medium. They're asking people to invest $1,500 to $2,000 or more for something that can be used only when staring at a screen in one room of the house. For that kind of investment, consumers need a fairly strong reason to buy. Fifteen hundred dollars will buy many books and gas enough for trips to the library when reference works are needed.

The Myth of the Home Computing Market

Mass-market CD-ROM may be as much of a dream as universal home computers, with as little chance of success. Those who expect mass markets for CD-ROM sound like those who (a few years ago) expected every household to have a personal computer. Some of the latter have moved into CD-ROM; curiously, some of them still believe that everybody will buy a PC when that "breakthrough program" emerges. Based on experience with home computers, this is a very doubtful scenario.

Will users of personal computers buy CD-ROM drives? Certainly. Will millions of PC users buy them? Almost certainly not, at least not in any great hurry. Will some publishers issue CD-ROMs that make money in the home market? Eventually, yes: it is possible to make money by selling a few hundred or a few thousand copies at a reasonable price. At $200, Microsoft's *Bookshelf* may be such a product. Will enough people buy CD-ROM players to make mass-market consumer CD-ROM profitable? That's impossible to say, but I would bet against it, at least if "mass market" means selling 100,000 copies or more.

The Mass Market Is Not the Only Market

CD-ROM can succeed as a product even if it fails in the mass market. Libraries should pay attention to the legitimate uses of CD-ROM, paying less attention to its potential for replacing print. *BiblioFile*, or some other set of MARC records, makes sense as a

CD-ROM product for some libraries, as do other CD-ROM products.

The arguments in favor of CD-ROM are clear:

1. CD-ROM can store enormous quantities of text and can include software, sound, and images (although sound and images take up much more space than text or software).

2. Shipping data or text in CD-ROM form is more economical than shipping it in any other form.

3. Although CD-ROM is still expensive to master, copies become quite inexpensive at relatively low numbers (in the hundreds). It is a good short-run publishing medium, well-suited to special products.

4. While CD-ROM access is much slower than hard-disk access, it is still relatively fast. With good indexes, CD-ROM can be a flexible and effective information retrieval medium, with no "line charges."

5. CD-ROM can only be used with a computer, making computer manipulation of CD-ROM data a natural part of CD-ROM use. Text retrieved from CD-ROM is already ready for word processing or other manipulation.

Many applications can already take advantage of these assets in a way that makes CD-ROM the best possible medium. More will in the future, as down-to-earth entrepreneurs and publishers seek effective uses for CD-ROM. CD-ROM has enormous potential to complement print, replace some microform sources, and either replace or complement online databases. Those publishers that search for best-sellers may fail, but those who recognize the special characteristics of CD-ROM should succeed. They will offer a new service with new advantages, one that can be offered at a reasonable price.

Libraries have already recognized the potential of CD-ROM to a surprising degree. When Research Publications, Inc. surveyed 20,443 library and information professionals, 4,859 said that they would have CD-ROM systems available at work by the end of 1987; 10,168, nearly 50 percent of those responding, said that CD-ROM would be in their libraries by the end of 1990. While the projections might be optimistic, 2,956 (more than 14 percent of those responding) already had CD-ROM available in the summer of 1987.

Overkill, Hype, and Reality

A cynic would say that the only people making money from CD-ROM are those holding conferences, selling special reports and newsletters, or consulting on its incredible potential. At least until recently, the cynic would generally be right.

Hype and overkill seem to come with every new technique and technology, particularly in these days when special-interest publications can pop up so rapidly and profitably. CD-ROM has had more than its share of "vaporware and paperware"--products that have no real market date or exist only on paper. It has also suffered from unrealistic expectations.

In 1988 it is possible that the cynical view will be wrong; as a sometime skeptic, I hope that is true. CD-ROM has much to offer, and its real strengths can be hidden or diffused by continuing hype. If too many people lose too much money through unrealistic expectations of the CD-ROM market, the whole marketplace could sour to the point where CD-ROM would become another Edsel or CED videodisc.

Many companies have announced CD-ROM products; quite a few even issued prototypes. Some companies have left the CD-ROM field as quickly as they entered it. For example, Digital Equipment Corporation issued a flurry of product announcements and prototypes not long before it decided that it should not be a CD-ROM publisher. Similar withdrawals from the market seem certain, as do failures of various magnitudes. Any new technology involves losses as well as gains; so far, CD-ROM appears to have fewer success stories than CD but a better history than teletext.

Some firms are making it work. Databases that would not work as well in another medium are appearing on CD-ROM. Good indexing schemes make CD-ROM valuable for many special uses, and further uses should grow. When people speak of CD-ROM replacing print, they are talking nonsense; when they speak of uniquely useful products on CD-ROM, they are seeing the future, a future that is largely available now.

What CD-ROM Should Do

Reference tools on CD-ROM can readily replace massive print sources, unwieldy microfilm, and usage-sensitive online databases, and libraries will find good ways to support such tools. Reference sources on CD-ROM offer the potential for access techniques nearly as powerful as online databases, access speed better than any microform product, and cost and space requirements much lower than print products.

Publishers of some print and online reference products may see CD-ROM as a threat rather than as an opportunity. Other publishers may see CD-ROM strictly as a new revenue source and may damage the medium by inappropriate attempts to maximize profits. Ideas such as charging for CD-ROM usage by retrieved citation could do much to stall its progress in libraries.

Fortunately, some publishers and vendors already recognize the ways in which CD-ROM can serve the mutual interests of publishers and libraries. Already, Bowker's *Books In Print Plus Reviews*, Wilson's *WilsonDisc* and Information Access's *InfoTrac II* show real uses for CD-ROM without imposing absurd charges. More specialized publications are also appearing, using the strengths of CD-ROM to good effect. We can expect many more in the future.

Most very large print reference products are rather clumsy to use and expensive to maintain. In many cases, the reference products are already computer-generated and could be produced on CD-ROM less expensively than in paper form, with more flexible access and more complete information. The disadvantages of CD-ROM don't matter for most large reference products. People don't browse *Readers' Guide* in a hammock in any case, and many such reference products use type that is so small that a computer screen may actually be easier to read. On the other hand, CD-ROM has real disadvantages when compared to print (see the following section).

It is reasonable to expect that CD-ROM will replace computer-generated microfilm for some library uses; CD-ROM is faster, more flexible, and much less annoying. It is also reasonable to expect that CD-ROM will replace many larger and more complicated print reference sources, where the printed product is unwieldy and expensive. Finally, CD-ROM should replace some online databases in Dialog, BRS, and other services--but only where patterns of use, creation, and time-sensitivity make CD-ROM a reasonable alternative.

PROBLEMS AND ISSUES

CD-ROM is currently a fledgling medium, scarcely surprising for a technology less than five years old. Beneath the hype and hoopla, some serious problems have continued to slow CD-ROM acceptance.

A Print Replacement

While a CD-ROM system (personal computer and drive) may take up less space than a set of *Readers' Guide,* and while an individual CD-ROM will certainly require much less space than the print equivalent, there are drawbacks to CD-ROM as a print re-placement, even for large reference products.

A multivolume reference set can be used by several people simultaneously, each working in a different part of the alphabet, just as dozens of people can use a card catalog simultaneously. For several people to use a single CD-ROM reference product simultaneously, a library must either invest in several players and several copies of the CD-ROM, or must install a networked CD-ROM system (given the slow retrieval speeds of CD-ROM, networked retrieval to a single disc may not even be realistic).

A library wishing to provide several CD-ROM services must also choose between purchasing a player and PC for each service, dealing with changing the discs, or using a "juke box" or multiple-player system. And unless the same software can be used for all of the CD-ROM services (unlikely, at least at this point), moving from one service to another will be difficult and disruptive.

These problems probably mean more to public libraries and smaller academic libraries than to large academic libraries (except that many large libraries are mainly clusters of smaller institutions). Smaller institutions cannot afford to have full-time CD-ROM specialists and may justifiably be wary of CD-ROM as a print replacement. If the publisher must prepare both print and CD-ROM versions, the price for CD-ROM is likely to be at least as high as for print. As with other "replacement" situations, the replacement becomes economical only when it becomes substantially complete.

An Online Replacement

CD-ROM has been touted as a medium to replace shared cataloging systems such as Online Computer Library Center (OCLC) and RLIN and as a replacement for online public access catalogs. In both cases, what should be a supplemental role has been marketed out of proportion to its real advantages and problems.

Both OCLC and RLIN provide much more member cataloging than LC cataloging, and much more information than will fit on a single CD-ROM or a small set of CD-ROM. RLIN, for example, would require as many as 70 discs to replicate its database and access mechanisms. OCLC, RLIN, and WLN (Western Library Network) all provide services going far beyond access to bibliographic data, and some of those services require online access to holdings, not simply bibliographic data. On the other hand, products such as WLN's CD-ROM sets can assist small and remote libraries in many tasks and can provide special resources for retrospective conversion: a supplement to and extension of the online system, not a replacement.

Similarly, CD-ROM catalogs can be effective interim measures on the road to online catalogs, can serve as effective backups, and can serve well for multi-institutional catalogs lacking online links. In other words, a CD-ROM catalog is basically a superior microform catalog. But CD-ROM catalogs do not replace online catalogs effectively; they can only provide current status information through links to an online circulation system and can only provide current acquisitions and cataloging information through hard-disk storage.

Even with such extensions, a CD-ROM catalog can rarely provide the flexibility and speed of access of a well-designed online catalog.

A Circulating Medium

Libraries should consider the possibility that they may eventually add CD-ROM discs to their array of circulating media, but should not be rushing out to establish circulation collections at this point.

Few libraries began to circulate compact discs until the last year or two, when there were already several million CD players in use. Few libraries began to circulate videocassettes until tens of millions of VCRs were in use, and relatively few libraries circulate software even now, with a few million Apple and several million MS-DOS computers in homes. As of early 1988 there may be a few thousand CD-ROM players in homes, or the total may be in the hundreds.

Libraries need not be in the business of moving ahead of public acceptance of a new media. The fate of CD-ROM in the consumer marketplace is still uncertain. Indeed, there is good reason to believe that CD-ROM will never succeed as a truly mass medium. If it does succeed to any real extent, it will take time and require resolution of the standards problems noted in the next section. For the next few years at least, it is unlikely that libraries would be offering any real service to their patrons by offering CD-ROM for circulation.

The Standards Problem

Before CD-ROM can be a successful publishing medium, it must be a *single* medium. If you need different players or even different software to use different discs, you don't have a coherent medium. The Philips-Sony *Yellow Book* sets forth a physical standard for CD-ROM discs and players: data format, track layout, disc diameter, type of rotation. That means that every CD-ROM disc is playable on every CD-ROM player, in the sense that the player can convert the pits and lands of the disc into a stream of characters or other information.

Early proponents say that CD-ROM works because it follows international standards; unfortunately, the international standards don't provide enough information to make discs interchangeable or readily useful. Several more levels of information are required to make CD-ROM useful:

1. Volume, file, and directory structure information: the "logical definition" of a disc. This level enables a microcomputer to find out what is on the disc and where it is.

2. Interfaces: the hardware connection between CD-ROM player and microcomputer, and the software that allows a microcomputer to control a CD-ROM player.

3. File content and data structure: what to do with the information on a disc. This is one level down from volume and file structure; it is the way that software can actually provide access to information.

4. Applications: indexes, command, and menu techniques, and how information will be presented to the user.

Standards are needed at the first two levels, if there is to be any hope of establishing CD-ROM as a flexible publishing medium. There should also be *available* standards for the third level, although some discs will necessarily use different standards. But until those three levels are sufficiently standardized to permit interchangeability, each CD-ROM is not only a different set of information but, potentially, requires its own special hardware and underlying software support (much as if each book was in a different language). The *Yellow Book* covers none of these levels and interchangeability is still quite limited among CD-ROM products.

The High Sierra Group

One such standard may be adopted and published by the time this book appears: a standard for the volume, file, and directory structure of a disc. A group of would-be publishers, vendors, and other interested parties met at the High Sierra Hotel and Casino in Stateline, Nevada, in early 1985 and began work on such a standard, calling itself the High Sierra Group or HSG.

The proposed HSG standard is detailed and extensive, and also open-ended enough to be used for storage systems other than CD-ROM. It includes specifications for a file structure volume descriptor, directory descriptor, file descriptor (directory record), and other basic information required to read individual files from a CD-ROM.

HSG gained recognition from NISO, the standards organization concerned with libraries, publishing, and information science. In 1987 the HSG proposal was balloted by the NISO membership as standard Z39.60; an identical proposal was balloted by the International Standards Organization (ISO). The published standard will establish the basis to develop additional standards and agreements so that publishers can create CD-ROM discs without having to establish complete CD-ROM systems.

SUMMARY

CD-ROM is a publishing medium, no more and no less. It may falter because of standards problems, unrealistic expectations on the part of publishers, or the failure to identify and target the proper markets. It may never succeed as a mass medium, but is likely to succeed within appropriate markets including libraries. Libraries have been uniquely important for CD-ROM since the beginning, and should continue to make good use of the medium while recognizing its limitations.

SELECTED READING

The following are just a sampling of the deluge of articles and books on CD-ROM, including those sources used in preparing this article.

Allen, Robert J. "The CD-ROM Services of SilverPlatter Information, Inc." *Library Hi Tech* 3, no. 4 (Winter 1985):49-60. (A vendor's view, but does show a typical library-oriented CD-ROM system in some detail.)

CD ROM. The New Papyrus. Redmond, Wash.: Microsoft Press, 1986. 619 pp. (A collection of articles, mostly by believers and proponents in CD-ROM. Presents a wide range of information and opinion, naturally slanted toward bright futures for CD-ROM. Only one writer seems to believe that CD-ROM will entirely replace paper, basically as an article of faith.)

Collier, Harry. "Optical publishing: a who-is-doing-what appraisal." *Electronic Publishing Review* 5, no. 4 (December 1985):245-256. (Good overview of CD-ROM principles and realities in late 1985.)

Helgerson, Linda W. "CD-ROM: A Revolution in the Making." *Library Hi Tech* 4, no. 1 (Spring 1986):23-27. (Brief, basic, clear.)

Jansson, Peter. "Patterning CD-ROM." *PC Tech Journal* 5, no. 7 (July 1978):163-73. (Detailed technical description of the High Sierra Group proposed standard, including some background. Not easy reading, but includes tables for the essential elements of the standard.)

Miller, David C. "Laser Disks at the Library Door: The Microsoft First International Conference on CD-ROM." *Library Hi Tech* 4, no. 2 (Summer 1986):55-68. (Extended report on the first Microsoft conference. Useful as background for Miller's *Special Report.*)

Miller, David C. *Special Report: Publishers, Libraries & CD-ROM: Implications of Digital Optical Printing* [available from the Library & Information Technology Association]. 1987. 99 pp. (Informal and very informative, if occasionally sloppy about facts not directly related to CD-ROM. Readable, interesting, reasonably well-balanced: Miller is not a "true believer.")

Murphy, Brower. "CD-ROM and Libraries." *Library Hi Tech* 3, no. 2 (Summer 1985):21-26. (Brief and somewhat a sales pitch, but a good basic introduction from a real producer.)

Schaub, John A. "CD-ROM for Public Access Catalogs." *Library Hi Tech* 3, no. 3 (Fall 1985):7-13. (Describes Brodart's *Le Pac*. The description seems to make it clear that, despite the author's statement, *Le Pac* is not really an alternative to an online public access catalog.)

Young, Jacky. "Integrating a CD-ROM into an Inhouse Library System: Sirsi's Lasertap." *Library Hi Tech* 4, no. 2 (Summer 1986):51-53. (Brief description of *BiblioFile* used as an integrated resource for cataloging on a local system.)

8

Digital Publishing and Optical Storage

CD-ROM is neither the first digital publishing medium nor the only current one; it is not even the first one to be used in libraries. A handful of other media, some in the marketplace and some still in the laboratory or in the minds of marketers, make up an alphabet soup of new possibilities. In addition to digital *publishing* media, some new technologies use lasers to provide storage (i.e., to allow users to save information).

The two most important digital publishing media have already been covered: compact disc and CD-ROM. Media and techniques included here fall into three general categories: alternatives to CD-ROM for distributing text and software, CD-based systems that go beyond text and software, and optical media that permit user-defined storage, not simply retrieval.

The first category includes one disc medium already used in some libraries (digital laser disc), two announced products that have not reached the market (OROM and DataRom), and one curious medium that combines low price and somewhat limited usefulness (the Cauzin data strip). The second category includes three variations on CD: compact disc-interactive (CDI), compact disc-video (CDV), and digital video interactive (DVI). The final category consists of two subcategories: write-once optical media and erasable media.

DIGITAL LASER DISC

Several vendors introduced laser discs for software, text, and other forms of storage before CD-ROM appeared. One such medium uses the same 12-inch videodisc as LaserVision and an industrial

LaserVision player, and several library applications have appeared using this technology, including the original *InfoTrac* and a 1985 version of *Mini Marc*.

LaserVision-based digital laser discs do not use a straightforward digital storage technique. Instead, digital information is transformed into a standard video format and recorded on the analog disc in the form of a television program.

Digital laser discs have much more capacity per disc than CD-ROM: about 40 percent more on one side of a disc, and both sides of a disc can be used. As with CD-ROM, digital laser discs and players are relatively inexpensive because they are essentially identical to LaserVision discs and players. That similarity is one strength of digital laser discs, but also a critical weakness. While LaserVision is sufficiently successful in industrial and special marketplaces to have an assured future, it has not achieved the consumer success of CD. As a result, players remain more expensive than CD equipment, particularly players with the digital interfaces needed for use with computers. Discs are also more expensive and likely to remain so.

At one point in the early 1980s, producers of digital laser discs promised a bright future and even suggested that libraries might wish to circulate such discs to their patrons. That future did not develop, and the introduction of CD-ROM seems sure to limit 12-inch digital laser discs to specialized markets. Note that 12-inch laser information systems *do* have a commercial presence, in the form of write-once optical discs, discussed later in this chapter.

OROM AND DATAROM

If OROM and DataROM were computer programs, they would be called vaporware: announced and publicized systems that may or may not exist, but can't be purchased.

OROM, optical read only memory, was announced by 3M (Minnesota Mining and Manufacturing) before CD-ROM came to market. 3M was to develop the medium, a 5.25-inch (diskette-sized) disc; others would build the drives and market the system. IBM has been thought to be involved in OROM development. 3M's activity in this area is natural, since the company operates one of the first optical disc pressing plants in the United States, and was the first to press CD-ROM domestically on a commercial scale.

OROM has about the same capacity as CD-ROM, but much better access speed: around 150 milliseconds compared to the 500 milliseconds of CD-ROM. The higher speed is roughly equivalent to floppy disk, still much slower than the 15 to 60 milliseconds of contemporary hard disks for personal computers.

A similar medium was announced by Sony under the name DataROM. Although Sony is a co-owner of the basic CD and CD-ROM technology, the company felt that a higher-performance medium made sense. The product has somewhat similar characteristics to OROM. There is no indication of when, or whether, either OROM or DataROM will ever be marketed. These media have no apparent significance for libraries, at least in the short term. If either one is eventually marketed, it will face tough competition from CD-ROM.

CAUZIN DATA STRIPS

Cauzin data strips use ink on paper to distribute digitally encoded text and software. Innovative and inexpensive, the technology has real but limited uses and an uncertain future. Cauzin strips carry machine-readable text and software as light and dark patches of ink on paper. The modestly priced reader translates the patterns back into data so that a computer can manipulate the text or run the software.

Specific Uses

Cauzin strips give periodicals a good way to provide small programs and manipulable text in machine-readable form, and offer flexible archiving capabilities. When Cauzin Systems was actively marketing the system, it published ads in computer magazines with small computer programs printed in each advertisement as Cauzin strips; if you purchased a reader, you could use the programs. Cauzin Systems clearly hoped that computer magazines would print programs as data strips.

PC World does exactly that, as do some smaller magazines. As with several other computer periodicals, *PC World* includes computer software in almost every issue: templates for spreadsheets, useful routines, complete utilities to make computing easier. Cauzin data strips enable users to load the programs without hours of tiresome keying or attempting to reach overloaded online bulletin boards--but only if users own Cauzin readers. It is a chicken-and-egg problem: most magazines won't add extra pages for Cauzin strips unless they know that a fair number of readers can use the information, and most readers won't buy Cauzin equipment unless they know that a steady stream of strips will appear.

Within the library field, *Library Hi Tech News* has publicized and used the format. The "Search Strategy Index" and "Information Technology Review" sections of each issue, consisting of bibliographic citations arranged by subject, also appear as Cauzin strips. Libraries with readers can build cumulative bibliographies in machine-readable form.

If a company has laser printers, Cauzin readers, and the appropriate Cauzin software, it can print its own strips; the strips can be photocopied and remain readable. It is possible to send machine-readable information from place to place using this technique, although that does not appear to be a good use. For small quantities of information, telecommunication is faster than mailing strips and not likely to be much more expensive. For large quantities of information, Cauzin strips are bulky and annoying; diskettes will work much better.

But companies don't keep every document active forever. Typically a document (or spreadsheet or other machine-readable text) is prepared, revised, and eventually filed away for historical records or possible later reuse. The paper copy is filed in a filing cabinet together with associated documents. The machine-readable copy represents a problem because it takes up space on a disk and may be difficult to associate with the paper copy. That's where Cauzin strips can be useful: the company can print out the strip version of a document and store it in the same folder as the paper copy.

Problems

The chicken-and-egg problem is difficult to overcome, particularly when a technology has a rather narrow area of use. After a flurry of early marketing activity, Cauzin Systems have almost disappeared from public view, which may be understandable. A typical home or business computer user is unlikely to find a great many occasions on which Cauzin data strips would be a perfect solution to a real problem.

For those librarians who think the technology is interesting and would like to experiment, the good news is that the equipment is inexpensive. If Cauzin disappears from view, the library will be out only $200 for the reader and software. If the library has a laser printer and adds the extra software, it can keep using the archiving capabilities. Libraries have at least one ongoing source of strips in *Library Hi Tech News* to use for experiments.

COMPACT DISC INTERACTIVE

The Philips-Sony team never stops looking for ways to exploit a technology. They dropped a bombshell at the first Microsoft CD-ROM conference in February 1986: compact disc-interactive (CDI). A new book, the *Green Book*, was made available to those wishing to license this new medium. Early news reports suggested that CD-ROM was dead now that CDI was on its way; those reports were wrong, as better-informed observers realized. The early announcement of CDI was a curious one for the co-founders of CD and CD-ROM, but it represented a set of technical standards, not a product entering the marketplace.

CDI combines text, software, audio, and video information on a single CD and can combine audio and video simultaneously, which CD-ROM cannot do. CDI can be used to store sound at various levels of quality, from CD quality (at the same 72 minutes as CD) down to very low quality with the ability to store hundreds of hours of voice-quality sound on a single disc.

The *Green Book* goes far beyond specifying recording standards. It also specifies data types, interfaces, and the microprocessor and operating system used to read CDI discs. The standard defines a complete playback system, one that permits the user to work interactively with the disc--thus the name. The microprocessor (the Motorola 68000) is a popular and powerful one, used in the Amiga, Atari ST, and some Macintosh computers; the operating system, a version of a system called OS-9, is not at all popular.

The Philips-Sony team considers CDI to be a home information appliance with commercial and educational uses--an appliance rather than a computer peripheral. Only computer users can use CD-ROM; CDI will be marketed to those who are not interested in computers. The powerful computer is built into the player.

CDI will be "downward compatible." A CDI player will also handle CD-ROM, although the reverse is not true. On the other hand, there is no assurance that CDI will actually make it to the marketplace. Two years after its introduction, it continues to be little more than a set of specifications. Libraries need not worry about CDI until and unless it reaches the marketplace. If it does, the discs will pose the same problems and potential as CD and CD-ROM, no more and no less.

COMPACT DISC VIDEO

Compact disc video (CDV) is yet another Philips flourish. A CDV disc combines 5 minutes of live-action video (with CD-quality sound) with 20 minutes of CD-quality sound without video. CDV won't play on a standard CD player since the player has to spin 10 times as fast for the video portion, but CD discs will play on a CDV player.

Five minutes of video and 20 minutes of sound are a curious combination, basically the equivalent of a "video single" (as might be seen on MTV) and one side of a typical popular album, or a complete extended play disc. CDV is no real threat to CD, no relation to CD-ROM, and not related to CDI. It isn't an information medium, but a peculiar form of entertainment.

The apparent market is teenagers, affluent teenagers, since CDV players will cost quite a bit more than CD players. A CDV player requires roughly the same properties as a LaserVision player. In fact, to date the "CDV" players on the market are really Laser-Vision-CD players, able to play 12-inch LV discs, 8-inch LV "singles," 12-centimeter CDV discs, and 12-centimeter CD discs.

That's good news for Pioneer and for LaserVision because CD caused more interest in laser media, considerably increasing sales of LV players, and CDV may continue that trend. On its own, CDV is a peculiar medium of no more (and, potentially, no less) use to libraries than 45rpm singles. Libraries that circulate such singles may eventually find themselves circulating CDV discs, but surely no sooner than they begin circulating LaserVision discs.

DIGITAL VIDEO INTERACTIVE

The sensation of the 1987 Microsoft CD-ROM conference was an announcement and demonstration from RCA Labs. Using special compression techniques and custom computer chips, RCA demonstrated full-motion video from a prototype CD-sized disc. The company asserted that one hour of color video with stereo sound could be stored on a single CD, and called it digital video interactive (DVI).

RCA recognized that video, like any other visual material, can be compressed quite heavily through the proper techniques. If you look closely at a still picture on a television screen--or at a printed image--you will see that relatively little of the image changes from one horizontal row to the next. If a way can be found to store *changes* between adjacent lines, rather than storing complete lines, it should be possible to store 10 to 100 times as many video frames on a single disc. That technique, called "delta compression" (*delta* representing the *difference* between lines), is one of several effective means of compressing visual data and other highly repetitive data.

RCA clearly stated that it was not demonstrating a market-ready system; it wished to "solicit early feedback on the technology and its future commercial developments." The company was also, almost certainly, out to slow down the progress of CDI.

When will DVI be available? Possibly not for several years, and maybe never. If DVI ever does reach the market, it will have the same significance as any other entertainment medium: libraries may, at some point, find it worthwhile to offer the medium for circulation. But it has no special uses for libraries.

WRITE-ONCE OPTICAL DISCS

Philips produced the first write-once optical digital disc recorder in 1978. Many other optical recording systems have been developed since then, and some libraries, notably the Library of Congress, have already used such recorders for a variety of purposes. Two prevalent terms can be used for all write-once optical media: direct read after write (DRAW) and write-once read mostly or write-once read many (WORM). This discussion will use either DRAW or write-once.

How DRAW Works

Write-once media come in several sizes, usually 12-inch diameter in early products, but including CD-size (12-centimeter or 4.72-inch), 5.25-inch, and other sizes up to 14-inch. Several materials can be used to support the recording medium: frequently plastic (as in CD), but also glass or aluminum. The supporting layer is called a substrate. The recording medium coats the substrate, usually a transparent protective layer (possibly more glass or plastic) covers the recording medium, and air or vacuum may separate the medium from the protective layer. In CDs, the information is pressed into the plastic itself and the reflective surface is added after the pressing. In write-once media, the plastic (or glass or aluminum) is simply a way of supporting the recording medium.

Recording media fall into three general categories:

1. Thin metal films based on tellurium, gold, and platinum or other compounds and alloys are evaporated or sputtered onto the substrate. The recording laser can cause pits or bubbles in the metal; tellurium suboxide will change to a crystalline form under the light. In either case, the reflectance of the material changes distinctly.

2. Plastic coatings containing light-sensitive dyes will show distinct changes after exposure to focused light, resulting in the optical equivalent of pits or bubbles.

3. Granular media of various sorts, including silver halide emulsions and textured media, also change reflectance upon exposure.

In each case a relatively powerful laser changes the recording surface; a weaker laser (or one not as sharply focused) can then read the changes. Information is read as it is written, or immediately thereafter, so that errors can be detected immediately. If a block of data shows errors, it will not appear in the disc index but will be rewritten elsewhere on the disc. Error-detection-and-correction codes such as those described in chapter 4 are also used to improve accuracy.

Once written, a write-once optical disc functions in a way that is similar to a read-only disc; it is even possible to use both types in a single player, if other physical characteristics are identical. As of this writing, there are no 12-centimeter writable discs readable on CD-ROM players, but such a configuration would have obvious advantages for the growth of DRAW.

Write-once media have definitely reached the marketplace, but with such a profusion of incompatible systems that prices have remained high and sales have remained small. There is no write-once equivalent of CD or CD-ROM, no single medium with detailed standards used by many companies and taking advantage of consumer product development. One March 1985 report on Japanese producers lists 9 different systems using two different sizes of disc, and 9 different combinations of substrate and recording medium and capacities ranging from 500 megabytes to 1.8 gigabytes (billion bytes) per side. Other systems range as high as nine gigabytes for a single disc. In all, at least two dozen different DRAW designs have been introduced or announced.

A DRAW system is in some ways like a slow magnetic disk, but with the peculiar quality that there is no direct way to erase or rewrite information. A file can be "rewritten" by writing a new version on a blank portion of the disc and providing directory information pointing to the new version, but the old version will always remain.

DRAW recorders store digital information, which can be text, software, graphics, or sound, just as in other digital media. Most current DRAW systems have even larger capacities than CD-ROM (because they typically use larger discs and both sides of a disc), making storage of graphics more realistic.

Potential Uses

Libraries can use write-once discs to preserve textual and visual information and to back up online databases. DRAW discs present a distinctive set of strengths and weaknesses with several attractions for libraries. If a library could be assured that discs and recorders for a particular version of write-once discs will be available for years to come, several uses make sense.

Archival

As an archival medium (i.e., a way to preserve text or images from brittle books or from materials that must be discarded), DRAW discs are imperfect but have clear uses. With a typical capacity of one billion characters or more, or 10,000 pages stored as images on a single disc, DRAW offers more compact capacity than microfilm; it also offers much faster access and more pleasant use.

The life expectancy of DRAW discs is unclear: almost certainly a decade or more, but possibly not more than 15 to 25 years. During that period, DRAW discs should stand up to heavy use. Thus, DRAW discs may be useful to make archival materials available while the originals are stored in a protected environment. Additionally, since DRAW storage is digital and can be copied without alteration, a relatively infrequent program of copying could assure an indefinite life span for the information on each DRAW disc.

Other

DRAW discs attached to microcomputers could serve as backup catalogs for online catalogs; write-once discs could also be used in place of CD-ROM where the number of copies to be created is small. These uses and others take advantage of the relatively good access speed and enormous storage capacity of DRAW. If a library can create a DRAW "snapshot" of its online catalog every week or every month, it can offer an acceptable alternative to the online catalog for two uses: system failure in the online catalog itself and, more likely, bibliographic access at sites where connection to the online system is unworkable. As with CD-ROM catalogs, the DRAW version will not be as good as the online catalog: it will have slower access and will either offer no information on circulation or, possibly worse, out-of-date information.

DRAW recorders could also be used to maintain audit trails in various library and computing applications, and for backup in the event of disastrous failure. For cases where auditability is needed, DRAW can be very valuable since the data can't be altered once it has been written. For backup, DRAW offers faster access than magnetic tape and much less chance of loss of the backup copy.

The adoption of DRAW for the most interesting potential use is dependent on pricing. There are a number of cases in which libraries wish to share information; many union lists are now produced on microfilm or paper, with a few on CD-ROM. CD-ROM is the best of these media in terms of ease of use and storage capacity but, as a publishing medium, it is ill-suited to applications where only a few copies are needed. If DRAW drives (or read-only drives able to read DRAW discs) become moderately priced and the discs themselves become inexpensive, DRAW discs could serve well in such applications.

Problems

If a library or group of libraries commits to DRAW technology for preservation, a crucial assumption is that blank discs will continue to be available and that the drives can be repaired or replaced over a long period. No such assurance can be made at the moment. Given the general chaos of the DRAW marketplace, it is fair to assume that many of the systems currently available will disappear. Philips introduced the technology but abandoned the field in 1982; others have come and gone.

Price is also a major problem. DRAW discs will probably always be much more expensive than CD-ROM or CD discs, since they require a much more complex manufacturing process. In the absence of a single, widely marketed standard, prices for DRAW drives and discs will stay high and systems may not stay on the market. Given this situation, libraries must be cautious about committing to DRAW.

This is not to say that write-once optical systems have all been failures. Several thousand document-image storage systems have been sold using several different write-once media, using drives that typically cost about $10,000. While no such system has been an overwhelming success, write-once optical systems do have a presence in the marketplace.

IBM introduced a DRAW drive in April 1987 as part of its PS/2 microcomputer announcement. The drive, to be available as an internal drive in PS/2 models or as an external drive for other computers, is expensive as PC components go (about $3,000) but relatively inexpensive for a DRAW system. If the IBM drive does come to market and IBM makes it widely available, it will be the first broad marketing of a DRAW system. That effort could lead to competitive but compatible drives, widespread acceptance (that is, tens of thousands or hundreds of thousands of drives), and the inevitable reduction of prices. The result could be to make DRAW a current technology of real use to libraries.

Such a result is in no way assured. The marketing has not begun, and IBM's record in the personal computer marketplace is mixed at best. It is not clear that most business users see any good use for DRAW; IBM needs to make the drives available, but also to show customers why they need them. IBM's commitment to any given product is also uncertain and, at this point, no other company seems to be in a position to make DRAW technology widely accepted and cost-effective.

Other Write-Once Media

Drexler Technology markets the LaserCard, a plastic credit card with an optical strip rather than a magnetic strip. The optical strip can hold two megabytes or a few images. Some information can be prerecorded when the cards are produced; other information is added in the field. Typical uses of LaserCards are to store extensive information on the holder of the card and store transactions and updates. Blue Cross of Maryland may be the first large-scale user of LaserCards. Other optical cards, some offering much higher storage capacity, are in development but not on the market.

LaserCards are relatively inexpensive compared to DRAW discs, but offer much smaller capacity. Two megabytes is roughly equivalent to three medium-length books, which is more than enough space to store a person's medical history and leave room for additional transactions against Blue Cross, but is certainly not enough space for "all the textbooks and assignment sheets a student would need for a semester's work," to cite one proposed use. Even if a student used only three 100,000-word books in one semester, which seems absurd, a typical textbook will contain graphs and illustrations. Illustrations require much more storage space than text: a *single* high-quality, full-page color illustration could not be stored on a single LaserCard without sophisticated compression techniques.

Several laboratories are apparently developing digital optical tape. The only advantage of digital optical tape would be enormous capacity. Access speed would be much worse than on CD-ROM or DRAW discs, and it would appear to be more expensive and difficult to reproduce digital tapes. Prices, availability, and uses for optical tape are all unknowns at this point.

ERASABLE DISCS

Think of an erasable optical disc as a hard disk with much slower access, higher capacity, better durability, and unknown prices (hard disks [magnetic disks] are discussed in chapter 15). Realistically, erasable optical discs simply represent a direct alternative to magnetic disks. Erasable optical discs have not yet emerged from the laboratory; when they do, their success and usefulness will depend on price, availability, and speed.

That's all that libraries need to know now, and all they need to think about if erasable discs do eventually emerge from the laboratory. An erasable disc is a random-access storage medium. It will have the following advantages and disadvantages when compared to magnetic storage media:

1. *Speed.* Current projections are that the fastest erasable optical discs will be slower than DRAW discs (i.e., probably well over 100 milliseconds). Moderately priced hard disks for home use now offer 28-millisecond access; those speeds are improving, and faster magnetic disks are already available. For direct access, an erasable optical disc will perform at speeds comparable to a floppy disk.

2. *Capacity.* If a small, modestly priced optical system can store one gigabyte per disc, it would have capacity advantages over small magnetic disks in 1988. But that advantage is precarious as scientists and engineers continue to improve magnetic disk capacity, with IBM already announcing laboratory demonstration of a potential tenfold increase in capacity.

3. *Durability.* Optical drives should be extremely crash-resistant since the recording medium is protected from physical contact.

4. *Density.* While optical drives may not offer a significant capacity advantage over magnetic media (for a given drive), they may offer better density, making them better suited for offline storage and for shipping large quantities of data from place to place. Assuming that erasable optical discs are removable, it should be possible to store incredible quantities of semi-archival information in very small spaces, something that is not possible with direct-access magnetic media. It should also be feasible to mail a disc containing a gigabyte (one billion characters) of information for a few dollars.

5. *Price.* This is the great unknown. It seems unlikely that erasable optical drives will be less expensive than typical hard-disk drives, but the removable erasable disks should

be much less expensive than removable hard disks or other magnetic media for equivalent capacity.

Curiously, the most advanced developmental systems for erasable optical discs are hybrid optomagnetic systems: they use both optical and magnetic technologies for recording and playback. In the meantime, pure magnetic disk systems continually improve in price, speed, capacity, and durability. In order for erasable optical discs to succeed, they must offer clear competitive advantages for more than a handful of users, which may be difficult to do.

SUMMARY

Digital media are no different from other forms of technology. Many technologies are introduced, few succeed, and even fewer have special significance for libraries. At this writing, of all the current and proposed digital publishing media, only CD-ROM seems to have a good chance of reaching a wide market.

Libraries have clear uses for economical optical disc recorders, either write-once or erasable. Cautious libraries are in the difficult position of deciding when a particular writable medium seems certain to survive for more than a year or two.

For this year and next, libraries need not concern themselves with any optical media other than compact discs and CD-ROM. With luck, the next five years will find an emerging write-once medium that libraries can use for preservation, archival, and other purposes. That future is not assured; a market with 24 incompatible systems is one with little chance for success. IBM's re-entry into the optical disc marketplace should be watched with cautious interest.

SELECTED READING

Hessler, David, and Jerry Miller. "Print: A New Medium for Distributing Machine-Readable Information." *Library Hi Tech News*

28 (June 1986): 1, 7-10. (Clear description of Cauzin Softstrips and reader, with examples of current and possible uses.)

Pezzanite, Frank A. "The LC MARC Database on Video Laserdisc: The MINI MARC System." *Library Hi Tech* 3, no. 1 (Spring 1985): 57-60. (Vendor's description of an early digital laser disc library publication, which replaced 2,800 diskettes with two laser discs.)

Slonim, Jacob, Dennis Mole, and Michael Bauer. "Write-Once Laser Technology." *Library Hi Tech* 3, no. 4 (Winter 1985): 27-42. (Good description of write-once optical media.)

Sources in the previous chapter may also be relevant for these media. Some of the information for this chapter came from David Miller's *Special Report* cited in the previous chapter.

9

Software for Lending

Should a library circulate computer software? Libraries that answer "no" can readily justify the decision. Software typically does not provide information, but tools to manipulate information; most programs have more in common with typewriters than with books.

Some libraries may wish to add software as an extra public service; others need to cope with software that comes along with books, a fairly common practice in books on specific microcomputer topics. Still others may be faced with an apparent demand for software lending and be unsure what steps to take. Libraries that add software to their circulating collections may find more problems than benefits; nothing will solve all the problems, but a few simple rules can avoid some problems.

SOME PROBLEMS WITH SOFTWARE FOR CIRCULATION

Software may cause more problems as a circulating medium than any other medium. This discussion includes some, but probably not all, of these problems. The problems range from minor to severe; at least one of them argues strongly against circulating most commercial software.

Which System?

Most patrons in most libraries don't have computers at home, and those who do have a number of different types of computers, which are incompatible (software for one type won't run on another type).

A music lover will probably have a cassette deck and a turntable and, by 1990, many will have CD players. But most computer users have one computer, and very few have computers of more than one type. As a result, any selection of software for a single type of computer inherently excludes the majority of computer users.

Consider some of the incompatible types of computers likely to be found in homes in 1987: MS-DOS or PC-DOS computers using 5.25-inch diskettes, including IBM PCs and hundreds of other brands; MS-DOS or PC-DOS computers using 2.5-inch microdiskettes, such as IBM PS/2 models and many portable computers; the Apple Macintosh series; the Commodore Amiga series; the Atari ST series; several partially compatible Apple II models, from II to IIGS; the Commodore 64 and 128; the Radio Shack Color Computer; and a bewildering variety of older computers. Varieties listed here--each type essentially incompatible with every other type--include only those currently available and likely to be in at least 100,000 homes. Older incompatible types that sold widely for home use include several Radio Shack TRS-80 models; the Timex/Sinclair computers, the Texas Instruments TI-99; CP/M computers from Osborne, Kaypro, and many other smaller companies; and earlier systems from Atari and Commodore.

The current list includes at least seven *major* categories of mutually incompatible computers. Including older units, the number jumps immediately to more than a dozen--requiring a dozen different sets of software. Which patrons will a library serve, and which will it exclude? If circulating software includes expensive items, a library's choices involve real discrimination in favor of one group of users and against others, and very few libraries can really afford to stock all available "flavors" of software.

More libraries probably use Apple IIs than any other type of computer, just as more schools use Apples than any other type. More Commodore 64s have been sold than any other single computer. There is no good way of predicting the most widely used computer in homes, although the general numbers suggest that MS-DOS compatibles may outnumber any other single category.

Is It Legal?

The biggest problems with software lending are legal and ethical. Most commercial programs come with license agreements that restrict use of the software to one computer or one user. The wording of the licenses states that the act of opening the package, either the shrink-wrapping around the binder or a sealed diskette envelope, constitutes agreement with the licensing provisions.

"Shrink-wrap licenses" (as such agreements are called) may or may not be binding; the issue has not been thoroughly tested in the courts. But if a program's single-computer license is legal, lending the program may be *inherently* illegal. Lending any program that carries such a license places the library in jeopardy, and some companies aggressively defend their licenses by prosecuting known violators.

Some programs have friendlier licenses. Borland may be the best example: its license makes an explicit comparison between the program and a book. The purchaser of a Borland program can sell it, lend it, take it from one computer to another--but must assure that the program is not used simultaneously on more than one computer. As the license says, it isn't possible for two people to read one copy of a book simultaneously.

Can a library lend Borland software such as Turbo Pascal, Sidekick, Turbo Basic, or Reflex? Legally, yes, at least as I read the license. The question that arises is why a patron would borrow a program. Sidekick, Reflex, and the Borland language compilers are tools that a computer user would use for months and years; it would be quite unusual to have a single three-week need for such a program. I can conceive of only three reasons for borrowing a productivity program:

1. To evaluate the program for purchase--a legitimate reason, but not typically the function of a library.

2. To carry out a special project--possible, but unlikely in most cases.

3. To copy the software for continued use--almost certainly the typical case.

The third reason demonstrates the ethical problem. The most plausible reason to borrow a productivity program is to copy it, and it is illegal to copy most commercial software. It violates copyright and constitutes direct theft of the software company's product.

A good lawyer could readily assert that any library maintaining a lending collection of commercial software does so with the near-certain knowledge that such software will be copied illegally. That may make the library an accessory to theft and violation of copyright, and it could be hard to defend against such a charge. In my mind, this single issue overshadows all other problems with software for circulation. It does not mean that a library cannot or should not circulate software; it does mean that a library should be cautious about circulating normal commercial software. The second portion of this chapter will discuss software that is suitable for lending, a field of circulation in which libraries can offer a real service at relatively low cost and low risk.

Technical Processing and Circulation

Software causes problems of technical processing and circulation that are not unlike the problems posed by other nonprint media. A particular program may have different titles on the box, the diskette, the manual, and the opening screen; new versions come out frequently and may or may not represent new editions requiring recataloging. Diskettes can appear as accompanying material in books, and many programs on diskette will themselves be accompanied by books--sometimes several books and a collection of other material with a single set of software. Security systems may damage software, and diskettes can be damaged accidentally or intentionally during use. None of these problems are unique to software.

SOLVING AND AVOIDING THE PROBLEMS

No easy solution exists for the sheer diversity of computer types; a library must decide which types it will support, and may wish to poll users as to their equipment.

There are three general solutions to the legal and ethical problems that surround the circulation of most commercial software. One solution is to post appropriate signs and leave the ethics to the users, trusting that software companies would not choose to sue libraries. A more cautious solution, if somewhat impractical, is to contact the software suppliers, inform them that your library wishes to circulate their software, and ask for appropriate permission or licensing guidelines. The third solution is to avoid circulating standard commercial software.

Avoiding the legal and ethical problems doesn't necessarily mean abandoning the idea of software for circulation. Thousands of programs can be circulated with no ethical or legal misgivings and at little cost to libraries. Many programs are in the public domain or copyrighted but free for copying, and many more programs can be freely distributed but ask for donations from those who continue to use them.

Demonstration Versions

Some software companies produce special demonstration or evaluation versions of their programs. These versions typically differ from the regular versions in one of two ways:

1. Demonstration versions lead the user through an explanation of the program's features and a sales pitch for the program, but don't actually let the user do any work.

2. Evaluation versions permit the user to use some or all of the functions of the program, but restrict the work in some manner. A word processing program may not support printing or saving to disk; a database manager may allow only 20 records to be entered; a program may have a counter that allows it to be used only 5 times. Most evaluation versions also have some instructions for use, since the full manuals won't be available.

Libraries may be able to circulate such versions without ethical or legal difficulty. On the contrary, companies might be delighted to make such programs available to libraries since they are essentially a form of advertising. Programs with use counters won't work well for circulation, but other forms could serve to help users evaluate programs. A library may not feel that distributing a form of advertising is part of its mission, but some libraries may find evaluation versions to be reasonable offerings.

Public Domain and User-Supported Software

Libraries can offer thousands of programs for every major computer in almost every category, free for the copying with no legal or ethical questions. A library may choose to circulate such programs knowing they will be copied, or may offer the programs for on-site copying rather than circulation.

Programs available for general copying fall into three categories: public domain software, where no rights are claimed by the author; free copyrighted software, which can be copied but typically not sold for profit or used in commercial software; and an important category called freeware, shareware, or user-supported software.

Producers of all three categories share the attitude that users should be able to try software before they buy it. All three typically come with documentation that can be printed out from disk files. Among them, the categories include a number of programming languages, business software, utilities to handle special jobs within a computer, and a surprising breadth of special-purpose programs such as the Yale Catalog of Bright Stars, a massive public-domain database of astronomical data. Games, graphics, and sound appear in these categories, too: thousands of games, and some remarkable efforts in graphics and sound.

Public Domain Software

In the early days of microcomputing Ward Christensen developed a simple telecommunications program called MODEM, and he wanted to be able to send program files, not simply data files. To do that reliably he needed an error-detection protocol, so he wrote one--XMODEM. The whole project was part of a hobby; he placed the routine and the program in the public domain. XMODEM continues as the most widely used error-detection protocol in microcomputer telecommunications; almost every commercial program incorporates it, as does the current version of MODEM. XMODEM is also the earliest well-known, public-domain software.

Many people who write microcomputer software do it for fun or for challenge. When they write something useful or entertaining they want to show others what they've done, but don't intend to market it. The results are public-domain software: programs made available with no copyright or claim of ownership. Good public domain programs become community projects: other programmers improve the code, incrementing version numbers and returning the new program to the public domain.

Public-domain software reaches computer users through online bulletin boards, user groups, a few small companies that copy such software, and other similar means. Commercial companies may take public-domain code and incorporate it into their programs, or may take a public-domain program and call it their own, selling it for profit. The distinguishing characteristic of public-domain software is that copyright notices do not appear; instead, some opening screens carry the name of the author and an explicit placement of the code into the public domain.

Free Copyrighted Software

The term public-domain software usually includes free copyrighted software, but this category is actually slightly different. Programmers and companies may choose to make software available free, but retain some control over it. The most common controls are that the software may not be resold as a commercial product and that the software may not be incorporated into other software without a specific license.

Programs of this nature will carry a copyright notice on the opening screen and usually in the printed documentation. The copyright notice will include wording that allows free or low-cost copying of the program and free use, but reserves certain other rights.

An extremely broad set of software falls into these two categories, with several thousand programs available for each of the most common types of computers. The distribution channels are the same as for public-domain software: bulletin boards, user groups, and small copying firms. Examples include hundreds of utilities, small programs that serve specific purposes for a given machine; many versions of the classic computer games "StarTrek," "Adventure," "Life," "Dungeon," and others; assemblers, interpreters, and compilers for Pascal, BASIC, FORTH, LISP, PILOT, and other languages; text editors; accounting and database management systems; telecommunications programs; templates for spreadsheets and commercial database managers; and almost anything else you might think of. Some possible channels for locating such programs include *PC Magazine*, which develops extremely useful utilities and makes them available as free copyrighted software; companies that release old versions of programs into the public arena; and programmers who offer "trial runs" of new ideas for comment and use.

User-Supported Software

The third category of software suitable for ethical copying uses the same distribution channels as the first two, but has two different characteristics:

1. This category includes quite a few programs as powerful and complete as most programs in the normal commercial sphere.

2. Programs in this category are, in fact, commercial; those who find the programs useful are asked and expected to pay a registration fee (typically $25 to $90), usually in return for printed documentation and support.

To put together one example, a PC-DOS computer owner could set up a fully powered system using nothing but PC-DOS itself and a group of user-supported programs such as PC-Write, a powerful word processor; PC-File+, a straightforward database management system with modest relational capabilities; PC-Calc, a spreadsheet program powerful enough for most home use; ProComm, one of the most powerful telecommunications programs; and PC-Outline, one of the best of the outline processing programs.

An ethical user will pay for these programs, but the companies both permit *and encourage* users to give free copies to other users. The request for registration appears on the opening screens or in some other place in the program; if users don't like the programs, they simply stop using them.

Providing Software that Can Be Copied

Libraries may choose to circulate disks of public domain and user supported software or to provide them for copying within the library. In either case the library should establish a coherent system for storing the disks and providing a list of available software. Some libraries may choose to provide full cataloging for the software; others may use a simple listing. Since this software typically will not come with printed documentation, libraries need be concerned only with the disks themselves.

Good sources of software include the distribution companies such as PC-SIG and local user groups. Libraries would do well to contact various local computer user groups; the groups may be willing to provide free organized sets of software to encourage computer use, and may even volunteer the labor to organize the collection and support its use. Academic libraries may find that computer science departments are good sources of software and will almost always have active user groups.

Programs from *PC Magazine* and similar sources must generally be obtained from electronic bulletin boards, and can be downloaded safely from those sources. In other cases bulletin boards may not be good sources of software. The microcomputer community has its own sociopaths, and some of these people get their kicks by putting out public-domain programs that will destroy the programs already on a user's computer. Typically, such programs are disguised as useful utilities or even as newer versions of established public-domain programs. Such programs, usually called "viruses" or "Trojan Horse programs," should not appear in user group libraries or in the catalogs of distribution companies, but will appear at times on electronic bulletin boards until the board operators have a chance to recognize and delete them.

The Glossbrenner book cited at the end of this chapter provides a wealth of information on public-domain and user-supported software, such as what it is and how to obtain it. The edition cited is old, but most of the ideas are still valid.

If a library has CD-ROM players and can attach one to an MS-DOS computer, the library can provide a special service for MS-DOS users. PC-SIG sells a $300 CD-ROM disc containing thousands of MS-DOS programs; that disc can serve as a master source to produce most of the public domain software an MS-DOS user would ever want. The disc also has the advantage that it can't be accidentally erased or damaged through normal error or clumsiness.

SUMMARY

When it comes to circulating most commercial software, the best advice for libraries is one word: don't. But libraries can serve their computer-using patrons at relatively low cost by obtaining public-domain, free copyrighted, and user-supported software and making it available for copying. Software freely available for copying covers most categories of computer use, with very high quality offerings in many areas. Such software eliminates legal and ethical problems for libraries, leaving only the problems of technical processing, circulation, and deciding what computer systems to support.

SELECTED READING

Except for the Strauss article, all citations below deal with freely copyable software.

Crawford, Walt. "Common Sense and Free Software: or, If It's Free, Can It Be Any Good?" *Library Hi Tech* 3, no. 3 (Fall 1985):47-56. (More details on free and user-supported software, with some examples.)

Glossbrenner, Alfred. *How to Get Free Software.* New York: St. Martin's, 1984. 436 pp. Index. (Clearly written and full of good information. Even if some sources may be outdated, the advice will steer a library toward good sources of legally copyable software. Highly recommended.)

Michels, Fredrick, Neil Harrison, and Douglas Smith. "User-Supported Software for the IBM PC." *Library Hi Tech* 3, no. 2 (Summer 1985):97-106. (Good brief discussion of shareware and descriptions of older versions of some important programs.)

Strauss, Dianne. "A Checklist of Issues to Be Considered Regarding the Addition of Microcomputer Data Disks to Academic Libraries." *Information Technology and Libraries* 5, no. 2 (June 1986):129-32. (An excellent list of issues to be considered in housing software for in-house use or for lending.)

10

Preservation

Books and other media preserve records of facts, thoughts, fantasies and accomplishments--in other words, the record of civilization. That preservation depends on the durability of the media themselves. One function of libraries is to disseminate these records; another is to maintain them for future use. The latter role requires conservation and preservation--two related areas that we will call preservation in this brief discussion.

Preservation works at three levels: artifact, image, and information. Technology plays a role at all three levels, in recognizing problems and finding ways to solve them.

Preservation is most successful when an artifact can be maintained in its original form and kept useful. A book is more than the sum of the pages within; the physical artifact has its own value, although it is a different sort of value than that of the text. Preserving books in their original state may be expensive, difficult, or even impossible, but is a goal worth seeking when conditions permit.

If maintaining the artifact is not feasible, good preservation maintains the exact images contained within the artifact. There are many ways of preserving images, with different definitions of what constitutes an image and what constitutes adequacy. The most obvious ways to preserve the images within a book are to rebind pages that are themselves durable and to produce high-quality facsimile editions. Most other image preservation techniques lose some qualities of the original, descending to a level where image preservation overlaps the third level.

The lowest level of preservation retains the characters contained within a book or periodical, but loses the image and the artifact. Those who see books as nothing more than ways of transmitting information see this level as ideal, particularly if the information becomes machine-readable. For sound recordings, the distinction between image and information is difficult to make and may be irrelevant.

THE PROBLEM: DETERIORATING MEDIA

A book is useless if the print is not visible, and nearly useless when the pages crumble, crack, or fall out of the binding as they are turned. Scratches reduce usefulness in microfilm and vinyl recordings and could make software totally useless. Other forms of damage make materials harder to use or, as with stained and discolored photographs, intrinsically less useful.

Damage can happen in a devastating manner--the Los Angeles library fires and the 1966 flood in Florence or, on a smaller scale, the many "minor" cases of library flooding. Most damage to library collections comes slowly, as paper becomes brittle through the "slow fire" of chemical deterioration, discussed in chapter 1.

Nothing lasts forever, and libraries commonly discard materials. But such destruction is planned destruction, not the wholesale unplanned elimination of a century's written record. There is surely nothing about the literature of 1830 that makes it inherently more lasting than the literature of 1930, except that it was printed on alkaline paper. Technicolor films of the 1930s and 1940s may not have more lasting significance than color films of the 1960s and 1970s, but they will have truer colors at the millennium, simply because the cheaper color processes that drove Technicolor out of the market are inherently susceptible to fading.

Paper and Bindings

Acidity promotes destruction in paper, but is only one of the factors that cause books to deteriorate. Light, particularly ultraviolet light, can discolor paper and make it brittle. Heat promotes chemical reactions, speeding up processes already taking place. Humidity causes problems when it is too high or too low, and particularly when conditions vary between dry and moist. Air pollution can help to oxidize paper; dirt and sand make the pages dirty and attract moisture. Mold and mildew will grow readily on books, destroying them in the process; insects will destroy bindings and pages. All these factors interact to make things worse.

Organic materials such as paper and most bindings tend to deteriorate more easily and more rapidly than inorganic materials, but alkaline paper properly bound and maintained in archival conditions can last for centuries. Typical acid paper will last one-half century, but various destructive forces can shorten the life of a book much more rapidly. Poor bindings play a part. Even the best bindings will deteriorate, but badly bound books fail more rapidly in use, as pages separate from the binding and too-tight bindings encourage readers to damage book spines.

Film

Film deteriorates in three ways: physical and chemical problems damage the image on the film; mishandling damages the image and the film itself; some films self-destruct. The third situation is most dramatic: most film produced between 1890 and 1930 used cellulose nitrate as a base, and cellulose nitrate decomposes. In the later stages of decomposition, particularly when tightly stored, the decomposition is dramatic: the film bursts into flame, providing oxygen to sustain its own fire and producing toxic gases that damage other materials.

That's the extreme case. The only solution is to copy the photographs to "safety" film and get rid of the originals. The cellulose acetate that replaced nitrate film also deteriorates, shrinking and separating from the emulsion (the image), but more slowly and without endangering surrounding materials. The polyester-based film used since 1965 appears to have good prospects for longevity.

A long-lived carrier does not assure long-lived images. When film is not processed carefully, processing chemicals may remain and cause the image to deteriorate. Light, heat, and the other enemies of paper will also damage film, and different forms of film (e.g., silver, diazo, vesicular) are susceptible to different forms of environmental damage. Most recent (post-1952) color motion picture film contains unstable images, as do many still color photographs, because the colors fade.

Films transferred to videocassette become magnetic recordings. The colors will not fade in a chemical sense, but videocassettes do wear out. Films transferred to optical disc become optical media and, as discussed in the next section, optical media are too new to have predictable life spans.

Sound Recordings

Opinion varies as to the life expectancy of cassette and reel-to-reel tape. The tape itself, typically polyethylene terepthalate or Mylar, is fairly long-lived, although cassette tape tends to stretch and break more often because it is thinner than reel-to-reel tape. Earlier recording tape used base materials such as acetate that could become brittle and break quite easily. Tape does warp when stored incorrectly, but the information on the tape is more of a problem. In addition to the problem of erasure, which can be caused by any strong electromagnetic field, there is the problem of print-through. The information on tape is itself an electromagnetic field; the recording on one layer of tape may influence the adjacent layers. For this and other reasons, most magnetic recordings deteriorate over time.

Vinyl is a fine archival medium but a terrible medium for use. Under proper storage conditions, a vinyl disc can be expected to last for decades, possibly centuries. But every time a needle contacts a groove, there is potential for damage. Every time the record is cleaned, the grooves may be abraded or chemicals may act on the vinyl. If the record is *not* cleaned, dirt will collect and be ground into the vinyl by the stylus. Heat will warp vinyl discs as will storage in anything other than an upright position. Every public library with a collection of sound recordings knows the situation: vinyl discs rarely survive many circulations or playings in good condition.

Compact discs, videodiscs, and other optical media may prove to have extremely good archival qualities, but it is too early to tell. The 10- to 25-year life span predicted for them is hardly archival. The materials used for optical media should have extended life spans, but experience already shows that some optical media can "delaminate," with different layers separating, thus making the recording useless. The great advantage of digital media, whether optical or magnetic, is that they can theoretically be re-recorded for many generations without any loss of information. The artifacts and the original recordings may have shorter life spans than vinyl, but the ability to make perfect copies can mean a virtually infinite life span for the information. Finally, optical media provide longer *useful* life than other sound recordings: ordinary use, even casual use, will not normally result in any damage.

PRESERVING THE ARTIFACTS

Circulation and preservation represent two library priorities at odds with one another. When the goal of preservation is to maintain the artifacts, one basic principle is to minimize disturbance: changes in temperature, changes in humidity, excess light, or excess handling. Any use of materials disturbs them, and circulation adds uncontrolled disturbances.

That conflict leads naturally to two types of library collection: those collections designed primarily to preserve the materials, and those collections (by far the majority) designed primarily for use. But the areas must overlap: preservation without use is pointless, and use without preservation is (in the long run) impossible.

Why It Matters, When It Matters

If you believe that libraries exist only to collect and disseminate information, and that information resides solely in the text of a book, this section will be meaningless. Why worry about the book itself? What matters is its contents.

Even the cheapest book club imprint says something about the economics and other conditions of a given era. Every book has some value as an artifact. The effort to conserve at least one copy of each dime novel is a sensible effort: such "trivial" publications say much about the way things were.

When should the artifact be preserved? First, when that is the cheapest and fastest way to preserve the contents. Second, when preservation of the artifact will aid future scholars. Third, when failing to do so will reduce the value of the contents. Unfortunately, there are no easy ways of knowing when any of the three apply.

Mass Deacidification

Damage is almost always irreversible, in paper as in other materials; if a book is already brittle, eliminating the acid will not make it less brittle. Deacidification makes most sense for relatively new books, where deterioration has not yet begun. The goal of deacidification is to neutralize the acid conditions existing in paper and to leave an alkaline balance or reserve, so that the paper will not return to an acid condition and continue to deteriorate.

Conservators can deacidify books one at a time, usually page-by-page, using aqueous chemical solutions. That process is slow and expensive. Several nonaqueous methods have been proposed and tried for mass deacidification--taking large quantities of books and converting the paper to an alkaline state--including vapor phase, morpholine, Wei T'o, and Diethyl Zinc. As we shall see, some were successful and others were not.

Vapor Phase

Vapor phase deacidification (VPD) involved pellets in pouches to be placed in boxes, or envelopes used to interleave a book. In either case the pellets or envelopes created an alkaline gas that permeated the paper. Unfortunately the gas itself appeared to pose a health hazard, and did not create any alkaline reserve in the paper.

Morpholine

The Barrow labs, where the research was done that identified acid (rather than wood pulp as such) as the culprit in self-destructing paper, also worked on solutions to the problem. They developed a mass deacidification process using morpholine, an organic ammonia-based solvent.

Unfortunately, morpholine did not stand up well under extended testing. It does deacidify paper, but the morpholine will leave the paper in a week or two with no alkaline residue; there may be health hazards as well. The process has disappeared from active investigation.

Wei T'o

The Wei T'o process begins as books are dried in air, then vacuum-dried. The books are soaked in a solution containing methoxyl magnesium carbonate, forced into the pages under pressure. Flash drying and evacuation recover most of the solvent; the books are then warmed and restored to air. They recover normal levels of moisture before leaving the treatment facility.

Wei T'o requires vacuum chambers and will damage some inks and binding. Wei T'o can cause slight yellowing of wood-pulp paper, can damage sized paper slightly, and can cause some inks to feather or smudge. The solvent itself is not explosive or apparently hazardous. The Wei T'o process has been used in Canada for several years.

Diethyl Zinc

The Library of Congress has, for some time, been studying the use of diethyl zinc (DEZ) for mass deacidification. Like Wei T'o, the process requires drying and a vacuum chamber. Unlike Wei T'o, the process does not involve soaking the books: the agent is used in gaseous form. The treatment cycle is lengthy (eight days--much longer than Wei T'o) and somewhat expensive (as is Wei T'o), but appears to yield good results.

The big problem with DEZ is that it ignites when it contacts air and explodes when it contacts water. That makes it difficult to transport; mixing the liquid form half-and-half with mineral oil appears to ease the problem. It is also dangerous to handle, and a major fire occurred at LC's first DEZ test facility.

Both DEZ and Wei T'o show some promise, and some problems. DEZ has yet to reach production stages, but strengthens paper more than Wei T'o and has no apparent side effects on paper or binding.

Mass deacidification and individual means of conserving and preserving books will work only before extensive damage has been done. Damage can't be reversed except by copying or transforming the object. Even mass processes are expensive: the lowest estimates are $3 to $6 per volume, not including transport. That is much cheaper than microfilming, but is still a significant added cost.

Nonprint Materials

For most nonprint materials, preservation means proper storage and minimal use: film, vinyl discs, and magnetic tape all last longer when stored in a controlled environment. The proper environments differ, but for each medium the greatest enemies of long life are use and changing environmental conditions. Optical discs may be the exception to this rule, but only time will tell.

It is not enough to store preservation copies and forget about them. Magnetic tape will last longer if it is wound and rewound (at playing speed) every year or two. This process helps to prevent both physical deterioration (packing and deformation of the tape) and magnetic deterioration through print-through. Some experts believe that vinyl discs should be rotated every few years--turned so that a different part of the disc rests on the shelf--because vinyl may flow very slowly, just as very old windowpanes show the effects of the slow flow of glass.

Nonprint materials as artifacts fall into strikingly different categories. Few would argue that cassette tapes have strong aesthetic value apart from their sound. The labels on some vinyl and other discs have special value, and record jackets have definite aesthetic values, but relatively few discs have any special meaning as objects. Photographs and prints, on the other hand, couple artifact and content: a copy of a photograph or lithograph is not the same as the item itself.

PRESERVING IMAGES OR INFORMATION

When books can't be preserved in readable condition, the next best solution is to preserve their contents, both the intellectual content and, if possible, the images within the book.

Images of Print

If a deteriorating book is still in print, or is available in a new edition, the logical choice is to purchase a new copy to replace one that is no longer usable. Where preservation of images is an issue, current editions are unlikely to be available. In the case of historically important editions, newer versions of the same *text* may not have the same *images*, and the distinction may be important.

Facsimile Reproduction or Reprint

Reprints may not fully preserve images, but good reprints and facsimile editions offer very good means of preserving images. But facsimile production and reprinting is expensive. Few libraries can take on such projects internally, and unless a publisher sees a large market, facsimile editions may be expensive or economically unfeasible. Reprints and facsimiles should themselves be long-lasting. They should use paper that meets the requirements for alkalinity and strength stated in *American National Standard for Information Sciences--Permanence of Paper for Printed Library Materials, ANSI Z39.48-1984*, and should be properly bound for long life.

Photocopy

Any library can copy items that are deteriorating and have the copies bound. For an item of significant local interest, particularly one that will be heavily used and is not available in printed form, this method of preservation may be ideal. When properly done, a photocopied book or magazine may have a long life; Xerox estimates that properly fused Xerographic images should survive for a century or more, since the fused toner is relatively insensitive to the environment. Presumably, other good-quality electrostatic plain-paper copies should do about as well. Acid-free, archival-quality paper is readily available for plain-paper copiers. Wet-process copiers and other copiers that use special paper are *not* likely to produce long-lasting copies; in any case, the resulting books will be unpleasant to use.

Good photocopies will retain the complete image of black-and-white text pages and line illustrations, but will generally lose some of the quality of halftone photographs in books. Color copiers are becoming more available, but are unlikely to be found in every library in the near future, particularly with reproduction quality sufficient for true image preservation. But when circumstances permit and the costs are reasonable, photocopied books offer a good preservation option.

Microfilm

Microfilm is definitely the preservation method of choice for the large-scale coordinated projects now taking place. Once a book has been filmed, new working microfilm copies can be made from preservation masters easily and cheaply. One library can film a book that may eventually be needed by dozens or hundreds of libraries. Unfortunately, microfilm does a poor job of preserving subtleties; illustrations other than line drawings will not usually reproduce well on common microfilm, since it is high-contrast and will eliminate most shades of gray. It is possible to produce color microfilm and microfilm capable of reproducing images more perfectly, but most in-library and commercial microfilming projects do not do so--and there is no economical way to produce paper prints on demand from color microfilm. The other weaknesses of microfilm were discussed in chapter 2; while it is an essential preservation medium, it will never be the most desirable one.

Optical Media

Libraries should soon be able to store images on optical disc, preserving the images with some loss of resolution. In the near future a library could reasonably use an optical scanner to convert page images into digital information, then store that information on an optical disc. Scanners limited to black-and-white are already quite inexpensive ($1,500 for high-quality units in early 1988); color scanners have appeared at $3,000 or so. Optical scanning--digitizing--is not the same as character scanning, where the text of a book is converted to machine-readable characters. Simple scanning results in images, not characters; the reader can then view page images on a screen or reproduce them on a laser printer.

Optical media may provide more compact storage than microforms, the media are easier to work with, and use should not cause deterioration. On the other hand, the cost of production is currently much higher than for microfilm; writable optical discs cannot currently be reproduced as easily as microfilm; and optical discs may not last as long as microfilm. Both microfilm and optical scanning reduce image clarity from that of the original page.

Text Without Images

If the text is all that matters, optical character recognition offers the most compact, cheapest to reproduce, and most easily manipulated form of preservation.

An image of one page of this book, stored at 300 dots per inch resolution, requires roughly 420 thousand characters of stored information. The *text* of a typical page consists of some 2,000 characters; thus, you can store the text of 210 pages in the space required to store the image of one page. Image compression will reduce that ratio but will never make it a small ratio. You could also manipulate the text, looking for words or phrases in the book and viewing text in any desired arrangement. What you could not do is accurately replicate the typography or arrangement of the original.

Optical character recognition is growing in sophistication and coming down in price. In the next few years it may be a reasonable alternative to other preservation techniques when the text is all that matters. The economics of the situation are unmistakable: once a book has been converted to a stream of characters, it can be transmitted or copied easily, quickly, and cheaply. It can be stored in an incredibly compact form--between 500 and 1,000 typical books on a single compact disc.

The question is whether preserving the text constitutes full preservation. In many cases it is perfectly adequate; in others, it is less adequate. But libraries have often made questionable decisions regarding content. For example, some library binders traditionally remove advertising pages from magazines when preparing them for binding. The presumption must be that only the articles are of any lasting interest; a social historian will tell you that the presumption is absolutely false. The presumption that typography, illustrations, and the like are unimportant to a reader seems no less severe than this other long-standing presumption, and in many cases it is equally false.

Destroying to Preserve

Preserving the image frequently means destroying the artifact. Many, if not most, methods for microfilming, photocopying, or scanning pages require that the page be absolutely flat against a lens, which usually means opening a book in a way that will destroy its binding. In practice, some preservation techniques simply destroy the binding *before* filming or copying, since separate pages can be handled more rapidly and consistently.

Special cameras and copiers have been developed for preservation use, but the term "disbinding" still has a place in the preservation vocabulary. The good news is that disbinding is not necessary; the bad news is that it will always take more time and money to preserve images from a bound volume. With contemporary automatic sheet feeders, the difference is dramatic: single sheets can be copied at 50 pages per minute or more, while no operator can possibly prepare bound pages at more than a few pages per minute.

Sound Recordings

It is tempting to say that digital recording can make a perfect copy of a sound recording, but that may not be true. There are those who assert that the process of digitizing introduces audible imperfection and reduces low-level clarity.

What is definitely true, however, is that further copying of a digital recording should not introduce *further* loss of information. Even the best photocopy of a book page loses some small amount of clarity; a copy of that copy will typically lose a little more clarity. After several generations, the image will be much coarser than the original. Similarly, a fifth-generation audiocassette or videocassette copy will be distinctly lower in quality than the original. The same is not true of digital sound (or any other digitally stored information): when copying is done properly, the 100th generation should be identical to the original.

Digital encoding also offers the possibility of modifying the original sound, although the propriety of such modification can be argued. The RCA/SoundStream "reconstructed" recordings of Enrico Caruso offer much clearer and more listenable performances than were ever previously available in recorded form, but there is some question as to whether they offer accurate performances.

SUMMARY

Libraries must preserve as well as disseminate. The need for preservation is well known, though not universally accepted. Almost every library has some special materials that require preserving, although research libraries properly devote more resources to the process.

Improved technology can make preservation more effective, but also makes it more complicated. New means for storing information require decisions: should the artifact, the image, or only the content be preserved? There are no easy answers; what is right for some users and some materials will be wrong for others.

SELECTED READING

Anyone who cares about conservation and preservation should begin by reading Carolyn Clark Morrow's *The Preservation Challenge*. Rarely does an expert write about a field with such clarity and interest; the book is informative and a pleasure.

American National Standards Institute. *American National Standard for Information Sciences--Permanence of Paper for Printed Library Materials, ANSI Z39.48-1984.* New York: ANSI, January 1985. 8 pp.

Cunha, George Martin. "Mass Deacidification for Libraries." *Library Technology Reports* 23, no. 3 (May-June 1987):361-440. (Very good treatment of a number of possibilities, including extended discussion of Wei T'o and DEZ. Detailed and apparently neutral in tone.)

Henderson, Kathryn Luther, and William T. Henderson, eds. *Conserving and Preserving Library Materials.* Urbana-Champaign: University of Illinois Graduate School of Library and Information Science, 1983. 207 pp. Index. (Papers from the 1981 Allerton Park Institute. Good, varied treatment of preservation issues.)

Minter, William. "Polyester Encapsulation Using Ultrasonic Welding." *Library Hi Tech* 1, no. 3 (Winter 1983):53-54. (Brief discussion of a method for preserving fragile documents. Not suited to book preservation.)

Morrow, Carolyn Clark. *The Preservation Challenge: A Guide to Conserving Library Materials.* White Plains: Knowledge Industry Publications, 1983. 231 pp. Bibliography; index. (Clear, well-written, interesting treatment: a remarkably readable and well-informed discussion of the subject.)

Parker, Elisabeth Betz. "The Library of Congress Non-Print Optical Disk Pilot Program." *Information Technology and Libraries* 44, no. 4 (December 1985):289-299. (Some details on the technology of videodisc and its possible use for preservation.)

Russell, Joyce R., ed. *Preservation of Library Materials.* New York: Special Libraries Association, 1980. 96 pp. (Proceedings of a 1979 seminar. Brief, but with some interesting insights. Too early for good discussion of the technology of mass deacidification or preservation problems in newer materials.)

Part 2

Computers and Communications

Computers are tools; libraries use computers and related technologies to carry out operations more effectively. Many librarians probably think of computer-related technologies when they think of technology in the library. In practice, however, these technologies are much less important to libraries than those covered in the previous section.

Chapters 11-15 cover the tools themselves. Beginning with computers and some historical notes on the line of developments that led from abacus to computer, part 2 moves to the ways that people communicate with computers: human-machine interface devices, to use current jargon. One chapter concerns mass storage devices, the permanent and semi-permanent memories for computer-processed information.

The second half of part 2 discusses communications technologies, the ways that computers and computer-related systems send information back and forth. An overview of telecommunications in general is followed by two chapters dealing with specific technologies that depend on communications. The first of these covers two related technologies that have never (to date) lived up to their promise: teletext and videotex; the second covers point-to-point message communication in the form of electronic mail and telefacsimile. The last chapter in part 2 focuses on local area networks, closely-linked sets of computers and related devices.

11

Computers

Computers pervade society in ways that would surely astonish those who first created them. From a contemporary perspective, some of us find it hard to imagine a world without computers. My own job did not exist before there were computers, and the organization I work for would not exist in anything like its present form without computers.

All but the smallest libraries rely on computers, for cataloging information and for online databases, if not for circulation control and online catalogs. Without computers, libraries would suffer--and the American economy would break down almost entirely. For all of that, I've been around (slightly) longer than computers, and so has everyone born before, or in the first part of, the Baby Boom: the first fully electronic stored-program computer--the first machine that can really be considered a computer--went into operation in June 1948, only 40 years ago.

HISTORICAL NOTES

Like the printing press, the computer arose from many separate strains of development and, like the printing press, the computer fundamentally changed society. The history of computers and calculators is fascinating. The tables and paragraphs that follow include a few of the highlights of that history.

Calculations go back as far as numbers; calculating devices date back at least to the first abacus, possibly 5,000 years ago. Table 11.1 includes some of the significant dates during the last four centuries. Wilhelm Schickard invented and built the first mechanical calculator, the Calculating Clock, in Tubingen, Germany in 1623, 20 years before Pascal's more famous independent invention of a similar device. The Stepped Reckoner established the principles that would lead to successful mechanical calculators, but more than a century passed before Charles Xavier Thomas de Colmar developed Arithmometers, the first mass-produced calculators.

Developer & Development	Date
Wilhelm Schickard: Calculating Clock	1623
Blaise Pascal: Pascaline	1643
von Leibniz: Stepped Reckoner	1672
de Colmar: Mass-produced Calculators	1820
Babbage: Design for Difference Engine	1823
Babbage: Analytical Engine (basic design)	1836
Pehr Scheutz: Working Difference Engine	1853
Babbage: Partial working Analytical Engine	1871
Lord Kelvin: Tide predictor	1873
Hollerith: Punched-card sorting & counting	1884
MIT: Differential analyzer	1927
Konrad Zuse: Prototype binary calculator	1939
Bell Labs: Complex number calculator	1939
Konrad Zuse: Programmable calculator Z3	1941
IBM: Mark I programmable calculator	1943

Table 11.1: Calculating Engines Before Computers

Later in the nineteenth century Charles Babbage designed at least two different devices to do much more powerful calculations. The Difference Engine would have prepared various mathematical tables, producing printing plates directly to avoid transcription error. Babbage never completed the device, but a similar device was developed later by Pehr George Scheutz in Stockholm. Meanwhile, Babbage went on to design the much more ambitious Analytical Engine, which would have been programmed with punched cards. Only a small portion of the device was ever built.

Herman Hollerith began to file patents in 1884 for a system to sort and count punched cards through electromechanical means.

That system saw its first great success in the 1890 census, leading to the founding of the Tabulating Machine Company, later merged into CTR (Computing-Tabulating-Recording Company), which later became International Business Machines (IBM).

As World War II neared, different developers worked on the idea of universal calculators, moving closer to the idea of the modern computer. Konrad Zuse completed the first successful *general-purpose* programmable calculator, the model Z3, in December 1941. IBM's Mark I, completed in January 1943, was an enormous programmable calculator; it and several other units built during the 1940s could compute rapidly, but were neither electronic nor proper computers.

If we define a computer as an electronic general-purpose computing device with stored programs and internal memory, the first units did not appear until the end of World War II. Those first units appeared in Britain, not the United States, and IBM had nothing to do with them--or with the fully electronic calculators that preceded them. Table 11.2 and the following section note significant dates in the history of true computers.

Developers & Development	Date
Atanasoff: Binary electronic calculator	1942
Moore School: ENIAC decimal elect. calculator	1945
Manchester U.: Mark I, full computer	1948
Mauchly/Eckert: BINAC	1949
Ferranti Mark I: First commercial computer	1951
Mauchly/Eckert: UNIVAC decimal computer	1951
Moore School: EDVAC completed	1952
IBM: First IBM computer, Model 701	1953
DEC: PDP-1	1960
DEC: PDP-8: first real minicomputer	1963
IBM: System/360, solid-state mainframe	1964

Table 11.2: Highlights of Post-WWII Computer History

Before there were electronic computers, there were programmable electronic calculators; in the United States, those calculators were generally regarded as the first computers. The University of Pennsylvania's Moore School of Engineering led the way when the team of John W. Mauchly and J. Prosper Eckert developed ENIAC (the Electronic Numerator, Integrator, Analyzer, and Computer). John V. Atanasoff at Iowa State built a binary-notation electronic calculator earlier (in 1942), but the completion of ENIAC (a decimal calculator) in November 1945 yielded a faster calculator that was probably more significant in the long run. But ENIAC was not a computer because it lacked stored programs.

The next project at the Moore School was the Electronic Discrete Variable Computer (EDVAC). Although EDVAC may have been the first contemporary computer design, it was *not* the first fully electronic stored-program computer to be built. That honor, according to Stan Augarten (author of *Bit by Bit: An Illustrated History of Computers*, listed at the end of this chapter), goes to the Manchester Mark I, completed in June 1948 at Manchester University in England. The first *commercial* computer in Britain, the Ferranti Mark I, was installed in February 1951.

Mauchly and Eckert left Pennsylvania to start a private company, working toward UNIVAC, the Universal Automatic Computer. The company's first product was BINAC, completed in August 1949; by the time the first UNIVAC was installed in March 1951, UNIVAC was part of Remington Rand. UNIVAC was a true computer but was based on decimal arithmetic; most computers since then have used binary arithmetic. The Moore School finally completed EDVAC, a binary computer, in 1952.

Some early computers used analog techniques, using different voltages to represent different values. Almost all recent computers use digital techniques, where all information is stored in the form of *binary digits* or *bits*. A bit is either on or off, one or zero.

The first IBM computer, the IBM 701, reached the market in March 1953; from that slightly late start, IBM went on to dominate the industry. The 1950s and 1960s saw transistors replace tubes, making computers smaller and faster. In April 1964 IBM introduced the System/360, its most expensive development effort (by far) up to that date and the first wide-ranging set of compatible mainframes. In the 1970s integrated circuits replaced transistors, making computers still smaller and faster; the System/370 replaced the 360 but retained compatibility.

Other names and companies enter into recent computing history, too many to mention here. Kenneth H. Olsen founded Digital Equipment Corporation (DEC) in 1957 and introduced the PDP-1 in 1960. The PDP-8, coming in 1963, opened the minicomputer industry, bringing computing power to hundreds of thousands of businesses and other concerns, as DEC machines made computing affordable for small operations. Other companies followed DEC with minicomputers, though none as successfully.

Personal Computers

The heart of every computer is a central processing unit (CPU). Until 1969 every CPU was made up of many different physical units using tubes, transistors, or integrated circuits. In 1969 Intel engineers developed a general-purpose microprocessor on a single integrated circuit: a one-chip CPU, the 4004. The 4004 was not powerful enough for real computers (it was designed for programmable calculators), but another development contract (for Datapoint Corporation) resulted in the Intel 8008, which could serve as the basis for a computer. The 8008 and single-chip CPUs in general made it possible to build microcomputers and personal computers. Table 11.3 shows some of the developments in the early years of personal computing.

Development	Date
Intel: 4004, single-chip microprocessor	1969
Intel: 8008, eight-bit microprocessor	Nov. 1972
Intel: 8080, first CPU widely used in PCs	1973
Motorola: 6800 CPU introduced	1974
Radio-Electronics: "Mark-8"	July 1974
MITS: Altair 8800	Jan. 1975
Zilog: Z80 CPU, basis for many PCs	1975
Sphere: first single-case PC	1975
CP/M: first disk operating system for PCs	1976
MOS Technology: 6502, basis for Apple II	1976
Texas Instruments: TMS9900, 16-bit CPU	1976
Wozniak: Apple I kit computer	1976
Processor Technology: Sol	1976

Table 11.3: Early Developments in Personal Computing

The Apple II was not the first PC--that much is fairly clear. Less clear is what computer deserves that distinction. Table 11.3 includes some claimants to the title, including the Sphere--the first affordable computer to put the keyboard and display in the same box as the processor--and the Sol, a sleek little box with solid walnut side panels combining keyboard, processor, and expansion cards. By the end of 1976 more than 100 companies offered small computers or accessories for other computers.

This book includes more detailed figures for the brief history of personal computers than for the longer history of computers in general. This is because personal computers have had a very different impact than minicomputers and mainframe computers: they bring computing power to individuals and even the smallest libraries and businesses. Table 11.4 shows some significant product introductions between April 1977, when the Apple II and Commodore Pet first appeared, and August 1981, when IBM entered the personal computing field.

Development	Date
Commodore Pet	April 1977
Apple II	April 1977
Radio Shack TRS-80	August 1977
Atari 400 and 800	1978
Epson MX-80 dot-matrix printer	1978
CompuServe and The Source	1979
VisiCalc, first successful spreadsheet	1979
Texas Instruments TI-99/4	1979
WordStar	1979
Sinclair ZX80: first under-$200 PC	1980
Commodore VIC-20, Radio Shack Color Comp.	1980
Apple III	1980
Osborne I portable computer	1981
Epson HX-20 laptop computer	1981
IBM PC	Aug. 1981

Table 11.4: Highlights from 1978 to 1981

Personal Computing Since 1981

The first IBM PC in August 1981 was impressive more for its name than its value. With 64K of RAM (random access memory), 40K of ROM (read only memory), one single-sided diskette (180K), and a cassette port, the unit cost $3,005 without monitor or software. IBM even had a model with no diskette drive at all; the company thought some people would run software from cassettes. (So did Apple, Commodore, and Radio Shack--but in 1977, not 1981.) IBM did not take over the marketplace, but did establish a leading role in business PCs and gained more *dollar* volume than any other manufacturer. Table 11.5 shows a few of the significant introductions since August 1981.

Development	Date
Grid Compass: powerful portable ($8,150)	1982
Apple LISA	1982
Columbia PC: first "clone"	June 1982
Compaq portable "clone"	Nov. 1982
Commodore 64	1982
Lotus 1-2-3	1982
IBM PC/XT	Feb. 1983
Radio Shack TRS-80 100	Mar. 1983
"Toy computers": Mattel and Coleco	1983
Hewlett-Packard touch-screen PC	1983
IBM PCjr	Oct. 1983
Apple Macintosh	Jan. 1984
IBM PC AT	Aug. 1984
Commodore Amiga	1986
Atari ST series	1986
Apple IIGS, vastly upgraded "Apple II"	1986
IBM PS/2	Apr. 1987

Table 11.5: A Few Interesting PCs, 1981-1987

The history of personal computing is a history of change: not continuous, not always for the better, but change nonetheless. Users live with uncertainty, and libraries must live with a complex range of currently available computers and those no longer sold, but still in use.

HANDLING COMPUTERS

The important questions about a computer are whether it will do the job you need, how much special care it will need, how much it will cost to buy and run, and whether you can expand it if and as your needs expand. The notes that follow treat a few aspects of computers lightly.

In Libraries

Librarians know symbols and abstraction: books contain text, symbolic representations of ideas and the world; catalog records contain abstract information about books--information about information. Computers are tools for processing symbols and information in abstract form. Libraries and library organizations adopted computers almost as soon as computers became available, and have been leaders in computer usage for some time.

Libraries use computers for many functions. Turnkey circulation systems, serials management systems, online catalogs, acquisitions systems, and integrated local systems are based on computers within the library or centralized computers serving groups of libraries. Librarians use terminals and personal computers to access Dialog, BRS, SDC/Orbit, and other online databases over telephone lines, using massive computer resources to find current information on a variety of topics. Similarly, librarians use terminals and personal computers to reach OCLC, RLIN, or WLN over leased lines, so that they can use cataloging done by other libraries for the great majority of new books and other items. Interlibrary lending may use some combination of OCLC, WLN, RLIN, telecommunications, and mail networks such as Tymnet and ALANET, or regional computer networks such as the Illinois LCS system, all in order to get information from where it is housed to where it is needed.

Library computer use frequently spans the boundaries of commercial computer support. The MARC (machine-readable cataloging) format originated more than 20 years ago, but you can still surprise most commercial computer people by describing the demands and flexibility of the MARC format, and the database support needed to use it effectively. More recently libraries have been the first real market for CD-ROM and the first widespread market for other optical disc storage.

Libraries can make good use of personal computers for a variety of functions, most of them not requiring special library-related software. Every library has uses for word processing, and almost every library can make effective use of spreadsheet software, outline processors, and PC databases.

Libraries also offer friendly, neutral places for people to learn about personal computers and improve their skills. Many public and academic libraries already offer computer areas, and more will do so in the future. If your library has space and money available, you may be able to offer a substantial public service by establishing a public-access computer area, and local businesses or computer user groups may be willing to contribute part or all of the equipment and software needed for such an area. The library may need to establish signup sheets or other scheduling mechanisms and may wish to have a special collection of software to be used in-house. The rewards can be considerable; the library becomes a center for dealing with new information-handling systems as well as the home of the traditional information systems, books and other printed media.

Computers, Processors, and Systems

A computer processes symbols, almost always encoded into long strings of on and off signals, binary 0 and binary 1. It is possible to turn almost any symbolic representation into binary numbers: text, sound, and graphics. The instructions that tell a computer how to manipulate the binary numbers are also binary numbers. A central processing unit reads instructions stored in memory and data stored in memory and manipulates data, storing it back into memory. Data and instructions also come from outside sources--tape, disk, keyboard, and other input devices--and data goes back to outside sources such as tape, disk, display, and printer.

Software makes computers something more than inert objects. On a disk or tape, software looks just like data (i.e., a series of binary numbers); some programming languages even treat data and program code interchangeably. The distinction at any instant is that program code acts and data is acted on: program code tells the computer what to do, and the computer manipulates data.

Computers gain much of their flexibility by loading software into direct-access memory; a computer can jump from place to place in a stored program without reading the program from external storage at each jump. Memory typically comes in two flavors: ROM and RAM. ROM contains program code and data that never change--for example, the basic instructions for handling input and output (BIOS, or basic input-output system). RAM contains information that can change. The term is a misnomer, since ROM can also be accessed randomly. RAM is really read-write memory, but RWM is unpronounceable.

Computers don't think. Computers do make mistakes, but very rarely, and a computer can generally recognize computational mistakes and electromechanical errors in memory or other storage. Most computer errors come about because of bad data or erroneous programs. Any professional programmer/analyst knows that a complex program will probably have some errors, certainly when first written and quite probably even after a decade of operation.

Futurists of the last decade proclaimed that every household would have at least one computer in the very near future. Some of those futurists now say they were right--every household (or almost every one) does have a computer. That assertion degrades the definition of computer by failing to distinguish between microprocessors and computers.

Microprocessors such as the Intel 80286 and Motorola 68000 process data--but those two chips are not computers, in and of themselves. They are CPUs or processors. When combined in systems with memory, input, and output devices they become computers. A computer is a *general-purpose* device that can be programmed for different tasks using replaceable stored programs.

Most households do indeed have one or more microprocessors, some of the same power and generality as personal computer CPUs. Most are simpler or more specialized, and most of these microprocessors lack general programmability. The chip in your modern TV tuner runs only one program: a program to select stations and carry out related functions. The chip in your microwave oven runs a program to turn the klystron microwave tube on and off at specified times, for specified durations, and with specified on/off cycles. You provide data to the programs through keyboards, but you don't really program the devices. Even "programming" a videocassette recorder is actually providing data: what days and hours to switch to which channels, and how long to record. You can't tell your VCR to read in a paragraph of text and change "Sue" to "Linda" throughout the text; the microprocessor is dedicated to a single task.

That distinction is important. A computer is a general-purpose system; given enough time and the right input and output devices, any computer can carry out the same task as any other computer. Theoretically, you could do global meteorological analysis on an Apple II connected to the right devices. It might take several years to come up with one day's forecast, but the computer can carry out the same steps as the Cray supercomputers actually used for meteorological computing. But your VCR, your microwave, your TV set, and your digital watch could not carry out such processes. They contain *dedicated processors* which are not computers in any useful sense of the term.

Mainframe, Minicomputer, or Microcomputer?

How do you tell if a computer is a mainframe, a minicomputer, or a microcomputer? Different writers have offered different criteria over the years, including word size, amount of memory, and speed. The *word size* of a computer is the amount of information (expressed in bits) processed or read from memory in one instruction: all else being equal, a larger word size will result in faster processing. The *internal memory* of a computer is the quantity of direct-access memory, RAM and ROM, available to the computer (as opposed to disk-based memory or other external memory). There is no single reliable way to measure the *processing speed* of a computer, but speeds are frequently stated in MIPS (millions of instructions per second).

None of these criteria will serve to distinguish classes of computers in 1988. Word size doesn't work: most mainframes use 32-bit words, but so do some personal computers such as the Compaq Deskpro 386 and the Macintosh II--and the first minicomputer, the PDP-8, used an 8-bit word. Internal memory doesn't properly differentiate either: Macintosh personal computers usually have 1 to 4 megabytes of RAM, well into the minicomputer range, and most IBM-compatible computers intended to run OS/2 will have 4 to 16 megabytes of RAM, traditionally in the mainframe range. Raw computing speed doesn't distinguish classes of computers; the DEC VAX 11/780 is considered a minicomputer, but is faster than early mainframes and slower (considering only the central processor) than some contemporary microcomputers.

There are differences, however, between mainframes and microcomputers. A microcomputer typically contains a single processor, whereas most mainframes contain several processors, with subordinate processors handling input/output and other secondary tasks. Minicomputers fall into a gray area because there simply are no clear dividing lines. My own division is a practical one, having to do with environment. I think of a mainframe as a computer that requires a computer room (i.e., special air conditioning, raised floors, and special power). A minicomputer, by these criteria, is a computer that doesn't require a special room and that normally serves multiple users simultaneously, using terminals and a time-sharing operating system. A personal computer is any computer that is dedicated to one person. If you take a personal computer, add a robust time-sharing operating system, and connect terminals, you have the functional equivalent of a minicomputer.

Don't take that (or any other) breakdown very seriously. Some multi-user library computer systems are built on microcomputers or groups of microcomputers; others use minicomputers; others use mainframes. Usually mainframes have greater overall system capacities than minicomputers: they can handle more terminals, more storage, and more peripherals with good response time. They also cost much more.

When considering a possible library computer, the crucial questions are those stated earlier. You *must* care whether you need to build a computer room, whether the system can meet peak load gracefully, whether you need computer operators, and whether the software (operating system and application programs) is robust. You should *not* care whether the central processing unit is a single chip (one traditional sign of a microcomputer) or whether the computer would be considered a supermicro, mini, supermini, or mainframe. By and large the terms no longer have much meaning.

Keeping Up

The Library and Information Technology Association (LITA) of the American Library Association (ALA) is more than two decades old. It was founded (as the Information Systems and Automation Division [ISAD]) after libraries had started on the road to automation, and has served as a forum for discussion and education ever since. It continues to be an important way for people concerned with technology in libraries to deal with those concerns. Interest groups focus on various aspects of personal computing, computer applications, and other aspects of information technology.

LITA is a major source of information on library uses for personal computers, as it is for most aspects of current technology in libraries. Several interest groups within LITA concern themselves entirely with PC-related issues, including the Microcomputer Users Interest Group and the Library Templates Interest Group. Other divisions of ALA also deal with PC-related issues, as do subgroups within state associations.

People who use personal computers successfully generally love to share their experiences. A great amount of expertise and ingenuity is available in the library community for those willing to look for it.

SUMMARY

A dumb, fast, consistent machine can make people more productive and make life easier. It can work rapidly for good or work rapidly for pointless or evil ends. A computer is neutral; it does what it is told--quite literally. Try as we might, we still have not made a computer that can execute the instruction DWIM, Do What I Mean.

This book does not celebrate the computer, but it was written on computers and would not have been written without them. A computer is only a tool, but it is a tool unlike any other in the course of history. It can manipulate any set of symbols at staggering speeds, with incredible consistency, and in ways that can create new ways of looking at old information.

The miracle of computers is their ability to do simple tasks very rapidly and consistently. Most complex tasks can be broken down into many smaller, simpler tasks; in some but certainly not all cases, those tasks can be translated to computer programs, removing mechanical burdens from people. But computers don't create, and there are whole classes of activity that can't (at least so far) be defined in terms that can translate into computer programs. People create, people think; people and libraries should use computers to amplify their own capabilities.

SELECTED READING

Any number of good books deal with the history of computers and the way computers work. Almost every issue of *Information Technology and Libraries* and *Library Hi Tech* deals with computers and libraries. The citations below represent some samples of different ways of looking at computers.

Augarten, Stan. *Bit by Bit: An Illustrated History of Computers*. New York: Ticknor & Fields, 1984. 322 pp. Bibliography; index. (Well-written and lavishly illustrated. Strongest on the early history and weakest on minicomputers and personal computers. Makes critical distinctions and covers the technology well and understandably.)

Branscomb, Lewis. "The Computer's Debt to Science." *Library Hi Tech* 2, no. 3 (Fall 1984):7-18. (A philosophic view, well worth reading.)

Crawford, Walt. *Common Sense Personal Computing: A Handbook for Professionals*. Ann Arbor: Pierian Press, 1986. 204 pp. Bibliography; glossary; index. (Some prices and comments on CP/M are outdated, but the philosophy is still valid.)

Duke, John K., and Arnold Hirshon. "Policies for Microcomputers in Libraries: An Administrative Model." *Information Technology and Libraries* 5, no. 3 (September 1986):193-203. (One approach to controlling organizational PC use.)

Manspeaker, William C. et al. "Microcomputer Installation and Support at the University of Michigan Library." *Information Technology and Libraries* 5, no. 4 (December 1986):295-306. (Useful article on real-life integration of personal computers in a large library.)

McCorduck, Pamela. *The Universal Machine: Confessions of a Technological Optimist*. New York: McGraw-Hill, 1985. 305 pp. Chapter bibliographies; index. (Reflections on computing. A well-informed and very personal view. You may find it thought-provoking or maddening.)

Reid, T. R. *The Chip*. New York: Simon & Schuster, 1984. 243 pp. Bibliography; index. (Interesting, well-written, but parochial at times, with some inaccurate baiting of Japanese companies as copycats.)

12

Input and Display

Computers process information. That information must come from somewhere outside the computer and the results must go somewhere outside the computer, if computer processing is to be of any use in the real world. Several of the following chapters discuss technologies used to supply computers with information and receive results. This chapter focuses primarily on the most common ways that people work *directly* with a computer, providing data using keyboards (and related devices) and receiving information on a display. This chapter considers keyboards and displays separately. Since a terminal is nothing more than a keyboard and display combined into a single unit, everything said about keyboards and displays separately applies also to terminals.

COMPUTER AND TERMINAL KEYBOARDS

The predecessors to computer keyboards are typewriter keyboards. The original keyboards were actually sets of levers: when a typist pushed down on a key, a relatively simple mechanical linkage conveyed the force to a type bar, causing it to strike a ribbon and transfer ink to paper. Contemporary keyboards for typewriters, terminals, or computers substitute an electrical impulse for the mechanical linkage. Different keyboard designs use different means for sensing keystrokes, responding to keystrokes, and informing users that the keystrokes have been received.

Design Characteristics

Well-designed contemporary keyboards have much in common, although they also differ in important characteristics. Some characteristics are so nearly standardized that any deviation will cause problems for experienced typists. For example, alphabetic keys are usually 13 millimeters to 16 millimeters from edge to edge and 19 millimeters from the center of one key to the center of the next; each row of a keyboard should be level, but physically a little lower than the row above it on the keyboard; it should be possible to strike several keys in rapid succession without losing keystrokes; and the space bar should respond at any point along its width.

Any good keyboard should have keys that move, that are neutral in color with matte (not shiny) surfaces and clear labels, and that are slightly concave. The Enter key should be much larger than alphabetic keys; it and other keys outside the normal alphabetic area should usually have a contrasting (but relatively neutral) color. Any keyboard not meeting these criteria will cause problems--as will any keyboard with keys that repeat or are exceptionally noisy (particularly if used in public areas).

The best modern keyboards can be detached from the display so that users can adjust them. They are relatively thin, typically measuring no more than 1.5 inches from the keytops in the "ASDFG" row to the desktop (in a normal sloping position), and will repeat any key if it is held down more than a second or two. While these criteria can make use more pleasant, they are less crucial than the characteristics discussed previously.

The biggest variations are in touch or feel. Some keyboards simulate the positive mechanical contact of typewriters, although usually with much less pressure. Keys on these keyboards give positive "tactile feedback"--usually a sudden lessening of resistance as the key passes a certain point, possibly accompanied by a click generated by the keyboard itself. Other keyboard designs offer steady resistance or some different approach to resistance; some keyboards offer very little resistance. A click may be generated by the keyboard or computer, or the keyboard may be silent.

The feel of a keyboard is very much a personal matter. Many people find the firm touch and distinct "click" of IBM keyboards to be highly desirable, others find them punishing for extended use. What some people call a "soft, fast" keyboard, others call "mushy."

The best keyboard for a given user is the one that user is happiest with; there is no best keyboard for all uses and users.

Alphabetic Layout

The first widely successful typewriters used a layout that is familiar today: the top row of alphabetic keys read *QWERTYUIOP*, the second *ASDFGHJKL*. According to some histories, the layout (typically called *Qwerty*) was designed deliberately to slow down typists, because the early mechanisms could not respond fast enough to avoid jamming. While some nonalphabetic keys have moved since the nineteenth century (e.g., the single and double quotes) and others have been added for computer keyboards (specifically ^~'{}[]|\< >), most keys are just where they were on early typewriters.

There have been other designs, but none has seriously threatened the dominance of Qwerty, and none seems likely to in the future. Qwerty keyboards dominate (and should probably be the only keyboard layouts considered for library use) because they are everywhere, and almost everyone who has used a keyboard is familiar with the layout. They also dominate because no other layout has been shown to be superior enough to justify the costs of retraining typists and replacing keyboards.

The longest-lived competitor to Qwerty is the Dvorak keyboard, in existence for decades. The Dvorak layout places more commonly used characters on the home row; early tests suggested that the redesign required much less finger motion, thus allowing faster typing with less fatigue. More recent tests suggest that the actual advantages of Dvorak are very small. The British Maltron keyboard arranged keys in two curved areas offset from each other to match the resting position of hands. The keyboard was interesting as an object, but was never even as successful as Dvorak. Purely alphabetic keyboards (with *ABCDEFG...* on the first row) have appeared on specialized devices, but have never been seriously considered for keyboards.

Computers and electronic typewriters make keyboard redesign relatively easy--and at least one Apple II mode has a simple switch on the keyboard to change it to Dvorak layout. But few users ever make the switch, apparently, and most typists find that speed and fatigue depend more on other aspects of the keyboard than on the Qwerty layout. While Qwerty may not be ideal, it is omnipresent-- and is not "broken" enough that attempts to "fix it" seem likely to succeed.

Function Keys and Other Extensions

Most computer and terminal keyboards have quite a few more keys than typewriter keyboards, including from 4 to 8 or more cursor control keys, keys such as Alt and Ctrl (or, on other keyboards, Open-Apple or Cloverleaf) that modify other keys, and a range of "programmable function keys"--possibly 10, 12, or even more. Some contemporary keyboards have 101 keys, more than twice as many as a typical typewriter keyboard.

A keyboard may have too many keys, particularly if it is intended for public use. Libraries may choose to remove keytops from certain keys or buy special keyboards to avoid problems with keys that should not be used. Public access terminals usually use a minimal set of special functions, which should boil down to one per key, with very clear labels on or near the keys themselves or, at worst, on the screen. The most useful function keys will have special labels, with the two most important labels being HELP and START (or START OVER).

Keyboards definitely have faults: the layouts are inconsistent, there is no single ideal feel or feedback, the keys and springs can wear out, and there are still millions of people who find keyboards threatening or difficult to use. They are nonetheless the dominant form for specific, flexible input, for good reason. Properly built keyboards never create accidental input, can be used rapidly with relatively little training, and maintain the uniquely compact flexibility of the written language.

OTHER INPUT DEVICES

Most library input requirements involve text, and for interactive text entry, nothing seems likely to replace keyboards. There are other input devices, however, most of them serving different and more specialized purposes. Optical scanners are discussed in chapter 14; two other devices are worth mentioning briefly.

Mice and Other Pointing Devices

Macintosh users swear by mice; so do many Atari ST users, Commodore Amiga users, and PC users who run Microsoft Windows or various graphics programs. Mice and other special input devices serve non-textual input needs; given the right application, they can serve such needs extremely well. These devices basically do one or more of three things: point, move, and draw. Some nonkeyboard devices only point; some only point and move; most can do all three. Cursor keys on a keyboard can point quite effectively and can move text quite well, but move graphics less effectively and are nearly useless for drawing.

A mouse is a mechanical or optical device that can transmit a vector (direction and distance) to the computer. You establish a direction and speed by rolling the mouse across a surface and take action by pressing a button (some mice have one button, some have two or three). As you move the mouse, a pointer on the screen moves with it and, in some cases, draws by leaving a line.

Several alternatives to mice exist, each with its advantages and disadvantages. Touch screens are direct and intuitive as pointing devices, but poor for moving or drawing. As many libraries know, they have real drawbacks even as pointing devices--messing up the screen with fingerprints, poor resolution (your finger is bigger than a single character), and possible muscle fatigue (reaching out to touch the screen is not natural). Light pens--devices used to touch a pen to the screen--behave much like touch screens, although with better precision. They are adequate as pointers, poor for other uses, and involve unnatural and somewhat strenuous movement.

Finally drawing tablets--separate tablets used with special pens or other instruments--take up more space and typically cost much more than mice, but allow much more natural and precise drawing. They can also be used well for pointing and moving, but make sense only for graphically oriented applications.

Bar Code Readers

Many library circulation systems use bar code readers as specialized computer input devices. A bar code reader reads a sequence of light and dark lines and convert that into a short message using a small character set. Because readers and codes follow established rules, reading is fast, easy, and error-tolerant.

A bar code reader can either shine a light on the bar code and read the reflection, or work with only a photocell, dealing strictly with differences in reflection of background lighting. Laser readers, usually stationary and used for high-quantity, high-speed operations, do the former; hand-held readers may work either way. Typically, a hand-held reader can scan a code in either direction, at almost any angle, at almost any speed. Similarly, laser readers can scan codes from a surprising variety of angles and at almost any orientation.

The secret is in the codes, which include distinctive preset patterns for the beginning and end of a code. There are a few different commercial standards for bar codes; some readers and applications use only one standard, but other readers can handle all of the standards currently in use, switching automatically in some cases. The reader and its electronics can recognize which is which, store all the codes in between, and reconstruct the complete bar code in its proper sequence.

DISPLAYS

Most computer systems will work with a variety of terminals. Even when a system needs a special keyboard, it is likely that the keyboard can be combined with any of several different screens. Literally hundreds of different displays are available for personal computers; while the range of terminal offerings may be declining, there are still dozens if not hundreds of options. For some applications, libraries may even choose a technology other than cathode ray tubes (CRT) or something other than the standard 25 line by 80 character monochrome display.

A turnkey computer system may be offered with only one display. If that is the case, it is the library's responsibility to insist that the display meet all its needs and provide good visual ergonomic qualities. Good displays need not be expensive and there is no longer any reason for libraries to accept displays with bad glare problems, fuzzy characters, poor contrast, or other defects. When a library installs an online public access catalog, the display and keyboard represent the image of the catalog and the library to the patrons. That image should be clear, precise, and effective; if not, the vendor is shortchanging the library and the library is being unfair to its patrons.

Screen and Character Size

Most contemporary desktop displays range in screen size from 11 to 14 inches measured diagonally, and most displays show 25 lines, with each line containing 80 columns. Characters are typically about five millimeters high (one-fifth of an inch), including spacing between lines, and about 2.5 millimeters (one-tenth of an inch) wide.

Some library terminals, not intended for extended reading, used screens as small as five inches, and some portable computers still use screens as small as nine inches diagonal, yielding characters that are just large enough to be easily readable. Characters much shorter than four millimeters or much narrower than two millimeters become difficult to read and tiring for extended use, although smaller characters are useful for special purposes (such as previewing the appearance of a complete printed page).

Larger screens are becoming more common, although larger is not always better. Almost all computer displays use small dots or lines known as picture elements or *pixels* to form characters. If a large screen uses more pixels per character (as the best ones do), it can display larger and clearer characters for easier use by those with poor eyesight, or more small characters for special uses. If a large screen uses the same number of pixels as a small screen, the characters may turn into patterns of very visible dots and be harder to read.

While 25 by 80 is the most common character array, modern PC displays can show much denser text. For example, most contemporary PC displays can be used to show 43 lines of text with 132 characters per line, using some software. The characters on a typical 43-line screen are uncomfortably small, but the larger display is valuable for working with spreadsheets and for some other special purposes.

Color Combinations for Monochrome Displays

Most text displays should be monochromatic, but the best color combination for monochrome displays is largely a matter of taste. Early computer displays used mostly white on black, which was a poor combination largely because of the phosphors used at the time. Characters were legible only under ideal lighting conditions, and the display tended to fatigue users. Part of the fatigue may have come about because the phosphors were either too "fast," causing flicker, or too "slow," causing ghosts when displays changed.

Green on black came to dominate the field some years ago. Green phosphors with proper delay characteristics (neither flickery nor causing ghosts) are available, and they can be fairly good. Even the early (and generally poor) amber-on-black displays suggested better solutions, however. Since the eye is unusually sensitive to amber, an amber-on-black display can be legible without being very bright. All else being equal, brighter displays cause more fatigue; thus, properly adjusted amber displays tend to be less fatiguing.

High-quality amber displays have become inexpensive and quite popular; meanwhile, some very good white-on-black and black-on-white displays have also emerged over the past few years, using new "paper white" phosphors. The Apple Macintosh was one of the first computers to use a relatively nonfatiguing black-on-white display and Zenith, Thomson, and others have followed.

Recent experience suggests that the engineering quality of a specific display may be more important than the choice of colors. A good green display will be more comfortable than a mediocre amber display, and an excellent black-on-white display may be better than any other combination. Personal preference is also important; while most people eventually prefer amber to green, some people find the color disturbing or distracting.

Legibility

Good legibility means that users can see the screen and the information on it; that the characters and graphics are clear; and that the characters are distinctive. Users should read words and numbers and should not have to take time to determine what the characters are, nor should they have difficulty reading the text because of glare, reflection, inadequate character definition, or other problems.

One factor in minimizing glare is minimizing the curvature of the screen. Curved screens, like convex mirrors, reflect light in more directions and from more sources than do flat screens. Many newer displays use nearly flat screens, and Zenith recently introduced a color display using a radically new color-tube technology with a completely flat screen. That display is expensive, but some of the monochrome "flat tube" displays are quite inexpensive.

Glare and reflection can also be reduced by using a darker screen surface or by any number of the following treatments. The screen can be etched, roughening the outer surface to scatter light rather than reflect it; a thin film may be sprayed on the screen to reduce reflection; a micromesh filter, usually of nylon, may be applied to the screen or used as an addition to the screen; or a tinted glass, plastic screen, or polarized screen may be added.

Each of these treatments has its drawbacks, however: etching can reduce clarity; micromesh filters reduce the amount of transmitted light and may reduce clarity; thin films may reduce clarity and can be highly sensitive to dust and fingerprints; and glass and plastic screens may make reflection worse while they reduce glare. When treatments take place at the factory, the rest of the display should be designed to work with the treatment; when they are added on, there will almost always be compromises.

Legibility also requires crisp, distinctive characters. Crispness is a result of properly built displays, with true focus and edge-to-edge linearity (the lines should be straight, not curved), and a proper balance of display design and character-set design. If there are not enough pixels in each character, the characters will not be crisp; if the balance of character elements to screen size and pixel size is wrong, users may see groups of dots rather than well-formed characters.

Characters must be distinctive. Even some of the best-known modern displays can cause confusion between character pairs such as **1 & l, 0 & O, I & T, 0 & 8, m & n, g & q, i & j, u & v, v & w, 2 & Z, 6 & b, O & Q, T & Y,** and **S & 5.** Whenever a user must stop to be sure what a character is, the user loses track of the words and stream of text. These problems should not be regarded as inevitable, because they do not have to be.

Special Displays

Most displays for most library applications show text in a single color. Color displays and monochrome displays capable of display graphics are replacing text-only displays in most personal computers, but terminals still tend to display text only. Graphics, or at least the higher resolution needed for good graphics, may be needed for special situations--for example, showing diacritical marks in conjunction with characters or showing bibliographic information in Chinese, Japanese, Korean, Cyrillic, Hebrew, or other textual systems. There are also special applications where special displays may be useful, including the types mentioned in the following sections.

Full-Color Displays

Full-color displays raise two questions: do they serve a real purpose for the application, and do they make economic sense? Until recently a full-color display either cost much more than a monochrome display, or displayed text at unacceptably low resolution, or both. You will still pay $500 or more to equip a personal computer with a full-color display subsystem that shows text almost as clearly as a $150 monochrome display subsystem (in 1988), but that's much better than the $1,500-to-$250 ratio of 1985 prices.

If the economics make more sense, do the displays serve a purpose? Full-color displays can be valuable for some graphics applications, but the virtues of full color for text are harder to demonstrate, and most attempts have not been very convincing. We all learn to read text in a single color, and there are no generally accepted relationships between color and meaning, with the possible exception of red for caution, warning, or danger. A person seeing a multicolored text display will assume that the colors have some significance, but will *not* come to the display with any idea of what that significance is.

Eight percent of men and a small percentage of women are color blind. That makes it inefficient to use color for important purposes, since a significant proportion of users won't get the message. Further, relatively few color combinations yield legible text. For example, most people will find text displayed in red, light yellow, or blue difficult to read on a typical color display. Given those problems, it is not surprising that full-color textual displays have not caught on for general use, and there is little reason to believe that they ever will.

Full-Page and Ultra-High-Resolution Displays

Displays used for functions such as online catalogs can already show more text than should reasonably appear on a single screen: 2,000 characters is a great deal of text, equal to a typical page of this book. Even for text editing, a 24-line screen shows nearly as many lines as a typical double-spaced manuscript page, and can show more characters per line than any reasonable manuscript.

But a typical display cannot replicate the appearance of a printed page, and cannot show as many characters as a typical newsletter page or single-spaced manuscript. For some applications such as desktop publishing and typesetting, users can be much more effective if they can view an entire page without printing it out. Displays have appeared that make this possible; some even have the proportions of a printed page, being significantly taller than they are wide. All have many more pixels than normal displays: it takes *at least* one million pixels to show a reasonable facsimile of a full page, as compared to the quarter-million pixels of a normal monochrome display.

Full-page displays don't come cheap: in 1988, such a display and its electronics may cost $1,500 to $2,300 or much more. They can pay for themselves in full-time publishing operations and in some other applications, but are neither necessary nor desirable in most operations. When you're editing or reading text, 50 or 60 lines is just too much to have on the screen at once. Reading from a screen is not the same as reading from a printed page (and, for that matter, 50-line pages tend to be less pleasant than smaller pages).

All full-page displays are ultra-high-resolution, displaying at least one million pixels. Ultra-high-resolution displays also have many uses in graphics, particularly for computer-assisted design (CAD) and similar fields. They also have somewhat specialized uses in libraries. For example, the second-generation Chinese, Japanese, Korean (CJK) terminals for the Research Libraries Information Network use Wyse 700 displays (much less expensive than full-page displays, but still ultra-high-resolution) to show very well-defined characters.

Health Hazards, Problems, and Ergonomics

Some of the references at the end of this chapter deal with potential health hazards and the studies that have been done on CRT displays. There *are* potential health problems for those who use displays and keyboards for hours each day, but the problems have more to do with inadequate workstation design than with problems inherent in the displays. There have been no findings that terminals emit any dangerous radiation; in fact, recent tests show that even when display electronics are deliberately driven to the point of failure, modern displays will not emit measurable X-ray or other hazardous radiation.

Displays can cause problems, either because they are faulty or because they are badly used. Some displays emit high-pitched noise (15.7 kiloHertz), usually only subliminally audible and totally inaudible to most adult men. The constant whine is rarely recognized consciously, but will definitely cause fatigue, headaches, and other problems in some people who use such displays extensively. No modern display should emit such noise; it is always the sign of a poorly designed display or one that is breaking down. Other defects are more obvious: if a display flickers, shows distortion, or is unstable in any way, it is defective and should be repaired or replaced.

Good displays should be used properly. That means placing them out of direct sunlight and in such a position that bright lights don't shine directly on the screen. It also means providing adequate work space around the display, and situating the display in such a way that a user will find it comfortable to use. In most cases, the most comfortable viewing position for a display is a few degrees below level (i.e., so the user is looking down just slightly at the display). As a rule of thumb, if the top of the display is a few inches below eye level, the display is in a good position.

The best modern displays offer built-in flexibility for users. Different users sit differently, have different heights, and have different preferences as to the angle of vision they prefer. One easy answer is a tilt-and-swivel display. You can add tilt-and-swivel stands to any display for $20 or so, giving users the option to set the display the way they want it. Some displays come with the tilt-and-swivel ability built into the display; that usually means lower overall expense, a more compact design, and fewer separate parts to deal with.

Display Technologies

Most modern displays use CRTs, which is surprising in some ways since the first textual displays for computers used CRTs and the technology predates computers by decades. The first digital computers used tubes for all operations, but the only tubes used in modern computers are in displays.

There have been and are many alternatives to CRTs. Tube technology saw its glory days many years ago; CRTs seem to be a vestigial reminder of an obsolete technology. The 1950s saw predictions that electroluminescent displays would replace CRTs. In the 1960s some observers saw plasma displays as a definite replacement for CRTs. Both display technologies work, as do liquid crystal displays (LCD) and light-emitting diodes (LED). But for most applications CRTs are not only the best-*selling* displays but the best *available* displays.

Why CRTs Dominate

Cathode ray tubes have a long history. William Crookes invented the CRT in 1879, and Ferdinand Braun conceived of using the CRT as a display or indicator device in 1896. When the first all-electronic television systems were developed in 1926 and 1929, the inventors used the existing technology of CRTs as the display device. The first color CRT emerged in 1949; rare-earth phosphors added brightness and purer color in 1964. Sony revolutionized tube design with the Trinitron in 1968, and Zenith may revolutionize it again with its flat high-resolution color CRT introduced in 1987.

By contemporary standards, cathode ray tubes are clumsy--large, heavy, and cumbersome. They require precision glass-blowing, creation of a vacuum, and all the heat and bother of other vacuum tubes. But the wide market for CRTs, in television sets as well as computer displays, leads to ongoing improvements and manufacturing efficiencies that continue to make CRTs dominant.

As compared to most flat-panel displays, CRTs can work better in bright light, have broader and purer color capabilities, respond faster, offer higher resolution, and are distinctly cheaper. Alternative technologies perform better in certain areas but fall down in others. Primary display technologies other than CRTs include the following:

1. Electroluminescent (ELD) displays, exciting thin-film phosphors by direct electrical connection, started in laboratories in the 1940s. The first Grid computer used ELD technology; some current portable personal computers use ELD displays or use ELD backlighting for LCD displays.

2. Gas plasma displays work by gas discharge, the glow of certain gases when subjected to electricity. Gas discharges have been studied since 1675; the first display system based on gas discharge was created by the Bell System in 1927 as an early alternative to CRT television receivers. Several portable per-

sonal computers (such as the Toshiba T3100 and Compaq Portable III) now use plasma displays, with good success. As with ELDs, plasma displays are flat and highly legible but very expensive to produce compared to CRTs.

3. Fundamental research leading to light-emitting diodes (LEDs) dates back to 1907, but Bell Labs only made LEDs practical between 1966 and 1971. LEDs dominated small calculator displays for a few years before being displaced by LCDs (see number four), and LEDs have important roles as indicators and for various other display uses, including alarm clocks and microwave displays. For very small textual and numeric displays LEDs seem ideal; larger displays do exist, but only for specialized purposes.

4. Liquid crystal displays (LCDs) and other "non-emissive" displays work by *altering* light rather than generating light. LCDs change from opaque to transparent, or reflective to nonreflective, depending on their electrical charge. Commercial LCD development appears to date back only to 1968. LCDs dominate the display market for hand-held calculators and electronic watches, and find use in many laptop and portable computers. LCDs in computers show the problems of LCDs. Typical displays react much more slowly than CRTs, making fast screen redisplay difficult or impossible; LCD screens lack contrast and can't be read except in the proper light; and most LCD screens have lower resolution than similar-sized CRT displays.

Note the distinction between LCD and LED. LCDs modify light and require external lighting to be visible in a dim room or in the dark. LEDs generate light. Your microwave probably uses LEDs to show functions; most modern inexpensive watches use LCD numbers. No personal computer displays use LEDs (except as indicator lights), but many portable computers use LCDs.

For full-size, textual displays, the role of non-CRT technologies is very minor. When depth, weight, and power requirements are not overriding characteristics, almost any computer designer will prefer a cathode ray tube: it works faster, offers better resolution, can be used in a wider variety of light, and is much cheaper. Although the technology is quite old, it continues to improve.

SUMMARY

The best way to work interactively with a computer is through a keyboard and a display, most probably a cathode ray tube. The oldest keyboard layout and the oldest display technology continue to dominate, because they work: they are proven, reliable, and inexpensive. Alternatives do exist, but are most useful for special applications.

Librarians should pay attention to the quality of keyboards and display; while inexpensive units can provide excellent performance, mediocre keyboards and displays do exist and should be avoided.

SELECTED READING

Cakir, A., D. J. Hart, and T. F. M. Stewart. *Visual Display Terminals*. Chichester: John Wiley & Sons, 1980. 253 pp. plus appendices. Glossary; bibliography. (A manual on ergonomics, workplace design, health and safety, proper use of terminals. Good, if dated and occasionally inaccurate.)

Miller, R. Bruce. "Radiation, Ergonomics, Ion Depletion, and VDTs: Healthful Use of Visual Display Terminals." *Information Technology and Libraries* 2, no. 2 (June 1983):151-58. (Still one of the best brief discussions of the topic; includes a good bibliography.)

Murray, William E. "Video Display Terminals: Radiation Issues." *Library Hi Tech* 3, no. 4 (Winter 1985):43-47. (Explicit report of radiation studies, none of which appear to show any hazard.)

Tannas, Lawrence E., Jr. *Flat-Panel Displays and CRTs*. New York: Van Nostrand Reinhold, 1985. 468 pp. Chapter bibliographies; index. (Exhaustive technical review of alternative displays with extensive discussion of CRTs and why they continue to dominate the display field. Detailed, very technical, quite readable for its depth of coverage.)

Chapter 5 of my book *Patron Access: Issues for Online Catalogs* (Boston: G.K. Hall, 1987) is also relevant to this chapter. Chapter 3 of my book *Common Sense Personal Computing* (Ann Arbor: Pierian Press, 1986) covers some of the same ground from a somewhat different perspective.

13
Printers

Some theorists suggest that computers and other technological advances could lead us to the paperless society, with online communications and magnetic storage taking the place of print. In practice, however, the end-product of most computing is paper, sometimes overwhelming quantities of it.

Most computers require at least one printer, in order for their users to share the results of computing with others. Libraries use printers in conjunction with personal computers and, to some extent, as part of online patron-access catalogs.

PRINT BASICS

All computer printers have two things in common: they accept information from other devices and turn that information into fixed visible output on paper or some paperlike medium. As with displays and input, most printing produces monochrome text; graphics and color printing have widespread but more specialized uses.

Most printers produce black type on white paper, typically paper similar to either typing paper or that used in plain-paper copiers and for offset lithography. The black type can be ink, a carbon compound pressed onto the paper, or mixed with plastic in a "toner" and fused to the paper. The black type may also be a waxy substance melted onto the paper. Some printers avoid adding black to the paper, instead removing a layer from specially coated paper or heating specially treated paper to produce images. Finally, some printers produce multiple colors, either through several colors of ink, several colors of toner, or several colors of waxy pigment.

Most contemporary computer printers form characters from dots. Some produce whole characters by impressing a fully formed image and some produce solid characters by drawing them. Some printers generate individual characters on paper in the order that they are received from the computer; some deal with a line at a time; some produce an entire page at a time.

Printer Selection

There is no single best printer for all purposes and all users. Choosing the right printer for a particular application means taking into account the needs of the application and the characteristics of various printers. Some important considerations follow:

1. *Noise.* Some printers are nearly silent while some have about the same noise as a copier. Most printers make more noise than any other computing equipment, to the point that acoustic hoods may be needed for use even in the back room of a library. When choosing a printer for use in public areas, noise may be more important than many other considerations.

2. *Speed.* Typical small printers range in speed from 10 characters per second to 10 pages per minute (as many as 500 characters per second). Printers for large computers may range from 600 lines per minute (about 10 pages per minute) to 120 pages per minute or more. Fast printers may also move paper rapidly, which, in some cases, may cause problems for forms handling.

3. *Convenience and complexity.* Printers vary enormously in ease of paper loading and handling, number and type of controls available, difficulty of use, and other convenience factors.

4. *Software support.* A printer can't do its best work unless the software being used recognizes the printer. Popular printers have widespread support; less popular printers generally try to imitate (emulate) the functions of popular printers, but do not always emulate the other printers perfectly.

5. *Versatility.* Many printers can do only one thing well: printing text in a single font on fan-fold plain paper. Many printers

can't handle envelopes except by printing self-adhesive labels to place on the envelopes. Many printers cannot print multi-part forms, and some really can't handle preprinted forms at all unless they were specifically designed for the printer.

6. *Print quality*. Printers vary enormously in print quality, and the same printer may offer several levels of quality. Some printers produce output that fades with use or is barely legible; others produce output that requires careful attention to distinguish it from typeset material.

7. *Paper quality*. Some printers require special paper; this may pose an extra expense and may yield unpleasant results.

8. *Cost of operation*. Printer ribbons and other supplies can vary such that the total cost of a printed page, including the paper, is as little as 1¢ or as much as 25¢ or more. Printers may also waste paper, if it is necessary to eject one page in order to remove the printed page ahead of it. Printers vary widely in use of electricity, although electricity is rarely a major cost factor unless the printer is used continuously.

9. *Maintenance, use cycle, and durability*. Most printers are fairly durable, but some are more prone to jamming and failure than others. Some printers require periodic maintenance of one sort or another; others require little or no attention. Durability is directly related to use cycles: some printers are designed to be used continuously, while others can be expected to break down regularly if used much more than an hour or two each day.

10. *Price*. The initial cost for a small-computer printer may be from $100 to $10,000 or more. A library may even have legitimate uses for printers costing anywhere from $10,000 to $300,000. Depending on a library's needs and the expected length and intensity of printer use, the total cost of the printer during its life can vary even more widely.

PRINTING TECHNOLOGIES

Printers use and have used many different techniques to produce readable text or graphics on paper. The most common printer technologies appear here.

Line Printers

The biggest (physically) entry in the Printer Hall of Fame must be the IBM 1403. It may be the most successful and, in some ways, best, of a class of printers known as line printers--printers that produce a line of characters at a time, at relatively high speeds.

Traditional line printers such as the IBM 1403 are big, expensive devices, typically with massive covers that raise and lower on command. A 1403 prints at 1,000 lines per minute when printing only uppercase; about half that speed for upper and lower case, and even slower when printing the full ALA character set.

Most line printers don't actually print an entire line at once. Instead, the line is retained in the printer's memory. A chain, drum, or other moving device places different letters in each print position and a hammer forces the appropriate letter forward to strike a ribbon and place ink on paper when the right character is in the right place. Several hammers may strike simultaneously or--in the worst case, a line consisting of the same character repeated over and over --all the hammers may strike sequentially.

Line printers use different mechanisms. The most precise mechanism, yielding the best print quality, is the print chain or print train mechanism used by the IBM 1403. Other line-printer mechanisms yield wavery lines, with characters appearing slightly above and slightly below the normal baseline.

Libraries rarely own high-speed line printers these days, but may have lower-speed line printers using similar technology. Libraries continue to benefit from the IBM 1403. Its chief virtues appear to be print quality and durability: the printers seem to go on forever. OCLC still produces catalog cards using IBM 1403s or equivalent printers; RLG still uses such printers to produce orders, claims, and cancellations. The 1403 was the first device to support the full ALA character set, including diacritics. In fact, IBM produced a special print chain to support library functions.

Line printers tend to be big, expensive, and noisy. They will rarely be found in contemporary small-computer installations: page printers are nearly as fast, much quieter, and much less expensive, and character printers can handle the occasional need for multipart printing.

Typewriters, Daisywheel, and Thimble Printers

Some early computers used interfaces to traditional electric typewriters, with one type bar for each letter or pair of symbols. That technique never worked well, and type-bar typewriters have almost disappeared from the marketplace.

The typical definition of "letter-quality" computer printing refers to the output produced by Selectric typewriters, their electronic successors and competitors, and computer-driven printers that use the same mechanism. Computer printers using this mechanism are typically called either daisywheel or thimble printers, depending on one detail of the print methodology.

Like line printers, daisywheel and thimble printers use fully formed characters and hammers to drive the characters into ribbons, pressing ink onto paper. Unlike line printers, daisywheel and thimble printers move the character set and a single hammer across a page, rather than having one hammer for each print position and a very wide ribbon.

Both daisywheel and thimble printers combine a spinning plastic or metal character mechanism, a single hammer, and a ribbon into a moving print device. As the print device comes to a column, the character mechanism spins until the right letter is in place. At that point, the hammer forces the mechanism into the ribbon.

Many daisywheel and thimble printers accept a full line at a time from the computer. That allows them to print bidirectionally: one line is printed from beginning to end; the next line is printed from end to beginning, right to left. Since horizontal motion is one of the slower aspects of daisywheel printing, bidirectionality can significantly improve the overall print speed.

The difference between a daisywheel and a thimble printer is the shape of the print mechanism. A daisywheel is a flat plastic or metal circle, a wheel, with each character or character pair on a different spoke. A thimble is a large cup, with the character spokes around the raised perimeter of the cup. Nippon Electric (NEC) pioneered thimble printers and largely controls the market; most other letter-quality printers use daisywheels.

Selectrics use a golfball print mechanism, somewhat different in principle and typically not able to perform at the same speeds. The golfball is a truncated sphere with letters all over its surface. For each print position, the golfball must be positioned properly, then moved forward into the ribbon. While the golfball is smaller than either a daisywheel or thimble, the mechanism is more complex and clumsier.

Daisywheel and thimble printers tend to be noisy and slow and to cost quite a bit per page. Speed ranges from 10 to 60 characters per second. Not only are daisywheel printers noisier than most others (and more difficult to shield, because they tend to produce a lot of heat), the noise goes on much longer because the printers are so slow. Material costs are high only if Mylar ribbons are used, but there is little point in using daisywheel printers except to get the best possible print quality, which means using Mylar ribbons. Such ribbons may cost anywhere from 3¢ to 10¢ (or more) per single-spaced page of print. Also, daisywheel and thimble printers are almost totally incapable of handling graphics: the only possibility is to use the period over and over again. Such printers can handle multiple typefaces, but only by stopping and having an operator change the daisywheel or thimble.

The benefits of daisywheel and thimble printing are print quality and flexibility. These printers have fully formed characters and typically use very good ribbons; they produce output indistinguishable from a quality electronic typewriter, since they are effectively no different. They can, with proper program support, also handle envelopes, special paper, multipart forms, and other special needs as effectively as typewriters.

Daisywheel printers have been around for roughly two decades. They are gradually disappearing from the computer printer market, while taking over the typewriter market. It seems likely that, by the next decade the only use of daisywheel printers for computer output will be low-cost electronic typewriters that can connect to computers for occasional light use. Dot-matrix printers have overtaken daisywheels on one side and laser printers have squeezed them on the other, leaving little room in between.

Impact Dot-Matrix Printers

Impact dot-matrix printers use hammers to drive metal into ribbons, like daisywheel printers. That similarity means that dot-matrix printers can also produce multipart forms and, if well designed, offer good forms versatility. It also means that impact dot-matrix printers are noisy: not quite as noisy as daisywheels, and easier to muffle, but noisy nonetheless.

The differences between the two types of printers are more important than the similarity. Where a daisywheel has a single hammer driving one of many single-character spokes, a dot-matrix printer has many hammers, each driving a single metal pin. Dot-matrix printers are characterized by the number of pins. Originally, there were seven-pin printers, with seven hammers driving seven pins. Today, printers are typically 9-pin, 18-pin, or 24-pin.

A seven-pin printer or nine-pin printer has a single narrow column of pins. To create a letter, the print head (hammers, pins, and ribbon) will move very slightly many times, with various pins struck at each position. The crudest dot-matrix printers used seven-by-five matrices: each character consisted of some combination of the seven vertical elements over five horizontal positions.

Seven-by-five matrices are extremely crude. The lowercase letters "g," "y," "j," and "q" must be raised above the usual line, since seven vertical elements does not leave room for dots descending below the line. Years ago, better dot-matrix printers moved to nine pins and a matrix typically consisting of nine vertical elements by seven horizontal positions. That level of detail supports legible characters, although the characters are still simple.

Most recent designs use more pins: 2 rows of 9 pins each, or 2 rows of 12 pins each. These 18-pin and 24-pin printers can print simple characters at much higher speed or, by putting down intermediate points, print more finely detailed characters at lower speeds. Some nine-pin printers can also produce very detailed characters, usually by making several passes for each line of characters.

The best impact dot-matrix printers can produce output that is very nearly letter-quality, although a trained eye can almost always tell the difference. The 24-pin printers have smaller pins, thus allowing more finely detailed characters, but the characters are still made up of slightly visible distinct dots.

Impact dot-matrix printers tend to be cheap to buy and run, using plain paper and (usually) inexpensive ribbons. The basic design has been around for decades, and good dot-matrix printers are extremely durable and easy to maintain. Dot-matrix printers range in speed from 40 to 400 characters per second, with typical models actually printing 100 to 200 draft-quality characters per second or as few as 25 to 50 near-letter-quality characters. Unlike daisywheel printers, dot-matrix printers can print special characters or graphics since the pins can be struck in almost any pattern under software control. The disadvantages of dot-matrix printers are primarily print quality and noise.

Thermal Printers

Thermal printers typically work in one of three ways, all of which combine near silence with quality typical of dot-matrix printers. Most thermal printers are dot-matrix printers, but the dots are not produced by physical impact.

Some low-cost thermal printers use aluminized paper; the printer elements (electrically charged dots) burn off a layer of the special paper, exposing the aluminum layer. These printers produce output that is only marginally useful because the paper is peculiar and hard to handle and the print tends to fade over time. Some other thermal printers use heated pins to darken specially treated paper. While the paper with this method is a bit less peculiar, the output is still neither attractive nor very permanent.

A few contemporary thermal printers work in such a way that allows use of plain paper. These printers use a special, rather expensive ribbon with wax-encapsulated pigment. The thermal elements heat the ribbon, causing the pigment to transfer to the paper. The results can be quite attractive (e.g., the IBM Quietwriter produces very nearly letter-quality output). The results can also be expensive: the Quietwriter can require 25¢ worth of ribbon to produce a single page, and color thermal-transfer printers can cost $1 or more per page.

The primary advantage of thermal printers is nearly silent printing. Speed can vary from that of a fast daisywheel to that of a slow impact dot-matrix printer. As with impact dot-matrix printers, thermal printers can produce graphics or special characters under software control. Except for transfer printers, thermal printers require special paper that is expensive and usually somewhat odd to the touch. Many experienced librarians are familiar with Texas Instruments Silent 700 terminals, which use thermal printers. There have been worse thermal printers since then, as well as better ones, but for general-purpose printing the devices have never been ideal.

Ink-Jet Printers

Ink-jet printers use ink but not impact. Instead, the ink reaches the paper through one of several means. In some cases, electricity forces drops of ink out of nozzles when required. In others, drops spray out continuously but are deflected electronically into a recycling area except when ink is actually needed. A third method uses solid sticks of waxy or plastic ink, melting dots on demand.

An ink-jet printer is a dot-matrix printer, using a row of nozzles to produce characters. These printers are about as silent as thermal printers but generally produce better-quality output on somewhat more familiar paper. Color ink-jet printers can produce vivid output at moderate speeds; monochrome printers can combine decent print quality, high speed, low cost, and low noise.

Until the early 1980s ink-jet printers were known as expensive, troublesome devices, offering good quality but with high maintenance costs. Hewlett-Packard revolutionized the market segment with the HP ThinkJet: a cheap, very compact, decent-quality printer that ran quietly, required little maintenance, and worked. The ThinkJet is still, in some ways, an anomaly: it is far simpler and much less expensive than almost any other ink-jet printer on the market, and sells in enormous quantities. HP has since introduced the PaintJet, a color printer with similar quantities.

During 1987 and early 1988 Hewlett-Packard has continued to transform ink-jet printing into an almost ideal technology for applications in which neither very high speed nor multiple copies are required. One problem with all ink-jet printers had been the special paper required for good print quality: somewhat slick on one side, absorbent on the other, and nearly impossible to write on with most pens. New ink-jet mechanisms introduced by HP in late 1987 solved that problem, making it possible to use plain paper with existing ThinkJet printers. The second introduction was the DeskJet, an under-$1,000 (in 1988) printer producing almost laser-quality (300-dot-per-inch) output at reasonable speed on plain paper.

The ThinkJet and other printers of its ilk may be the most useful compact printers on the market They are also some of the lightest, cheapest (to buy and use), and quietest. Before very late 1987 the special paper requirement represented a serious drawback. As of this writing, the only real drawbacks are that ink-jet printers are not as fast as page printers and that they cannot produce multipart forms, since the ink does not hit the printer with any real force.

Ink-jet printers are particularly well-suited to public areas of a library. The materials are inexpensive, the printers are about as quiet as printers can be, the printers are themselves inexpensive, easy to maintain and the print quality is, while not superb (except for the DeskJet), adequate.

Plotters

Plotters draw lines on paper to produce text or, more typically, images. Plotters involve complex paper-handling, pen-handling, and pen selection mechanisms. They are special-purpose devices, suited to drafting, computer-assisted design, high-quality graphic output, and other similar purposes. They can print text, slowly and at high cost, but they are not really designed for text printing. As with ink-jet printers, Hewlett-Packard may be the most important single name in plotters, to such an extent that some IBM personal computer plotters are actually Hewlett-Packard products with the IBM name attached.

Plotters can produce some of the best multicolor output, using several pens to achieve the desired effects. They tend to be fairly quiet, with paper motion and mechanical noises involved with pen selection creating the most significant noises. They serve uniquely well for their special purpose, and seem likely to continue as an important technology with little or no relevance to the library field.

Laser and Other Page Printers

The last category of computer printers applicable to library work is page printers: printers that produce an entire page of output at once. Page printers are commonly called laser printers, and the great majority of page printers do use laser imaging.

Most modern page printers work in the same way. A photosensitive drum or band is exposed to light. The light may either sensitize it so that it *does* pick up toner (a mixture of plastic and pigment) or so that it *does not*. The drum or band then picks up toner and transfers it to paper through electrical charges. The paper goes through a heated area that fuses the toner to the paper. That process is the basis for plain-paper copying (Xerox copiers and similar copiers), and is also the basis for most page printers.

Most desktop laser printers use print mechanisms based on photocopier mechanisms. The primary difference is that there is no glass plate and no light bar. Instead, a laser and mirror combination uses computer-generated information to scan line-by-line over the drum, causing charges equivalent to those caused by a copier's light bar. It is a form of copying, but without a physical original.

Not all page printers are laser printers. Some use a row of liquid crystal diodes to shut out or transmit light to the drum or band, others use light emitting diodes. The results are the same: dots on the drum or band are sensitized or desensitized, resulting in toner being permanently affixed to paper.

Laser printers have many advantages. They are about as noisy as copiers, which is to say much quieter than any other printers except thermal and ink-jet printers. They are fast: for straight text, 6 to 12 pages of text per minute, no matter how much copy is on the page. They use ordinary copier paper and can be relatively cheap to operate--usually 4¢ to 5¢ per page, more expensive than some dot-matrix printers but cheaper than most other printers. They produce extremely high-quality output. While they are dot-matrix printers, the matrix is so dense (usually 300 dots per inch in each direction, perhaps 30-by-40 dot matrices for typical characters) that their output looks better than daisywheel output.

They also provide remarkable flexibility for graphics and multiple character fonts. The high print density makes it reasonable to use proportional fonts and multiple typefaces and fonts on a single page, possibly mixed in with graphics. Desktop publishing makes sense only on laser printers or typesetting equipment. Whereas the best dot-matrix printers produce near-*letter*-quality output, laser printers produce near-*typeset* output.

The disadvantages of laser printers are fourfold. First, they cannot print multipart forms because there is no impact. Second, they cannot typically use as wide a range of paper sizes and thicknesses as impact printers. They can print only on individual sheets, and can only handle envelopes or thick paper with some difficulty. Third, they tend to be more expensive than other printers, although that disadvantage is declining: a $1,000 laser printer (at discount) is already available, and others will follow. Finally, inexpensive desktop laser printers are not designed for continuous use, day-in and day-out. A laser printer that prints 200 pages each business day will probably last for years with little or no maintenance--that's a fairly typical use rating (4,000 pages per month). But at 8 pages per minute, 200 pages is less than a half-hour's work; if a desktop laser printer prints continuously for 8 hours a day (conceivably almost 4,000 pages), it will almost certainly break down quite often, as would a desktop copier used continuously all day every day.

Hewlett-Packard also dominates this market, but in this case HP does not actually build the printer. Canon, a well-known Japanese firm, builds the print engine and HP adds electronics. HP's dominance comes from its early introduction of a reasonably priced printer, its reputation for quality, and its aggressive pricing. The current HP LaserJet, the Series II, with better-quality output than almost any other laser printer, can be purchased for as little as $1,700 at discount. This book was produced using a Hewlett-Packard LaserJet Series II to print camera-ready originals. When I say "near-typeset-quality," I'm also saying that it's good enough quality for some books. The second most important desktop laser printer, the Apple LaserWriter, is also based on the Canon print engine, with substantially more sophisticated electronics (in most models) to enable more flexible desktop publishing, at a higher price.

More expensive laser printers run at higher speeds and can run all day, every day without breaking down. The Research Libraries Group and the Library of Congress produce catalog cards on Xerox 9700 laser printers, able to print 120 pages per minute, 15 times the speed of an HP LaserJet. They are almost 150 times the price, at about $300,000. They will stand up to continuous use, something that desktop laser printers could never do. The Xerox 9700 actually has the same resolution (300 dots per inch) as the HP LaserJet, and if anything, slightly lower print quality.

Full-color laser printing requires much more complex printers. Such printing will be available by the end of this decade, but is unlikely to be practical for typical small-computer use for a few years to come.

Typesetting Equipment

Laser printers produce *near*-typeset quality. Computers can also generate output to drive real typesetting equipment. Such equipment is really not designed to be part of a personal computing installation, and would almost never make economic sense for any but the largest libraries. Typesetting equipment can also use several technologies; computer-driven typesetting is most likely to expose photosensitive paper through computer-driven light sources, although other techniques may be used.

Typesetting equipment is much more expensive, starting in the tens of thousands of dollars. It is not necessarily faster than laser printing, but it is much more detailed: 1,200 to 2,400 lines or dots per inch compared to 300 dots per inch.

The only relevance of typesetting equipment to typical library computing applications is that many personal computer programs can now generate output files that will drive phototypesetting systems directly. A library can prepare a publication using a laser printer for test runs and proofs, then produce the final output on a phototypesetter. The library prepares disks that drive the photo-typesetter directly, usually at much lower cost than any normal typesetting. A growing number of service shops offer rental time on laser printers and relatively inexpensive typesetting from the same disks.

Future Possibilities

It is safe to assume that computer-generated printing will be with us for decades to come. Some new technologies may arise, and some older ones may fall into disuse. Daisywheel printers already appear to be on the road to oblivion, although daisywheels will survive in some applications.

Page printers get better as time goes by. Higher-resolution desktop laser printers are already available, and coming down in price. Doubling the resolution to 600 dots per inch makes it extremely difficult even for experts to tell laser output from photo-typesetting. Doubling once more, to 1,200 dots per inch, will erase the distinction entirely. Twelve hundred dots per inch is considered true typeset quality. Six hundred dot-per-inch printers now cost $10,000 or so, and will surely become less expensive. Twelve hundred dots per inch may be harder to achieve, because toner particles must be very fine and paper movement extremely accurate for such high-density printing to work properly. Those are engineering problems, and will almost certainly be solved fairly soon.

It is clear that laser printers will become more and more popular as prices come down. It is also fairly clear that impact dot-matrix printers will continue to do well for some years. In many cases, they are much cheaper. They can handle jobs that laser printers cannot. There will continue to be a maddening variety of printers, frustrating for software developers but offering special capabilities to meet special needs.

SUMMARY

The best printer for a library application is the one that suits the application best. If money is not an object, laser printers will do very well for public access and most staff use. Where money is an object, ink-jet printers (and specifically the HP ThinkJet) may be the best choice for public use; a variety of other technologies may suit other needs.

Printers can be noisy, irritating, expensive, and low quality. Attaching printers to computers may sometimes seem like a black art. But most printers work, and work well. Even though they are more mechanically complex than most elements of computing, they seem to survive as well as some purely electronic elements.

SELECTED READING

The most useful material for those considering small printers may be the series of special Printer Survey issues published by *PC Magazine*. This series began in 1984 (vol. 3, no. 3 [November 27, 1984]) and has continued with a special issue each fall. Each issue contains more than 100 individual printer reviews and detailed comparative charts. The issues cover all printers released within the previous year that are designed for use with MS-DOS personal computers-- which means very nearly all personal computer printers, except for a handful specifically designed for Apple or other computers.

14

Graphics and Speech

Most of the time computers are used to manipulate words and numbers. But for almost three decades, some people have used computers to manipulate visual images, and mechanical speech began long before computers. Today's computers offer powerful, flexible handling of graphics and visual images for a variety of purposes, from the simple bar charts created with spreadsheet programs to the planet-transforming sequence in *Star Trek II*, wholly computer-generated by Industrial Light and Magic. Speech synthesis has very clear functions, narrowly useful for most people and vitally important for some; speech recognition, however, has yet to live up to the early promises of developers and futurists.

This chapter mentions only a few aspects of computer graphics, image processing, speech synthesis, and speech recognition. Several recent books in this chapter's Selected Reading section offer much more detailed overviews.

COMPUTER GRAPHICS

The right graphics can enhance many presentations or constitute its own art form; the wrong graphics can mislead the viewer and distract from effective textual communication. Until recently computer graphics cost too much and required too much time for the typical user. Now the primary limitations are skill and appropriateness.

Historical Notes

The first computer-generated plots began around 1950. At about that time John Whitney Sr. began to experiment with computer graphics and animation. Two years later the Whirlwind I at MIT included a CRT specifically for plotting. Six years after that computer graphics became fundamental to a specific computing application: the SAGE air defense system.

The year 1960 saw considerable expansion in computer graphics, including computer animation at Bell Labs and a computer graphics lab at the New York Institute of Technology. Computer-aided design and drafting (CADD), a major industrial use of computer graphics, began no later than 1965.

Computer graphics reached the masses, in a very limited way, in 1972 when Nolan Bushnell invented PONG, the first video game. Minicomputer-based CADD systems--powerful computers dedicated to that single use--appeared around the same time. The Xerox Palo Alto Research Center, better known as PARC, worked on visual interfaces for computers for some time before releasing the Alto computer in 1974. The Alto used icons, windows, a mouse, and other elements that would reappear in the Apple Macintosh a decade later.

Good computer graphics require good displays, and inexpensive displays help to spread graphics processing. Relatively inexpensive raster-based graphics displays (i.e., computer-driven cathode ray tubes) became available around 1975. Since then, displays have continued to become cheaper and better in resolution, color availability, size, and other attributes. Computer and software developments have made graphics available to almost everybody who owns a computer.

Graphic and Image Processing Basics

Graphics can be displayed or printed in one of two manners: as vectors or as dot patterns. Graphics can also be processed in either manner, with some translation possible between the two.

Vectors

A vector is a line segment with a given length running in a given direction, and is defined by two points on a surface, the beginning and end. Line-drawing graphics usually define a set of curves in addition to straight lines.

Plotters are vector devices and produce printed output by drawing lines. There have also been vector display devices, such as those made by Tektronix, and some may still be used for special purposes. Vector displays actually "paint" lines on the screen with the cathode ray, deflecting the ray in specific ways under program command. Some vector displays use phosphors that retain an image until explicitly erased: these "storage displays" show a solid, un-flickering image that is usually rather dim. Other vector displays constantly refresh the set of vectors. Vector displays are almost un-heard of in personal computing and tend to be much more ex-pensive and more limited in uses than raster devices.

Vector *processing and storage* have real advantages. True vectors require only two items of information: the coordinates of each end point of the line. Curved lines require more information, but still much less than a map of every point to be displayed. Vectors can also be scaled and manipulated very easily. The line segments can be expanded or shrunk using relatively little computing power, and can be rotated relatively easily as well. (When speaking of vectors henceforth, I include curved lines; although these do involve more information, they can still be identified and stored compactly and processed easily.)

Most computer drawing programs use vectors as much as pos-sible, adding shading and fill patterns within defined spaces for en-hancement. That includes CADD systems for personal computers and larger computers. Good systems allow the user to identify a set of vectors as an object, storing the object and manipulating it inde-pendently of other objects. A vector-based object can be expanded, reduced, duplicated, and otherwise modified without becoming "grainy": it continues to be a set of lines and curves.

Most business graphics, such as the graphs produced from spreadsheet programs, are generated as vector graphics. Such graphs normally consist only of straight lines, arcs of circles (in pie charts), fill patterns or colors, and text.

Dots and Rasters

Most computer display devices and hard-copy devices don't draw solid lines and curves. Instead, they display all information (text and graphics) as dots: *picture elements* or *pixels*. (Technically, the term "pixel" should be reserved for displays; in practice, it applies equally well to hard-copy resolution. The term dates back to 1969, and is in *Webster's Ninth New Collegiate Dictionary*.)

For CRT displays (and sometimes for laser printers), another term comes into use: *raster* or *raster-scan display*. The raster is both the display area of a television or CRT and the set of scanning lines that form the image. A normal television or CRT image is created by a cathode ray that sweeps steadily back and forth in horizontal sweeps, moving down the screen with each sweep until it reaches the bottom and jumps back to the top. The position of the beam is always predictable as a function of time. The image is created by turning the beam on and off, lighting up or not lighting up portions of the phosphor. The only practical way to handle graphics on a raster-scan device is dot by dot, pixel by pixel. To use printer terminology, most raster-scan devices are treated as dot-matrix displays.

Virtually all computer displays other than CRTs are also dot-matrix displays, including plasma screens and LCD screens. So are most contemporary computer printers: dot-matrix printers, obviously, but also laser printers and thermal printers. The only vector printing devices in common use are plotters and the only other non-dot-matrix printing devices are solid-character printers such as daisywheel printers.

Every dot-matrix device is physically capable of producing graphics, limited in resolution to the number of dots per square inch. That may not be the way the device is used, of course. It is fair to assume that most dot-matrix displays and printers, most of the time, produce text--albeit text that is defined as a series of dots, either within the display or printer or within the computer. Displaying graphics requires addressing individual pixels rather than character matrices. Another term frequently used in discussing displays is *all-points addressability*: a graphics support system should be able to modify any given pixel on a screen independently of any other pixel.

Many graphics displays consist of vector graphics converted to pixels, a straightforward process that does not always yield perfect results. The vectors are mapped onto the field of bits--lighting up or printing the pixels that fall on each line or closest to it--creating a *bit-mapped display.* But graphics may also be read or created as a series of pixels. Painting programs (as opposed to drawing programs) generally produce bit-mapped images, and scanners convert images on paper into bit-mapped storage, as do devices for capturing images from video cameras.

Within a bit-mapped display, each pixel is (theoretically) independent of all adjacent pixels. That may mean storing each pixel as a bit on disk or in memory, leading to very large storage requirements. There are three ways of reducing the storage requirements:

1. Simplifying the image by reducing the resolution. Once reduced, the resolution can never be regained: if a full-page image scanned at 300 dots per inch (yielding a little more than 1 million characters or 8.4 million pixels) is reduced to the resolution of a Wyse 700 (1 million pixels) and stored at that resolution, 88 percent of the information originally captured will be lost. If restored to a full-sized display or printed image, the image will have an effective resolution of only 36.5 dots per inch, reducing high-quality scanning to coarse and ugly output. That doesn't usually happen, of course, because the image is typically stored at high resolution even if it is displayed at lower resolution.

2. Compressing the image by some technique that takes advantage of patterns--for example, converting a succession of white or black elements to a number, or storing only the differences between one scanned line and the next. A number of compression techniques exist, and some claim reduction to as little as one-tenth of the original storage. These techniques are also used in telefacsimile to reduce communications requirements.

3. Converting the image to vectors. In some ways, this is the ideal solution, but it makes sense only in certain cases. If an image really consists of line drawings, it may be possible to produce an effective vector equivalent. Alternatively, if the goal in processing an image is to create a line-drawing equiv-

alent, image processing and human intervention may make such conversion feasible.

Optical Scanning and Character Recognition

Unless a computer user or program creates graphics directly on the computer, the graphics must come from external sources. Two widespread techniques for converting visual material to digital form both work by scanning: in one case, by scanning a captured video image (typically from a videocamera); in the other and more common case, by scanning the image on a sheet of paper.

The latter technique can be used for graphics work, but also as a means of converting text to machine-readable form if the scanned image can be recognized as sets of characters. It is also a fundamental part of telefacsimile (discussed in chapter 18).

A scanner "reads" a printed page, turning the light and dark areas into off and on signals or numbers representing shades of gray or colors. Whatever the hardware technique, the result is a large quantity of information that constitutes a bit map of the page image--millions of picture elements. That bit map can be displayed as a graphics image and manipulated using graphics software; some software will attempt to convert the image into a set of vectors, usually with the help of the computer user.

Turning the bit map into text requires software to analyze the picture elements and recognize groups of them as letters. Libraries have used one of the most sophisticated optical scanning and character recognition systems, combined with speech synthesis, to aid blind and visually impaired patrons--the Kurzweil reading machine, made by a division of Xerox. The Kurzweil can "speak" the words in a book only by recognizing the characters on a page.

Character recognition software has gotten cheaper, but most of the cheap systems lack sophistication. Quite a few programs can achieve fairly high accuracy with typed text or (in some cases) text printed on a good-quality dot matrix printer. Very few can read proportional type, as is used in nearly all books and a great deal of contemporary computer output. The Kurzweil can, and so can one or two other expensive systems. Most software systems can read only a few sizes and faces of type, and most have very little tolerance for pages that are at an angle. A photocopied page, where the copy is slightly askew, may be totally unreadable.

Ideally character recognition and scanning can provide a fast, easy way to convert text to machine-readable form. That ideal comes closer to reality each year, leaving the problems of copyright and other aspects of converting text. But the ideal is still not cheap or certain. The human eye and mind are wonderfully flexible and forgiving; computers are neither.

Scanners certainly have current roles in some libraries as part of Kurzweil units, for telefacsimile, or for various forms of graphic input. Scanners as text acquisition systems can work now and should play more of a role in the future, but it is easy to oversell character recognition. Eighty percent accuracy sounds fairly impressive, but a system that converts with 80 percent accuracy will require more labor than retyping the text, according to most estimates. Would you accept a book in which one of every five letters or words was either misprinted, illegible, or absent?

Drawbacks and Problems with Graphics

The primary mechanical problem with image processing has already been mentioned: high-resolution images and particularly images with lifelike color require large amounts of memory and fairly expensive displays. In some cases graphics also force messy tradeoffs in purchase decisions. The worst case, now largely historic, is the suffering that IBM Color Graphics Adapter (CGA) users go through when handling text in order to use relatively low-resolution color graphics. Fortunately most contemporary graphics devices offer sufficient resolution for comfortable work with text. Good graphics still cost money, but the equipment becomes more affordable each year. Other problems with graphics are caused more by people than by technology.

Memory and Display

All computer-based image processing shares one common problem: images require much more storage and computer processing than text because they consist of light, dark, and color rather than a limited set of arbitrary symbols. A page of this book contains roughly 2,000 characters (16,000 bits), which can be displayed on a single screen. If that display is done as graphics (black and white only), it will require 31,500 characters (252,000 bits), 16 times as much storage. Adding 16 shades of gray or colors would quadruple the requirement to 126,000 characters or roughly 1 million bits.

The requirements increase as more sophisticated graphics add higher resolution and more colors and shades. Ten years ago those requirements--and the cost of high-quality displays capable of high resolution--limited computer graphics to very expensive systems. Memory was expensive, and it was not enough to simply store the pixels, they also had to be generated and maintained. High-resolution graphics require large quantities of memory and fast computing and display devices; fortunately, such devices are now relatively inexpensive. Nevertheless, graphics require substantially more disk space (to store images) than text processing does.

Talent and Appropriateness

The other major problem with graphics is a byproduct of powerful, inexpensive graphics hardware and software. Good graphics software doesn't make a person an artist, any more than good word processing software makes a person a novelist.

Most of us have sat through heavily illustrated talks in which the slides or transparencies didn't make sense or couldn't be read and most of us have encountered many flyers and other printed presentations in which poorly used graphics detract from the message rather than enhance it.

This problem is not, strictly speaking, a drawback of graphics, except to the extent that easily used tools encourage people to indulge in visual creation without taking the time to learn the basics of art or design. Most libraries can make good use of graphics, but need to remember that amateurish productions will damage the image of the library and probably fail to achieve the intended results.

TALKING WITH YOUR COMPUTER

Talking and listening computers have been a mainstay of science fiction on television and film for many years. Personal computers and larger computers can now be made to talk and listen, within limits. The speaking computer serves some very useful purposes. As with many other technologies, speaking computers found early use in libraries in the form of the Kurzweil reading machine. Voice input has certain specific uses today and may have more in the future, but has some real limitations, both technological and practical.

The Computer Speaks

There are times when reading a computer display is inconvenient or impossible. If you are using computer facilities over the phone, with the buttons serving as a limited input system, you have no display for output. If you can't see well enough to read a display, or can't see at all, you need some other means of output. Computer-generated speech can provide that output.

People have toyed with the idea of artificially produced speech for centuries. The first plausible speaking machine was apparently created by Wolfgang von Kempelen around 1791. Work toward understanding the mechanisms of speech and replicating human speech continued and, in the 1930s and 1940s, oscilloscopes and other instruments made it possible to analyze the patterns of speech as captured by microphones. The first electronic synthesized speech was demonstrated at the New York World's Fair in 1939 in the form of the Voder, created by Homer Dudley of Bell Labs. Controlled by an operator using a keyboard and pedal, the Voder could generate understandable speech in real time. Intel, Bell Labs, Texas Instruments, National Semiconductor, and General Instruments all introduced chip-based speech synthesis systems in the late 1970s and early 1980s. Perhaps the earliest major consumer example of digitally synthesized speech came from Texas Instruments at the end of the 1970s: Speak and Spell, a children's educational toy.

Approaches to Voice Synthesis

In order to synthesize speech, the computer must be able to recognize words and their pronunciation. The computer must also produce that pronunciation in a manner that makes sense to the listener. Research has gone into the elements of speech that make it understandable, in order to devise ways to store intelligible speech without using impossibly large quantities of memory. Research and development also work on different ways to produce synthesized speech so that it will be intelligible.

The special problems of speech synthesis have to do with stringing words together into understandable sentences and, in open-ended systems, putting phonemes (the basic elements of spoken language) together into understandable words. While pitch is relatively unimportant in English, intonation still plays a significant role in understanding; the same sentence may have several meanings depending on stress and intonation. Similarly, although there may be only 60 or so phonemes in the English language, the ways that phonemes fit together into words makes word synthesis relatively complex.

Set Vocabulary and Open Vocabulary

Many commercial speech synthesis chips and systems have it easy. They work with a limited vocabulary, probably store complete words, and need only put the right words in the right order. Examples are in "talking cars," telephone response systems, electronic banking systems, and other situations where the vocabulary can be predicted.

An intermediate level of complexity will become more popular as spoken output becomes part of more computer programs. Databases and other programs can generate spoken results, but the results will follow a predictable syntax and will not necessarily raise problems of full-sentence understanding. The synthetic speech mechanism may require an open vocabulary (i.e., it might need to store phonemes and be able to generate words given sets of letters). That ability requires sets of rules and exceptions: rules for common English spelling-pronunciation relationships, and exception dictionaries for the many words that don't follow the rules.

The most complex situation occurs in the Kurzweil reading machine and recently introduced computer attachments for the blind, which must generate speech from any textual stream. These systems provide the most powerful possibilities, particularly for general use of computers by the visually impaired, but also the most complex requirements. Not only must such a machine be able to turn any set of characters into either spoken characters or (preferably) a word, it should be able to form a sequence of words into a coherent, understandable sentence.

Speech synthesis already works well enough to serve visually impaired users in some cases. The voices may be "mechanical" and lack plausible intonation patterns, but with a patient listener the computer can indeed speak with fair intelligibility.

Library Uses for Voice Synthesis

The primary use for voice synthesis in libraries is also the most complex: providing access to information for visually impaired patrons. Such access can fall into three general categories: the printed word, the online catalog, and other computer-based information.

The history of the Kurzweil reading machine in libraries is not uniformly positive, but there are those who find it valuable. As similar devices get less expensive and more understandable, they should open the world of books to more patrons who can't read the print.

The online catalog presents another opportunity for better access, but also presents some special challenges. Some of the information on a catalog screen may be unusually difficult to speak, and the system must recognize which fields (for example, call numbers) should be spelled out rather than spoken as words. The sheer volume of information presented in a typical online catalog, particularly a menu-driven catalog, may also present a problem.

A speaking terminal for an online catalog should provide all the equipment needed for spoken access to other online and computer-based information. Most libraries will never find it easy to integrate such devices into their systems given the added cost and the need to provide headsets or other means of privacy. But with improving clarity of synthetic speech and more comprehensive systems for handling open-ended vocabularies, speaking terminals and computers may make sense for more libraries so that they can serve potential patrons not now being served.

The Computer Listens

Talking computers serve some very real needs (and provide entertainment in some cases), even if some uses of talking chips may seem frivolous or even annoying. Listening computers can also solve some very real problems: specific problems in industry and other areas, and general problems of those who cannot handle keyboards in any reasonable manner. But listening computers can also cause problems. Would a computer know when it was being spoken to and, more important, when it was not?

Technical Problems

Speech recognition systems work by comparing the sound patterns received over a microphone with stored sound patterns. Both stored sound patterns and received sound patterns may be processed (based on the results of speech synthesis research) in order to isolate those elements of speech that are crucial to understanding.

Speech recognition involves three serious problems in addition to those involved in speech synthesis:

1. Any two people have significantly different voices; patterns that work for one person won't work for another. General-purpose patterns to match all speakers are not available, and there is no good indication of whether such matching is possible. Current speech recognition systems cannot handle even a group of people who all have the same accent and same vocal range and recognize more than a few words. Even within that narrow spectrum, each person has his or her own idiolect (personal dialect) and unique vocal pattern. A recognition system that could recognize all common American accents equally well, let alone those of speakers throughout the English-speaking world, is far beyond current abilities; most recognition systems must be trained to recognize each voice.

2. A single person's voice changes over time and because of changing circumstances. A person with a cold sounds *substantially* different than the same person when well. Excitement, danger, and fatigue will all change a person's voice pattern. It is quite possible that, if you become frustrated by occasional errors in voice recognition, your voice will change sufficiently so that the recognition will become totally useless. Even with training the recognition system may not work perfectly, and retraining may be necessary over time.

3. It is one thing to recognize a distinct word, spoken with an artificial pause before and after the word, but that isn't the way people speak. Very few speech recognition systems can recognize continuous speech (as opposed to words isolated by lengthy pauses), and most of those can recognize only a small vocabulary. Dictating, to, an, isolated, speech, recognition, system, would, be, as, annoying, as, reading, this, sentence.

Continuous speech involves work on the part of the listener as well as the speaker: the listener brings an enormously sophisticated context to bear on the speech. In fact many combinations of syllables could be taken as different sets of words, if you either lacked or misunderstood the context. We record anecdotes of children's errors in this regard, mostly involving chants, songs, or prayers. The cross-eyed bear Gladly is only one of the better-known confusions of childhood.

Even children listening to hymns come with an enormous background in understanding speech and applying almost infinite context. Computers lack that extended background. When people speak, they do not enunciate each word as a wholly separate entity; they speak in phrases and sentences, with words coming in an unbroken stream. As far as speech recognition software has already come, it must go much further before you could expect to see reasonably accurate transcription of connected speech. Until then, you can expect to see some fairly ludicrous transcriptions. After all, children are much smarter than computers.

Current Speech Recognition Products

You can certainly purchase speech recognition systems in 1988, although none that will allow you to dictate a letter or article into your computer. A *PC Magazine* survey in late 1987 (cited at the end of this chapter) reviewed 15 systems that can be used with IBM PC and compatible computers, ranging from $199 to $8,995 in 1987 prices. All 15 claim 98% accuracy, but within severe limitations. Eleven can recognize only isolated words, typically from only one speaker, with the largest vocabulary reaching 1,000 words. Four attempt to deal with connected speech, but with very small vocabularies (50 to 200 words).

These systems and most other speech recognition products currently available have real uses for inventory, for replacing the keyboard on a keystroke-by-keystroke basis, and for limited sets of commands to speed processing. They do not have much general usefulness for converting speech into machine-readable text.

Do You Really Want to Talk to Your Computer?

Assume for the moment that artificial intelligence (AI) research has suddenly broken out of its decades-long "just around the corner" period. Assume that AI, faster computers, cheap, fast storage, and clever programming make it possible to build a computer interface that really can recognize 99.9 percent of words within connected speech from any English-speaking user. Would that be a good general-purpose replacement for a keyboard, and would it be a good thing?

Perhaps not. The keyboard offers controlled communication with the computer, where verbal communication in most settings is relatively uncontrolled. With a fully developed listening computer, you might have to shut off the microphone when another person walks into your office, when you receive a phone call, or when you feel like venting your frustration with a project. A listening computer may offer a more intimate interface than most of us choose to have. If you want a computer as a friend, vocal interaction may be part of that friendship. If you simply want it to be an effective, efficient tool, vocal interaction may not be desirable.

Voice Storage and Playback

A computer may be useful to store and play back speech without any recognition of the content of the speech. Computers can store vocal messages in the same way that they can convert any other sound to digital form and store it. Voice mail can be an interesting adjunct to electronic mail for an organization that can afford the disk storage required to store extended voice messages.

The technology of voice storage and playback is digital audio, although voice storage involves a much smaller bandwidth and a much narrower dynamic range. The voice is sampled and converted into digital streams which are recorded on magnetic disk or some other medium. When playback is requested, the digital stream is converted back into audio form.

Voice storage and playback do not involve any content analysis on the part of the computer. If messages are addressed, the addressing is done through specific input (such as the tones created by telephone buttons) and recognized on that basis. The message is simply a stream of digits; the computer makes no attempt to convert that stream into information or process it in any way. Effectively the computer is simply a fancy recorder which, in some cases, can be a reasonable use.

SUMMARY

Contemporary computer graphics offer enormous flexibility and power at relatively modest prices, but that power does nothing to assure competent, coherent results. Libraries can make good use of computer graphics, but should recognize that the computer does not guarantee good taste or skillful presentation.

For the right money and in the right circumstances, your computer can talk to you; that power can be useful in a number of specialized library settings. You can only talk to it (and have it pay attention) with a small vocabulary, at significant expense, and in special circumstances. For now and for the near future, the keyboard is still the best way of controlling and communicating with a computer.

SELECTED READING

Artwick, Bruce A. *Applied Concepts in Microcomputer Graphics*. Englewood Cliffs, N.J.: Prentice-Hall, 1984. 374 pp. Index. (Readable, thorough introduction by the creator of *Flight Simulator*. Intended for those who wish to design graphic systems.)

Boyne, Walter J., and Hernan Otano. "Direct Document Capture and Full Text Indexing: An Introduction to the National Air and Space Museum System." *Library Hi Tech* 2, no. 4 (Winter 1984): 7-14. (One ongoing experiment in image capture and character recognition.)

Gerald, Jeanette. "Voice Response Systems Technology." *Library Hi Tech* 2, no. 4 (Winter 1984):33-38. (Brief introduction to voice response.)

Linggard, R. *Electronic Synthesis of Speech*. Cambridge, England: Cambridge University Press, 1985. 149 pp. Exhaustive bibliography; index. (More scholarly than Morgan's *Talking Chips*, less readable and entertaining. Good historical background. Very technical through much of the text, but does provide some information not in Morgan.)

Marshall, George R. *Computer Graphics in Application*. Englewood Cliffs, N.J.: Prentice-Hall, 1987. (A Reston Book.) 454 pp. Bibliography; index. (Designed as a text. Includes [seemingly] every cliche and half-fact in the field. Readable and includes quite a bit of information, but must be approached carefully.)

Morgan, Nelson. *Talking Chips*. New York: McGraw-Hill, 1984. (National's Semiconductor Technology Series.) 178 pp. Glossary; bibliography; index. (Clear and frequently entertaining account of the technology of speech synthesis. Deeply technical in some passages, but most of the book is readable and informative. The author leaves in the wonderful and often snide footnotes that most of us automatically remove before a final draft.)

Rosch, Winn L. "Voice Recognition: Understanding the Master's Voice." *PC Magazine* 6, no. 18 (October 27, 1987):261-308.

(Clear, brief discussion of basic aspects of voice recognition, followed by careful reviews of 15 voice recognition products available for use with personal computers. A good survey of the current field.)

15

Magnetic Storage

Floppy disks, hard disks, and magnetic tape all use the same basic technology as audiocassettes and videocassettes. That technology typically begins with rust (i.e., ferric oxide, Fe_2O_3). Some magnetic media now use materials other than ferric oxide, but it's reasonable to say that computer memories tend to be rusty.

MAGNETIC RECORDING

In 1898 Valdemar Poulsen wound a steel piano wire in a spiral groove around the surface of a drum. A rod next to the drum held an electromagnet. By rotating the drum and pulling the electromagnet down the rod, current from a microphone would magnetize the steel wire. The signal could be played back over headphones. As demonstrated at the 1900 Paris Exposition, magnetic recording had begun.

Steel wires continued as the medium of choice until 1927, when J. A. O'Neill patented a recording tape--paper tape coated with magnetic liquid and dried. Fritz Pfleumer patented a similar tape in Germany using iron powder as a medium. The result was the Magnetophon, introduced in 1935 by AEG and IGF in Germany. After World War II Magnetophons came to the United States. 3M developed iron oxide (rust) coated tape in 1947; Ampex began to sell tape recorders in 1948.

All magnetic recording involves the use of an electromagnetic recording head to cause particles within a medium to take on a desired magnetic orientation, and the use of a playback head (which may be the same head) to sense the magnetic orientations. Those orientations may be read as patterns analogous to waveforms (as in audiotape and videotape), or may be treated as strictly zeros and ones (as in all magnetic storage for computers).

The constants are a magnetic coating, one or more recording heads, and motion. With one exception, magnetic media accept or feed back information only when the medium, the head, or both move. Beyond the constants, each application and each medium involves different details. As with audiocassettes, most computer recording media use moving media rather than moving heads to extract the information. While heads do indeed move in floppy and hard disks, the movement is to locate different portions of the data; the data is generated based on movement of the disk.

The single exception is core memory, consisting of wire grids with small magnetic rings at wire intersections. Signals sent through pairs of wires sensed and set the orientation of the rings. Core memory has essentially vanished as a technology, since semiconductor memory (RAM) requires much less space, operates much more rapidly, and costs much less to produce and operate.

MAGNETIC TAPE

Magnetic tape for computer storage functions in much the same way as does magnetic tape for audio recording. Fixed heads (one per channel) record, and playback information on moving tape. Even the tape coatings are similar, to the point that computer tape can, if slit to the width of audiotape, be used to make relatively low quality sound recordings.

Computer tape recording is both more difficult and simpler than audio recording. Audio recording requires linear (or predictably nonlinear) response over a wide range of frequencies and wide amplitude range, while digital recording requires nothing more than off-and-on sequences. But computer tape must start and stop rapidly and predictably, and minor errors in digital recordings will cause much more damage than in audiotape. Computer tape recording also involves much higher-speed motion and data transfer than audiotape, imposing more strenuous demands on the tape backing, the magnetic formulation (particularly the smoothness and durability of the coating), and the recorder mechanism.

Most contemporary computer tape units use nine tracks and heads, one for each bit in a character and a ninth for a parity bit. A parity bit is an extra bit that is set either so that every character has an odd number of "on" bits or an even number of "on" bits, for odd or even parity respectively. Parity bits provide a crude form of error-detection: if any one bit is read incorrectly, the parity will be wrong. Most open-reel computer tapes store information either at 1,600 characters per inch or 6,250 characters per inch, with a few older units still restricted to 800 characters per inch.

Computer tape represented an enormous improvement in storage density and handling speed over punched cards. In the years after computer tape recording became practical, it came to dominate mass storage and mass data communications applications. Tapes became higher quality and generally cheaper; tape mechanisms came down slowly in price and improved steadily in performance. But tape was never an ideal mechanism for direct data storage, for in order to get to a particular piece of information the computer must read through the tape from the beginning or end. Even though some modern computer tape subsystems can read an entire reel in two or three minutes, that's still an eternity when you're using information interactively.

For some years, hard disks represented the medium of choice for interactive applications but were so expensive that tape still seemed appropriate for operations in which immediate access was not required. As hard disk prices come down and capacities improve, the emphasis continues to shift to disk storage. Movies may still show spinning tape reels to illustrate computers processing information, but fewer and fewer applications use tape as a direct medium in data processing.

Advantages and Chief Uses

Tape still has its uses, some of which appear likely to remain for years to come. It is still the cheapest and most reliable way to save backup copies of hard disks, particularly since tapes can be sent to off-site locations for protection. It is still the best way to send large quantities of information from one computer to another when the two lack a direct high-speed connection. It is still the best way to store large quantities of information when the information is never needed instantaneously and rarely needed at all, particularly if those rare needs require processing most or all of the information rather than a single element.

The key advantages of tape are that it is cheap, compact, and proven. A single 2,400-foot reel of tape recorded at 6,250 bpi (bits per inch, or characters per inch on 9-track tape) using 32,000 characters per block, can store roughly 170 million characters, costs about $15 to $20, and can be mailed for a couple of dollars. For storage purposes, thousands of such reels can be stored in a single room, offering much denser storage than any other magnetic medium.

Disadvantages and Problems

The disadvantages of tape are that it is not a true archival medium and that access is slow and sequential. Slow and sequential access rule out tape for interactive retrieval. The other disadvantage only matters if people mistakenly use tape as an archival medium. It is not. While the backing and the magnetic material may stay intact for decades, a particular digital recording may deteriorate within a few years, frequently because of magnetic print-through. That doesn't matter for typical short-term backup uses, where a year's survival should be more than enough, but it does matter if you need to retrieve data stored 10 years earlier. If the tape is copied to a different tape every year, you should still have a good database after 10 years. If not, the database may or may not be intact.

Tapes cause problems in data communications when the sending agency and receiving agency don't understand what the other is doing. There are standards for tape but, unfortunately, there are several of them. While most modern tape drives can write or read 6,250 bpi and 1,600 bpi tapes interchangeably, many institutions still have tape drives that cannot read 6,250 bpi tapes. While there are ANSI standards for internal tape labels (readable by computer) and for tape format, the dominant company in large-scale computers, IBM, has its own standards--two of them. Fortunately, most IBM computers can also read and write ANSI tapes, and many non-IBM computers can read and write IBM-format tapes.

Librarians can find tape standards particularly tricky. Most transaction and archival tapes of bibliographic data (including those generated by OCLC and by RLG [Research Libraries Group] as of early 1988) are created using a tape format ("spanned but un-blocked") that no longer meets any national standard. The format used to write USMARC records to tape by both OCLC and RLG is the same format used by the Library of Congress prior to 1977. Since then ANSI has adopted and LC has moved to a new format. Some organizations within the library field can only read tapes produced using the pre-1977 format; many organizations outside the library field have never heard of or used that format.

Magnetic tape is a mature medium. Improvements continue within the field, but at a slower pace than in other computer-related fields. It should survive for years, but cheap write-once optical discs or reasonably priced erasable optical or optomagnetic discs could eventually make digital tape obsolete. That has not happened yet, but tape does not have any magical qualities that could prevent it from happening.

HARD DISKS

The computer industry recognized the need for random access early in its history. Rey Johnson of IBM began work toward a random-access data storage system in 1952, and in 1955 IBM announced the IBM 305 or RAMAC (Random Access Method of Accounting and Control) disk drive. This drive was 24 inches in diameter, with 50 disks rotating at 1,200 revolutions per minute. It had a total capacity of five million characters.

That was the start of the hard disk industry, and IBM continues to be a dominant supplier of hard disks and a leader in developing better hard disks. Hard disks made interactive computing possible and preceded online information services. In more than three decades of use, hard disks have continued to evolve toward smaller sizes, higher capacities, faster speeds, and better cost/performance ratios.

A relatively recent IBM model, the 3380, has only 16 disks (8 each on two spindles), and the disks are only 14 inches in diameter, but the capacity of the device is 2.5 gigabytes. A gigabyte is one billion characters (one thousand million--the prefix *giga* avoids the conflict between the British and American meanings of *billion*). A 3380 uses one-third as many disks, each having about one-third as much recording surface, to store 500 times as much information as the RAMAC. Retrieval for any character on a 3380 is many times faster than on the original RAMAC, but the principles of the device remain the same.

The Basics

A hard disk or disk pack typically consists of one or more aluminum alloy platters, coated on both sides with magnetic material and mounted on a common spindle with space between the platters. One or more recording/playback heads for each surface (two surfaces per platter) are mounted on arms, making up a comb that moves back and forth to access different portions of the disk. The disk spins at a constant speed, typically 3,600 revolutions per minute. The heads fly slightly above the surface on a cushion of air created by the spinning surface. Unlike tape recorders and diskette recorders, recording heads on hard disks never intentionally contact the recording surface: at 3,600 rpm, the friction created would rapidly wear out head and surface alike.

Each surface is logically formatted into tracks--concentric circles, separately addressable, rather than the single spiral track that makes up each surface of a vinyl disk, CD, or CD-ROM. Hard disks are CAV devices: the disk spins at a constant speed so that tracks at the inside of the disk must be more densely recorded than tracks at the outside. Each track is divided into sectors, the same number of sectors in each track, with physically smaller sectors nearer the spindle. The number of sectors per track and number of tracks on a surface vary enormously among different hard disk designs, as does the size of each platter and the number of bytes that can be recorded in each sector. The most popular hard disks for personal computers in 1988 are 3.25 inches and 5.25 inches, while larger computers still generally use 8 inch and 14 inch disks. Smaller hard disks will come to market in 1988 or 1989, but disks smaller than the two-inch models soon to be introduced may not make much sense.

The size of sectors is important because space on a hard disk is almost always allocated on a sector-by-sector basis or on some larger scale. If one file uses only one-quarter of a sector, the rest of the sector will be wasted, but the result is much more efficient processing since the computer need not keep track of each individual byte on the hard disk and can read or write a sector at a time. In practice, most systems allocate space in units larger than a sector, such as a "cluster" of 2, 4, 8, or 16 sectors; an entire track; or a "cylinder," which is the same track on all surfaces of a disk pack.

To give an example, one of the most popular hard disks for high-speed personal computers (in 1988) is the Seagate ST251. It consists of three platters and has six heads. Each of the 6 surfaces has 820 tracks and each track has 17 sectors. Each sector stores 512 characters (bytes). Thus, storage might be allocated by the sector (512 bytes), a cluster of four sectors (2,048 bytes or "2K"), a track of 17 sectors (8.5K) or a cylinder holding 51K (actually 52,224 bytes). The disk is considered a "40Meg" device and stores a total of 42,823,680 bytes. On a large computer using much larger disks, tracks and cylinders might be the most practical way to allocate storage, but clusters or even individual sectors are more frequently used on personal computers.

In addition to size and format, disk users must be concerned with speed and durability. Speed is influenced by at least five factors: the rotational speed of the disk itself; the speed of the head-moving mechanism and the rapidity with which it can find the right track and read it reliably; the number of heads used on each platter; the speed with which the computer and associated electronics can accept data from the hard disk; and the efficiency with which data is read, written, and organized. Discussions of these matters can become very technical, involving matters such as "interleaving"--reading every second or every third sector as sequential information rather than reading sectors sequentially, to allow time for the computer to accept one sector before sending the next. In real-world situations, the various factors tend to be lumped into average random-access speed and data transfer rate. For example, the Seagate ST251 shows an average random-access speed of about 39 milliseconds with the most common "interleave factor," and can transfer data at 5 megabits per second (625,000 characters per second).

Durability also involves several factors: contamination, "auto-parking," and the ability of the recording medium and the head to survive crashes. The heads on hard disks fly at distances above the disk much smaller than the diameter of a human hair, so contamination on the disk can strike the head, damage it, and possibly cause it to "crash" into the surface of the disk. In some disks the heads remain suspended over the recording surface when the power is off; if the disk is moved abruptly or some other untoward event occurs, the heads may come into contact with the surface, possibly damaging both surface and head. "Auto-parking" heads automatically retract outside of the disk area when power failure (accidental or by turning off the computer) occurs, thus substantially reducing the risk of damage. Modern disks are far more durable than earlier ones: the magnetic coatings are much harder, the heads are lighter, and auto-parking helps to avoid problems.

Furthermore, most modern disks are based on IBM's "Winchester technology," named for the original project code-name which apparently came from the intended capacity of the drive (30 megabytes on each of two surfaces, or 30-30, recalling the Winchester 30-30 rifle), or on some even more modern development from that technology. Winchester disks combine the platters and the head mechanisms into a single enclosed package that is either completely sealed or accepts air only through filters designed to eliminate all contamination. Virtually all PC disks and almost all modern large-computer disks use Winchester technology or some other sealed-drive technology.

As hard disks gain capacity and speed, they get smaller and cheaper. When personal computers first appeared, most hard disks were still large and expensive. The first hard disks for personal computers were five megabyte devices, the same capacity as RAMAC, though in a much smaller package and costing only a little more than the computer itself. As the personal computer field has grown, hard disks for PCs have become widely used and affordable.

The drive already used as an example typifies this trend. Where early 5- or 10- megabyte drives with 100 to 120 millisecond random access cost $2,000 to $3,000 less than a decade ago, the Seagate 251 in 1988 costs as little as $400. At the same time it offers four times the capacity, three times the speed, and one-fifth of the cost--and fits in the same space as a half-height diskette drive. (That drive was not chosen at random. In 1987 and early 1988, it is the most popular drive in the IBM AT-compatible market. That was not true a year earlier and probably won't be true in 1989, but does represent a useful sample in an ongoing trend.)

Uses and Advantages

Most library automation systems use hard disks, and any library personal computer that will be used heavily should probably have a hard disk. On an AT-compatible computer, a 40-megabyte hard disk will offer 34 times the capacity of a high-density diskette drive, 4 times the speed (39 milliseconds as compared to roughly 150 milliseconds), and much faster data transfer. It is not possible to maintain or manipulate large databases on diskettes, and increasingly difficult to use modern software without a hard disk.

There are no current alternatives to hard disks for very large databases, at least none with similar capacity, ease of updating, and speed of access. The technology is surprisingly old but seems likely to keep improving for many years to come: IBM scientists have already demonstrated the possibility of storing 10 times as much information in the same surface area as current disks, meaning that capacity and access speed should continue to improve.

Disadvantages and Problems

There are three basic problems with hard disks: they can crash, making large quantities of information unavailable; for personal computer use, the very large capacity may make it difficult to find files; and they cannot be removed and replaced as readily as diskettes or tapes.

All three can be alleviated. The information on hard disks should be copied (backed up) to floppies, tape, or other device regularly. On larger systems, it may also be possible to have an auditing mechanism that can reconstruct the transactions since the most recent backup. Most personal computer users will not do the daily backup that books and magazines advise, but every hard-disk user should back up critical data files at least weekly. That means that the user is willing to lose a week's worth of work; those not willing to lose that much work need to do more frequent backups.

You can think of backups as magic charms, in a way. It is quite possible that a personal computer hard disk will never fail over a decade of continuous use (in fact, 8 hours per day and 250 work days per year for 10 years totals 20,000 hours, which is a typical "mean time to failure" for good PC disk drives). But it always seems that the disk that isn't backed up is the one that fails--maybe just because that failure causes so much trouble to its owner.

There are good ways to organize files on hard disks, varying with the type of computer being used. The major requirement is to think about disk organization, not simply keep stuffing files onto the disk with randomly chosen names.

The next section deals with solutions to the third problem, removing and replacing hard disks.

Removable Hard Disks

Removable hard disks can be purchased for PCs and have long been used, in various forms, in larger systems. Removable disks for PCs are more expensive than fixed disks but can provide effectively infinite storage capacity. Another alternative for large storage capacity is Bernoulli-technology drives. These drives, using a combination of hard-disk speed and a flexible disk medium, use a variant of the air bearing. In a Bernoulli drive, a flexible disk spins at some distance above a recording head. The head is curved in such a way that the disk is deflected toward the head, bringing it close enough for high-density recording and playback.

One advantage of Bernoulli drives is that they are relatively unaffected by contamination. If dust or some other particle is on the disk, it breaks the airstream and the disk inherently moves away from the head. Bernoulli drives aren't crash-proof, but very nearly so. The medium is separate from the head and can be removed and replaced. Although not terribly cheap ($40 to $80 for a 20-megabyte Bernoulli cartridge), the cartridges do allow reasonably priced "infinite" storage.

Bernoulli drives have three disadvantages. First, they are slower than the best hard disks. Second, the drives are currently much more expensive than fixed disk drives. Third, the cartridges have a limited useful life, perhaps a year or so under heavy everyday use. Bernoulli drives have become quite successful for applications in which large quantities of data must be stored, where large databases must be interchanged, where security is important (the cartridge can be locked up at night), or where cost is not a critical factor and fast, reliable backup of hard-disk information is important. They do not appear to be generally competitive with hard disks for the reasons noted above.

FLOPPY DISKS

Skipping over some of the early magnetic computer media (such as magnetic drums), we come to the low-cost workhorse of personal computing: the floppy or flexible disk. Flexible disks combine some aspects of magnetic tape and some aspects of hard disks. Like magnetic tape, they use magnetic coating on a Mylar backing (but are coated on both sides of the plastic). Like magnetic tape, the head actually makes physical contact with the medium. Like hard disks, floppy disks spin during use and provide reasonably fast direct access to any information on the surface. IBM pioneered floppy disks, and the first floppy drives were 8-inch drives in various IBM computer peripherals, used to read in basic operating instructions.

Eight-inch drives and disks, usually called diskettes, spread into the minicomputer field in smaller minicomputers and workstations. They had the advantages of being small and cheap compared to hard disks of the same era, and made an excellent medium for transferring and distributing small and moderate quantities of information. A single floppy might hold only 500,000 characters, but that was quite enough for many applications.

The introduction of desktop and personal computers resulted in a much broader market for diskettes and rapid development of newer, cheaper, and better diskette drives. An odd thing happened during the late 1970s and early 1980s: instead of steady growth toward bigger and faster storage, many new drives plunged to much smaller capacity and slower speed. The reasons were size and price: the new drives were 5.25 inches rather than 8 inches, and were designed to be cheaply manufactured. (Eight-inch drives continue to be used in some dedicated word processing systems and in some minicomputers and multiuser microcomputers.)

The original disk drives for Apple and Commodore computers may have been the nadir of disk capacity, with less than 100,000 characters. The drives were cheap; they were also slow, relatively unreliable, and unique in their formatting requirements. Every brand of disk drive or brand of computer required a different arrangement of information on the disk, possibly even different disks. Some disks stored information on one side, some on both; some stored at "single (low) density," some at double density. (A double-density drive stores twice as much information as a single-density drive, either by using more and narrower tracks or by putting more information in each track. High-density drives carry this idea further.) Some used a single hole to offer a fixed point for locating information, some used multiple holes spaced around the inner margin of the disk.

Some drives still used eight-inch disks, but not for the more popular brands. Almost all 8-inch drives could read the original IBM disk format, but there were at least 50 and probably more than 100 mutually incompatible 5.25-inch formats. The introduction of the IBM PC changed that, to some extent, since all IBM-compatible computers could read and write IBM formats. Even though IBM introduced three different 5.25-inch formats within 4 years, it still had a stabilizing influence--although one that did not and does not extend to all parts of the computing community.

Capacities moved back upward, as did speed and reliability. The typical basic 5.25-inch diskette today stores 360,000 characters; more advanced drives store 1.2 million characters. Meanwhile, a smaller size has emerged--the 3.5 inch microdiskette developed by Sony, with the flexible medium stored and protected in a rigid plastic case. The plastic case provides protection and allows for closer, faster, and denser recording. Current 3.5-inch diskettes store 700,000 or 1.4 million characters.

A floppy disk begins as a circle of polyethylene terephthalate or PET--better known by the DuPont trademark Mylar--coated with iron oxide, cobalt-enhanced for high-density diskettes and 3.5-inch microfloppies. The Mylar disk itself is indeed floppy: if you remove a diskette from its case or jacket, it is as limp as a paper towel. The disk is sandwiched between two layers of a nonwoven polyester or rayon cloth bonded to the jacket, which is made of polyvinyl chloride or PVC. The cloth keeps the disk clean and the PVC jacket provides a stiff casing to protect the disk. Three and one-half-inch diskettes use an ABS plastic shell instead of a PVC jacket and have a sliding metal shutter over the read/write hole. The diskette itself is only accessible when it is in use, thus providing much better protection for the recording surface.

Uses, Advantages, and Problems

Diskettes provided the standard storage medium for the early years of personal computing, and still offer the best means of distributing programs and moving moderate amounts of information from one computer to another. They are reasonably durable, light, easy to mail or carry, and offer relatively good access. But hard disks continue to improve in speed, capacity, and price; for most serious personal computing, hard disks are now the medium of choice.

Diskettes work well in their limited role within hard-disk systems, but do not work nearly so well as general-purpose interactive storage mechanisms. The head contact and other factors require slower drives (around 300 to 360 rpm). In order to keep head and diskette wear to a minimum, most diskette drives stop spinning if not used for a two or three second period. The result is slow retrieval--faster than tape and roughly competitive with CD-ROM, but 4 to 10 times slower than hard disk. That slowness, and the limited data capacity of diskettes, reduces their general usefulness.

SELECTED READING

Camras, Marvin, ed. *Magnetic Tape Recording*. New York: Von Nostrand Reinhold, 1985. 445 pp. Indexes. (Lightly annotated collection of classic papers in the development of magnetic tape. Edited by the person who filed the major American patent for AC bias, assigned to Armour Research. Some interesting reading, mostly very technical and very detailed.)

Daniel, Eric. C., and C. Dennis Mee, eds. *Magnetic Recording. Volume 1: Technology*. New York: McGraw-Hill, 1987. 514 pp. Chapter bibliographies; index. (Quite readable, extremely thorough textbook. Concerns primarily the fundamental technology. Volume 2 will address actual recording systems such as tape and disk, and should be extremely good additional reading if it follows the standard set by Volume 1.)

Schenck, Thomas. "Magnetic Tape Care, Storage, and Error Recovery." *Library Hi Tech* 2, no. 4 (Winter 1984):51-54. (Brief description of tape technology and consideration of error recovery and prevention.)

White, Robert M., ed. *Introduction to Magnetic Recording*. New York: IEEE Press, 1985. 309 pp. Indexes. (Intended as a textbook for the field; a deeply technical 60-page introduction followed by a selection of reprints at various levels of technicality. A few pages can be read by the layperson.)

16

Telecommunications

Telecommunications is the process of communicating information over some link. The technology of telecommunications is as old as the telegraph and as new as optical fibers and linked systems. Telecommunications includes the telephone, television, satellite communications, microwave relays, and all the other tools and techniques for communicating over a distance. Contemporary libraries rely on telecommunications to enhance current services and provide new ones.

Telecommunications revolutionized society, probably more so than the automobile. The telephone and telegraph brought immediacy to news gathering, and radio and television extended that immediacy to reporting. When people working on a common project in New York and San Francisco or Grass Valley and White Plains can discuss questions on the telephone rather than sending letters back and forth, the project can proceed almost as rapidly and as effectively as if the entire team were in one place. Today, members of the team can work on the same computer program simultaneously or transmit plans (including detailed drawings) to one another in minutes. Those are minor examples of the fundamental importance of telecommunications to modern society.

The history of telecommunications is so long and complex that a summary treatment would be ludicrous. Instead, this chapter notes some of the fundamentals of telecommunications, discusses a few specific aspects briefly, and considers some ways that libraries do or should use telecommunications. The chapters that follow focus on specific aspects of telecommunications.

FUNDAMENTALS

A communications link always requires five elements: information to be communicated; a transmitting device that can make any needed modifications in the information to prepare it for transmission; a communications link or channel, either a physical connection or clear transmission path; a receiving device; and protocols or agreements such that the receiving device can recognize the transmission (i.e., separate the transmission from background noise or other irrelevant information) and restore the information, either to its original form or to an acceptable equivalent.

If any one of the five elements fails, there is no communication or garbled communication. Reliable two-way communication involves a sixth factor: verification, a way for the receiving system to inform the sending system that the message has been received correctly.

Information

Anything that can be turned into electrical signals can be communicated. Information suitable for telecommunications includes computer-stored text, voice, software, music, video, and compressed images of pages, to name a few. We cannot currently telecommunicate scent, texture, feeling, or physical nature.

A library can readily obtain a bibliographic citation to a book through telecommunications. It can, somewhat less easily, receive or send imperfect images of the pages of the book. There is no way to telecommunicate the physical qualities of the book itself.

Transmitters and Receivers

Transmission always transforms, but transformations may take on many types and levels of complexity. You can't send a voice over a wire, but it's easy to transform the sound of a voice into a signal suitable for transmission over a wire or through the air. A telephone handset represents one of the most straightforward combinations of receiver and transmitter. The transmitter--the mouthpiece--transforms the sound energy of a voice into electrical impulses through a simple microphone. The receiver--the earpiece--uses a simple speaker, in some cases identical to the microphone, to translate electrical impulses back into sound energy. Much more complex transformations may take place within the telephone system, but the basic transformation is simple. Most telecommunications involves more complex transformations, but the principles remain the same.

Communications Links

Theoretically a communications link is always the equivalent of a wire between the transmitter and receiver. In practice, a communications link may be a complex web of wires, optical fibers, intermediate receivers, and transmitters (repeaters or transponders). The communications link used for a five-minute communication may not even have one constant form: different portions of the communication may go through many different paths to get from transmitter to receiver.

The simplest links are pairs of wires. The lowest-quality direct-wire links carry teletype and telegraph information. Voice-grade links, somewhat higher quality, carry telephone conversations and digital information of many sorts. Specially tested "conditioned" lines carry computer information or other information at higher speed and with greater reliability.

Higher-capacity communications links include coaxial cables, fiber optic cables, and transmission over microwave or satellite links. These are discussed later in the chapter.

Protocols and Agreements

If you speak only English and a colleague speaks only Japanese, the clearest telephone connection will not allow you to telecommunicate properly because you have no common protocol for spoken information. A receiver can restore content only if it knows the rules. If you have an AM radio receiver that can be tuned to 97 mega-Hertz, you still can't use it to receive FM stations. The frequency may be the same, but the rules are different.

Every telecommunications system involves many protocols, from the RS232C standard of a connector to the elaborate protocols involved in the Linked Systems Project. There can be no telecommunication without absolute agreement as to the form of the information. If a transmitter sends nine bits for each character and the receiver expects seven, the best link in the world cannot provide proper communication.

HIGH-CAPACITY COMMUNICATIONS LINKS

Two physical media and two special broadcasting techniques offer high-capacity communications, from the equivalent of a few hundred telephone wires to the equivalent of hundreds of thousands.

Coaxial Cables

A coaxial cable typically has four layers. A thick copper wire or bundle of wires is wrapped in electrical insulation. A copper tube surrounds the insulation, and a protective shell surrounds the copper tube. The tube and central wire conduct signals; the name *coaxial* notes the shared axis of the two conductors. Thin coaxial cables connect modern television sets to antennas or to cable television systems; the cable systems use coaxial cables to distribute programs. Even thin coaxial cables carry several thousand times as much information as a single voice telephone line: a single television channel requires roughly 1,000 times the bandwidth of a voice conversation, and a thin coaxial cable can carry 80 or 90 television channels.

Microwave Communications

Microwaves are high-frequency electromagnetic waves. Any specific electromagnetic wave, including light, radio signals, and household current, can be characterized by its frequency or its wavelength. Since electromagnetic energy travels at 186,000 miles per second or 300,000 kilometers per second, the length of a wave is equal to that figure divided by its frequency, given in Hertz (cycles per second). Household current (60 Hertz) has a wavelength of 5,000 kilometers. Microwaves have wavelengths between 1 millimeter and 10 centimeters, corresponding to frequencies between 3 and 300 kilomegahertz (or gigaHertz). (By comparison, FM radio within the United States broadcasts in the range of 88 to 108 megaHertz, representing wavelengths from about 2.7 to 3.4 meters.)

Microwaves can be transmitted in a fairly narrow band using fairly little energy, and can carry large quantities of information. Microwave communication requires a line of sight between transmitter and receiver. It must be theoretically possible to see the transmitter from the receiver: any physical object between the transmitter and receiver will block the microwaves. Most microwave links are less than 30 miles apart, but each link can combine 2 antennas, serving as a relay station so that communications pass through a series of links.

Microwave links have greater carrying capacity than coaxial cable, and microwave is cheaper than coaxial cable when enough information is being transmitted. The chief disadvantage of microwave links are their susceptibility to disruption when a sufficiently large object interrupts the signal path; chief advantages are large capacity and the fact that they eliminate the need for cables strung from point to point.

Satellites

In 1945 the science fiction writer Arthur C. Clarke submitted a paper titled "The Space Station: Its Radio Applications" to the British Interplanetary Society. The paper dealt with orbital mechanics and the future possibility of artificial satellites. Clarke perceived that a satellite with a stable orbit at roughly 22,300 miles, orbiting over the equator, would have an orbital period of 24 hours. It would spin around the earth at the same angular velocity as the earth itself. The result, from an observer's perspective, is that such a satellite would hover in the same point overhead at all times: it would be "stationary" from the ground.

Such a satellite is called *geosynchronous* because its orbit is synchronized with the earth. Clarke's paper went on to note that a geosynchronous satellite would be useful to relay messages from one point on the ground to another, as long as both points were "visible" from the satellite. Clarke was 20 years ahead of his time, since it was not possible to launch a satellite in 1945. His invention--for that is effectively what it was--could not be patented, because you can't patent something that can't be done. Publication of his article made the idea public, and something cannot be patented after the idea has been published for more than a year. Just as von Neumann made digital computing an open technology, Clarke made geosynchronous satellites an open technology. More recently, he has written charming and only slightly rueful commentaries on the million-dollar idea he necessarily gave away.

In 1963 NASA turned Clarke's paper into reality with the launch of SYNCOM, the first geosynchronous communications satellite. It could relay one television signal or several telephone channels simultaneously. In 1965 the first international geosynchronous satellite was launched: Early Bird, owned by Intelsat, an international consortium. Since then, many geosynchronous satellites have been launched, some by governments and many by private industry. GE and Western Union both own geosynchronous satellites, as do other companies.

Satellite communications are effectively "distance-neutral": it should cost no more to transmit information between New York and San Francisco than between New York and Washington, D.C. As long as the transmitter and receiver both can "see" the satellite, the ground distance between the two locations is a minor (and essentially irrelevant) portion of the total transmission distance, since a minimum of 44,600 miles is required to get to and from the satellite. That makes satellite transmission particularly effective for long distance communications. In 1983 figures the cost of transmitting a one-hour television show from Los Angeles to New York by microwave was $2,000; by satellite, the same transmission cost $400.

A typical geosynchronous satellite carries a *transponder*--a receiver and transmitter working on different frequencies to avoid confusion. Modern ground transmission systems can be relatively inexpensive, in the tens of thousands of dollars. Ground receivers are quite cheap, and hundreds of thousands of homeowners have installed satellite dishes costing as little as $2,000.

The major advantages of satellite communications are large bandwidth and the elimination of greater costs for greater distances. The disadvantage for two-way computer-to-computer communications is that no communication can move faster than the speed of light. A satellite link imposes a delay of roughly one-quarter second, or a half-second for a message to be received and acknowledged. For most purposes, a quarter-second delay is trivial. But for some applications such as centrally polled networks, where each terminal is checked repeatedly for information, that delay can be significant.

Fiber Optics

Light will "follow" the path of a transparent medium if light moves more slowly in that medium than in the medium surrounding it. The speed of light is lower in water than in air, and a light shining into a stream of water will, to some extent, follow the path of the water. The effect is much more pronounced in glass: under the right circumstances, most of the light shining into one end of a curved rod of glass will shine out of the other end of the rod. This phenomenon is the basis of fiber optics: transparent fibers can carry light around curves. If you can modulate the light--turn it on and off rapidly or change its character in a controlled manner--you can carry information over the light beam and through the optical fiber.

Development	Date
Tyndall: Light follows water	1870
Wheeler: "light pipes"	1881
Standard Telecom: early optical fiber	1968
Corning: practical optical fiber	1971
AT&T: Chicago test of fiber-optic links	1977
Lake Placid: Winter Olympics communications network based on fiber optics	1980

Table 16.1: Some Developments in Fiber Optics

Table 16.1 shows a few of the developments that led to fiber-optic links. The British physicist John Tyndall demonstrated the internal reflection of light in 1870, showing that light would follow water into a container and out of the container. In 1881 William Wheeler filed a patent involving hollow reflective pipes to light buildings from a single source. Serious study of fiber optics for practical use began after World War II. From 1968 to the present, several companies including Britain's Standard Telecom, America's Corning Glass Works and Bell Labs, and Japan's Nippon Sheet Glass have developed increasingly effective glass and plastic optical fibers, or fibers that lose less and less of the light over a given distance.

An optical fiber is a two-layer cylinder combining different types of carefully manufactured glass or plastic. A transparent cylinder called *cladding* surrounds another transparent cylinder called the *core*. The core is "less transparent" than the cladding (i.e., light travels more slowly through the core than through the cladding). Technically the cladding has a lower *refractive index* than the core. Light entering the core at one end reflects off the cladding, continuing to reflect over and over again down the core until it reaches the other end. The reflections take the light around curves, as long as the curves are not too severe.

Fiber-optic cables carry information as modulations in the light or as rapid on-off cycles. Since most information-handling equipment relies on electrical information, fiber-optic systems require converters at both ends. At the sending end, an electrical signal is used to control either a light-emitting diode (LED) or a laser. At the receiving end a phototransistor or, more likely, a specialized light-sensitive diode converts light back into an electrical signal. Over long-distance connections, repeaters combine receivers and transmitters to boost the power of the light beam.

Advantages and Disadvantages

A light beam can carry much information through a very thin fiber. Typical fiber-optic links for telephone use carry 672 simultaneous voice-grade conversations over a single fiber, a capacity that requires 21 pairs of copper wires. Some fiber-optic links carry 4,032 conversations simultaneously (or the equivalent in other information): such links carry information at a rate equivalent to 32 million characters per second.

Since a tiny amount of glass can do the work of dozens or hundreds of copper wires (and all the shielding needed to keep the wires from interfering with one another), fiber-optic cables are much smaller and lighter than traditional communications cables. That means that much more information capacity can be carried along existing structures or through existing utility tunnels.

Until the introduction of fiber-optic links, copper was becoming much more expensive because, like many other metals, it is in relatively short supply. On the other hand, the major ingredient in fiber-optic links is silicon--sand--of which there is an essentially unlimited supply. Even though optical fibers are expensive to manufacture, the overall cost for a fiber-optic link is no higher than a traditional link, and will be less expensive in the future.

Optical fibers do not radiate electricity and are not subject to interference from electromagnetic sources. Electronic "noise" can be a problem for high-speed communication within computer rooms or on factory floors; replacing copper cables with optical fibers eliminates that problem. The lack of radiation also makes fiber-optic links more secure. It is essentially impossible to eavesdrop on a fiber-optic link without actually cutting into the cable, and nearly impossible to cut into a cable unobtrusively.

Fiber optics require extreme care in assembly and operation. A severed fiber-optic link requires much more intricate repair than a damaged copper cable. When a company is establishing a fiber-optic link, it knows what the losses over a single run of cable will be, since cable suppliers specify the loss for each variety of cable. But attenuation over the run of a cable is only one source of loss. Every time light passes from one material to another, even if only from the end of one cable to the beginning of another, losses may occur. If the two ends are not aligned properly, there may be no transmission at all; if there is dust between the two ends, serious losses will occur. Properly installed fiber-optic links have no apparent disadvantages when compared to other direct links, and the technology is spreading rapidly.

EQUIPMENT AND LONG-DISTANCE
TELECOMMUNICATIONS

This sampling includes two areas that deserve more than a paragraph but, given the confines of this book, less than a chapter.

Modems

The word *modem* comes from *mo*dulator-*dem*odulator. Serving as a transmitter, a modem modulates the on-off sequences of digital information into tones that can go over telephone lines. Serving as a receiver, a modem demodulates the tones and retrieves the digital information. All modems perform those functions. Early modems did nothing else. Thousands of librarians have used acoustic couplers with Texas Instruments Silent-700 series printing terminals, to connect to online information systems such as Dialog and perform searches. The acoustic couplers, small speaker-microphones contained in pads shaped to fit telephone handsets, connected to low-speed modems, typically communicating at 300 bps or 30 characters per second.

Three hundred bits per second is also called 300 baud, but baud and bps do not always mean the same thing. For a modulation technique that uses a single shift (for example, the difference between two tones) to differentiate zero and one bits, the baud rate--defined as the number of "state reversals" per second--is the same as the bits per second. However, all higher-speed modems use more complex techniques: a single state reversal may cover more than one bit of information. To avoid confusion, this discussion will use bps consistently.

Contemporary modems run at higher speeds and connect directly to the telephone line through modular jacks now used for almost all telephone connections. The spread of modems to personal computers has resulted in a larger and more competitive market; as a result, modems have become much cheaper and more sophisticated. Many modems now include their own microprocessors, enabling them to dial numbers, test for various conditions, and even store and execute complete logon procedures for online services.

As recently as 1985, a good 300 bps modem cost $70 and up and a 1,200 bps modem cost $300 to $700 or more. In early 1988 300 bps modems have almost disappeared from the market; 1,200 bps modems, all of which will also run at 300 bps, cost $80 to $400, usually including software for telecommunications. Modems of 2,400 bps, very expensive in 1985, are already down to as little as $175, with name brands available in the $200 to $600 range. Newer modems evaluate line quality and automatically step down to lower speeds as needed, making high-speed modems more reliable.

As noted previously, telecommunications requires protocols as well as equipment. The two lowest speeds have nearly universal protocols within the United States: Bell-103J for 300 bps modems, Bell-212A for 1,200 bps. Foreign standards may not be the same, for example the European CCITT (International Telephone and Telegraph Consultative Committee) standard for 1,200 bps is not identical to Bell-212A. However, almost all 2,400 bps modems use CCITT V.22*bis* protocols at their highest speed.

Higher speeds than 2,400 bps can be obtained for $1,000 or less, but only make sense if telecommunications will be with another user of the same equipment and if leased lines or high-quality telephone lines are available. As of early 1988 common protocols for high-speed modem-based telecommunications do not exist. As a result, a given brand of modem can typically communicate only with others of the same brand, unless it is built to be compatible with some other brand.

Packet Switching

A librarian searching BRS over a 1,200 bps modem can't possibly key in 120 characters per second continuously (the best typists key at only about one-tenth that rate). BRS may send back results at a full 120 characters per second but, most of the time, the communications link is idle. A librarian sends 20 or 40 characters; BRS responds with perhaps 100 characters; the librarian considers the response and formulates the next step.

If the library has a dedicated line solely devoted to that BRS link, the line is being wasted at least 90 percent of the time in a typical application. If the BRS system is a long distance from the library, the library must pay long-distance rates for the exclusive use of that line.

Most data transmissions are relatively short--100 characters or less. By packaging those 100-character transmissions and combining many different transmissions intelligently, the long-distance line could be used to full capacity, resulting in lower transmission costs for each package. That's part of the motive for packet switching, and is effectively how packet switching works.

A packet-switching system breaks messages down into fixed-length packets, including identification with each packet. Packets from different sources may be combined across the same link; different packets from the same source may travel across different paths. If all the critical elements in a communications network understand the protocols for packets, the network can provide high capacity at low cost.

Packet switching has its own set of special terms, such as X.25 (the packet protocol adopted by CCITT) and PAD, short for "packet assembler-disassembler." PAD is the electronic device that, much like a modem, turns information streams into packets and packets back into information streams. Tymnet and Telenet both use packet switching for telecommunications, making better and cheaper use of long distance lines. Some of the major private leased-line networks (such as OCLC and RLIN) are converting to packet switching and others are considering such moves. In Europe and Canada, packet switching forms a fundamental part of most long-distance data communications; it seems likely that this will be increasingly true in the United States.

TELECOMMUNICATIONS AND LIBRARIES

Consider your own institution: how many operations require communication outside your own walls? Telecommunications improves interlibrary lending, makes shared online catalogs possible, is at the heart of OCLC, WLN, RLIN and UTLAS, Dialog, BRS, CompuServe, The Source and all the other online information sources.

For most applications, most librarians need not concern themselves with the details of telecommunications. But you may be able to deal with vendors and services better if you understand something about the field. You should certainly know more about telecommunications than this book offers if you are involved in building a multi-location online catalog or other system that depends entirely on successful telecommunications.

Optical fibers have the potential to provide vastly increased communications capacity, within a campus or community and across long distances. As optical-fiber networks grow, libraries may benefit from cheaper, more readily available telecommunications.

Libraries can also benefit directly from communications links with lower error rates. To take one example of the effect of error rates, OCLC and RLIN both use telecommunications protocols that assure correct reception of messages. If the message is not received correctly, it must be transmitted again. Retransmission adds to the response time perceived by the user. Both systems use relatively "lean" communications networks, placing many terminals on each dedicated line, because the lines are so expensive. The load on the networks represents a *major* factor in response time: for example, in 1987 at least two-thirds of RLIN response time was network delay rather than actual computer time. Telecommunications networks with higher capacity (for the same price) and lower error rates will directly improve response time in such a situation. Similarly, lower prices for the same capacity would reduce the telecommunications cost for the networks and, thus, for libraries using the networks. The same should be true for other online services and telecommunications networks.

SUMMARY

The modern library depends on telecommunications, not to replace books and other physical objects but to enhance and extend services. Libraries certainly do more than provide data, and it is hard to conceive of any telecommunications system totally replacing the physical library. But telecommunications serves libraries in many ways, and librarians do well to consider new developments in the field. The chapters that follow deal with a few developments (some old, some new); the books and articles cited here provide more information on various aspects of telecommunications.

SELECTED READING

Boss, Richard W. *Telecommunications for Library Management.* White Plains: Knowledge Industry Publications, Inc., 1985. 180 pp. Extensive glossary; bibliography; index. (Brief, generally clear discussions of a range of telecommunications areas.)

Brownrigg, Edwin B. et al. "Packet Radio for Library Automation." *Information Technology and Libraries* 3, no. 3 (September 1984): 229-244. (Report on an actual experiment but also extensive information on packet-switching protocols and the like. Includes extensive bibliography.)

Koenig, Michael. "Fiber Optics and Library Technology." *Library Hi Tech* 2, no. 1 (Summer 1984):9-15. (A good quick summary of the advantages of fiber optics, marred by some truly inane questions on the future of paper "as a storage mechanism.")

Seippel, Robert G. *Fiber Optics.* Reston, Va.: Reston, 1984. 167 pp. Bibliography; glossary; index. (Very technical and quite thorough. The basis for much of the information on fiber optics in this chapter.)

Singleton, Loy A. *Telecommunications in the Information Age.* Cambridge, Mass.: Ballinger, 1983. 239 pp. Glossary; bibliography; index. (Concentrates on video-related technology including cable, satellites, videodisc, and videocassette, etc.; also some comments on teleconferencing and telecommuting. Light, interesting, reflects the general optimism of 1983.)

17
Teletext and Videotex

Foresighted information scientists have long been fascinated by the possibilities of interactive television--making more of the omnipresent medium than simply a broadcast form of entertainment and information. Two related technologies emerged in the 1970s that aim to do precisely that: turn the television (and, for videotex, the telephone) into a home information center.

Libraries are logical partners in such systems, providing information and using systems to encourage library use and reading in general. To the extent that videotex or teletext succeeds, libraries should be aware of possibilities for enhancing the role of the library in the community. On the other hand, it would be a mistake to commit time and money to systems with little or no chance of success in the marketplace. By now libraries should know better than to embrace new technologies simply because they are there.

This chapter is largely a cautionary tale. Videotex has been around for more than a decade, teletext for longer than that, but neither has become well established in the United States. Despite some success overseas, attempts to implement either technology in the United States have been expensive failures.

TELETEXT: THE TECHNOLOGY THAT NEVER WAS

Would you pay $300 to $900 (or $20 a month) so that you could choose 1 of 100 screens full of information and advertising on your TV? Would you pay $10 a month to be able to choose 1 of 5,000 screens? For most Americans, the answer is a flat no. That may be all that needs to be said about teletext: viewed as a gold mine by broadcasters and publishers, it has been a dismal failure in every general-market test to date.

How It Works

Many large hotels offer an extra channel on in-room televisions showing the events of the day, such as who is meeting where, interspersed with ads for hotel facilities and other items. Some cable systems offer similar channels with community information. The information scrolls slowly up the screen or appears screen-by-screen. If you watch such a service for a few minutes, you'll see a complete set of information and see the cycle begin again.

That is how teletext works, with three differences:

1. Instead of using an entire channel, normal teletext is broadcast along with a regular television signal during the vertical blanking interval (VBI), the time it takes to go from the bottom of one screen or "frame" to the top of the next.

2. Only a portion of a screen can be transmitted at once; a decoder (added to or built into the television) stores portions of the desired screen until it is complete, then displays it.

3. A keypad allows the viewer to select specific pages, rather than having to sit through all 80 or 100 pages in order to see the desired page.

The vertical blanking interval is overhead in television transmission. Television images consist of hundreds of horizontal lines (525 in the United States broadcast standard), broadcast and displayed from top to bottom at high speed. Twenty-one scan lines do not appear on the screen (unless the television is improperly adjusted, in which case they appear as a dark band).

Some of those 21 lines are used to synchronize scanning--to assure that the television is showing what the station is transmitting. Others are used for closed captions, an area where transmitted text does offer a useful and successful service in the United States. A few are open for other uses, and teletext can be transmitted on these lines. Teletext does not offer instantaneous response when a page number is keyed: on a 100-page "teletext magazine," it may take 20 seconds to get the desired page.

A Brief History

The British Broadcasting Corporation (BBC) developed Ceefax (for "see facts") in the early 1970s, originally as a means of adding captions for the deaf and multilingual captions to television programs. The system was extended to add pages of text and graphics, and began full operation in 1976.

BBC introduced two Ceefax services and British commercial stations added two more. With strong government backing, teletext grew in Britain so that more than one-half million TV sets were equipped with decoders by 1983, with the number growing fairly rapidly. France also developed teletext services with heavy government support, resulting in some specialized services and a very small "public magazine" all under the umbrella name "Antiope." Canada also experimented with teletext through the Canadian Broadcasting Corporation. In all these cases, teletext has involved large government subsidies from the beginning and continuing into the present.

Within the United States, teletext has been attempted off and on since 1979, but with no major effort at marketing and no apparent success. According to one account, both CBS and NBC transmit (or did transmit) teletext magazines as part of their network services, but few stations, if any, choose to actually broadcast the teletext, and no more than a handful of decoders have ever been sold. Other experiments have also taken place, on cable and on local stations. Time Inc. briefly experimented with an entire cable channel devoted to teletext, offering 5,000 pages instead of the usual 80 to 100. Time spent $35 million on a project that reached 400 homes, and canceled the experiment after a year. One experiment called "KNTM," KeyFax National Teletext Magazine, used the Atlanta "superstation" WTBS to broadcast 100 screens to subscribers who were asked to pay $20 a month for decoder and access. That service even included book reviews from ALA; every indication is that the service was an utter failure.

Where It Has Succeeded

Teletext has worked when governments have been determined to make it work. Even then, confirmation of the success of teletext seems vague. The major apparent success of teletext is in the United Kingdom, with four services operating with some success. The services resemble portions of newspapers: news, sports, weather, reviews, and schedules. The commercial service Oracle includes a heavy dose of advertising, and the services are heavy on jokes, puzzles, quizzes, and games.

Why It Has Failed

Teletext offers a solution for which there is no problem, at least for most people in the United States. Relatively few people buy new media and new technology simply because they are new. In order to succeed, a new technology must do something distinctly better or different than existing technologies. A new medium can be more up to date, cheaper, more pleasant to use, or more interesting than existing media. In any case, however, it must offer something distinctive that is perceived as worthwhile.

Teletext doesn't offer anything that most people are willing to pay for. Few people have much need of up-to-the-minute information on most aspects of life; for most of us, the daily newspaper is more current than we really require. The daily newspaper is also a much more capacious medium than teletext. A typical teletext system may offer 100 to 200 pages, each page having no more than 100 to 150 words of text (less, if graphics are included). Thus a system will provide no more than 10,000 to 30,000 words in all, and probably much less, given the need for index screens and graphics. (A more realistic figure might be 6,000 to 15,000 words.)

That is not much information when compared to a typical daily newspaper. Two full newspaper-sized pages carry as much text as an entire teletext system. Even *USA Today* conveys far more information than any teletext system and is much easier to read. Ads also work much better in the print medium: readers encounter them in the natural course of reading (rather than by calling them up specifically), and the ads can contain vastly more detail than is possible in a teletext screen.

There has never been a major national marketing effort for teletext in the United States, probably because local tests have failed so badly. People will agree to try decoders for free, and will use them out of curiosity, but when they are asked to pay for the decoders or for the teletext channels, they need some compelling reason. To date, no such reason has been found.

If teletext ever does succeed in a US market, either as a local or as a national service, libraries will and should be involved as information providers, just as libraries provide news of special events and the like to local information channels on cable systems. Libraries should not spend the time and money required to be *active* parts of teletext systems until such systems can show some record of success; the probability of such a record seems low, given the history and economics of teletext.

VIDEOTEX: MAJOR FAILURES AND MODEST SUCCESSES

Videotex is interactive and offers essentially unlimited amounts of information. People can request the information or features they want and get results fairly rapidly. But videotex is also inherently more expensive to provide and use than teletext. To date there is no indication that anybody has ever operated a profitable videotex system in the United States.

Videotex enthusiasts muddy the waters by including CompuServe, The Source, other online information systems, and even electronic bulletin boards as part of videotex. Even with this broad (and somewhat untenable) definition, profitability and sustained mass market use still evade the industry.

Any number of well-funded, expensive experiments have been tried and abandoned. One large videotex project continues to be alive, but is not yet healthy. Videotex has much more to offer than does teletext, but it is still not clear that people want or need what videotex can provide.

How It Works

A classic videotex system uses the telephone network or a two-way cable television system to transmit information requests from users to providers and information screens back to users.

The user must have a decoder and keypad attached to a television and either a cable or telephone link. The keypad is used to switch from television to videotex and to maneuver through videotex menus. In some cases, the keypad may be a full typewriter keyboard that can be used to do keyword searches.

A computer or network of computers receives keyed requests and sends back screens. The computer also maintains charges and generates billing information. Various information providers prepare the text and graphics that will be sent out as screens. In a fully functional commercial videotex system, the providers are paid for their efforts based on actual use of the information provided.

A strict definition of videotex always includes graphics as a basic part of the service: crude *mosaic graphics* made up of graphics characters taking the place of text characters; *geometric graphics* transmitted as predefined drawing instructions to create shapes and colors on the screens; or *photographic representation* transmitted as bit-mapped graphics.

Mosaic graphics, used in the British Prestel system, create relatively crude images but use relatively simple equipment and offer reasonably fast transmission (10 seconds a screen at 1,200 bits per second). Geometric graphics, used in Canada's Telidon system, require more sophisticated decoders and take 30 seconds per page to transmit, but offer better quality. Photographic or bit-mapped graphics appear relatively impractical for videotex because a full-screen color picture would take about one hour to transmit at 1,200 bits per second, and would require an expensive decoder to store the large amount of information.

For videotex to succeed, a given marketplace must have the following:

1. Vendors able and willing to establish the computer system and telecommunications connections needed.

2. Information providers committed to providing services that will appeal to the marketplace in a timely manner.

3. Telecommunications networks that have sufficient capacity and do not involve excessively high costs.

4. Users who find the services sufficiently worthwhile to justify initial and ongoing charges.

5. Marketing activity sufficient to locate the users and convince them of the worth of the service.

A Brief History

Like teletext, videotex started with government-funded experiments in Europe and Canada. The British Post Office demonstrated "viewdata" in 1976 and changed the name to Prestel in 1978. When the system was being developed, projections were that it would have at least 100,000 users by 1979. In fact, there were some 17,000 users as of 1983, with use growing at a few thousand a year.

The French government began an even more ambitious videotex operation around the same time. France began with a plan to equip all French homes with simple terminals, use those terminals for online telephone directories, and abandon printed directories. Since the terminals could be used for any videotex, the major equipment barrier to widespread use would be overcome by government fiat. While that plan has since been abandoned, the government continues to provide free terminals in certain areas and to subsidize videotex in various other ways. It is nearly impossible to evaluate French videotex as a marketplace success because the system is too tightly intertwined with government priorities.

The Canadian Department of Communications created Telidon, Canada's technology for high-quality videotex, and the government has subsidized systems to the tune of at least $40 million since 1978. Many services began in the late 1970s and early 1980s; some have ceased while others continue. There seems little to indicate that Canadian systems have succeeded in bringing videotex to the average household.

Many experiments have taken place in the United States over the last few years, most of them commercial and most of them resounding failures. The typical scenario begins with large market projections to justify heavy startup costs, followed by almost no market penetration and rather rapid shutdown. Knight-Ridder newspapers developed a system called Viewtron; at its peak, the system had fewer than 20,000 subscribers. The publishers of the *Los Angeles Times* also started a videotex system, Gateway, and abandoned it after it proved to be an expensive failure. Other experiments to date have also failed. The usual question does not yet have good answers: what can videotex provide that will entice consumers to pay for the equipment and pay either a monthly fee, an hourly connect fee, or a fee for each screen?

Previous Library Experiments

Libraries have been involved as information providers in many videotex experiments. Libraries continue to be involved with British and Canadian videotex systems as information providers, to some extent. In the United States, one extensive experiment involved a library organization as not merely an information provider, but as the *creator* of an experimental videotex system.

Channel 2000 was created by OCLC as an experimental system in cooperation with the Public Libraries of Columbus and Franklin County, Ohio State University, Banc One, and others. The system included the complete catalog of the public library, the complete text of the *Academic American Encyclopedia*, and many other items for a total of two million screens.

The test ran for two months, involved 200 households, and produced studies and reports. Those studies done independently of OCLC suggest that users tired of the system after the first flush of newness wore off. Since the system was only an experiment, it cannot be considered either a success or a failure in the marketplace. In some ways, it was an unrealistically advanced experiment: users who found books they wanted received the books, free of charge, with the library paying postage both ways. Such a system in widespread use would vastly increase the operational costs of libraries, unless service charges were instituted.

Trintex: The Last Great Hope?

Of all the ambitious U.S. videotex plans and experiments, only one major system remains alive: Trintex, a joint venture of IBM and Sears-Roebuck. Trintex began in 1984 when Sears, CBS, and IBM announced a joint venture to use the resources of all three corporations in a major national videotex system. With more than $450 million spent as of late 1987, the joint venture continues, although CBS has already pulled out of the project. The current Trintex system, called Prodigy, is be test marketed in 1988. It requires that users own PC-DOS computers and uses the low-resolution Color Graphics Adapter for graphics.

Prodigy departs from other videotex systems in requiring a full business-oriented computer, not merely a keypad to be used with a television and telephone. That departure further narrows the market, and really moves away from videotex toward a related but separate field, online databases. Prodigy will include graphics and rely heavily on advertising, giving it some of the trappings of videotex. It is probably the last hope for consumer videotex in the United States, and seems unlikely to be a major success.

That is not to say that there are no successes in videotex. Special systems serving special markets do exist, some of them publicly accessible. For example, Teleguide systems are available in several areas of the U.S., offering tourist information heavily oriented to advertisers at free public terminals. Some libraries have Teleguide terminals that are interesting and can be useful, although most do not seem to offer as much up-to-date information as the usual free tourist magazines published in major tourist areas. Teleguide systems are, at best, modestly successful, and bear no relationship to home videotex.

Redefining the Field

The dismal history of videotex has led proponents to a semantic solution: they now treat all online databases as being part of videotex.

Thus, according to this view, Dialog, BRS, CompuServe and The Source are all videotex. Taking this to extreme, OCLC and RLIN could also be called videotex systems because people key information requests into a remote system and get back screens of information. Proponents also consider electronic bulletin boards to be a form of videotex.

This shift in definition simply muddies the water Online information sources accessed by home computers or terminals are not the same as videotex. Most such services have limited graphics or none at all; most of the income for such services comes from business and library use at fairly high hourly rates; most home use is from personal computers; and none of these services relies on advertising revenue.

Electronic Bulletin Boards

Electronic bulletin boards are also not videotex, but can provide some of the same services with less risk and less overhead. An electronic bulletin board is a personal computer or set of computers with sets of incoming telephone lines and modems, and special software. People dialing in (using personal computers or terminals) can look up information and, on many systems, participate in ongoing conferences, respond to surveys, contribute and obtain free software, and send and receive electronic mail (discussed further in chapter 18). In a way, an electronic bulletin board is a miniature version of an online database.

A number of libraries already operate electronic bulletin boards, and more are likely to do so in the future. The costs are moderately low: a few thousand dollars for the computer, hard disks and modems, and ongoing costs for the incoming telephone lines. Electronic bulletin board software can be free or may be a few hundred dollars. Thus, libraries can make information available to personal computer users with a relatively small investment, but must recognize that they are giving special treatment to a small group of usually affluent users, presumably with funds that would otherwise be used for services more generally available.

Videotex for Library Use

Libraries should keep track of videotex experiments, but should not commit large sums of time or money to participation until some market penetration can be proved. Any community-oriented videotex system should include, at the very least, library hours and news of special events. At best, a videotex system might provide access to the library catalog or to reference sources provided by the library; if videotex systems use full keyboards, it would even be possible to offer reference assistance through a videotex system.

These and other services will improve the library's role in the community, *if* the videotex system is successful. Library participation in failing systems can be a drain on time and money that does substantial damage to the library. If a videotex system proves successful, but only to the business community and an affluent minority in the community, the library must consider where its energy and finances belong. At present, the best course for most libraries would seem to be interest but not activity.

SUMMARY

Videotex in the United States has a dreary past and troubled present; teletext presents a far more dismal picture. Libraries should embrace new technology, but not at the expense of proper service to the community. The pattern of videotex and teletext experiments in the United States suggests strongly that teletext is a failure, and raises serious questions about the potential of videotex. Until the picture becomes clearer and brighter, libraries should be wary of extensive involvement. Electronic bulletin boards offer a relatively low-cost way for libraries to provide current information to patrons who have personal computers, but also represent allocation of resources to a small, affluent portion of library users.

SELECTED READING

Binder, Michael B. *Videotex and Teletext: New Online Resources for Libraries*. Greenwich, Conn.: JAI Press, 1985. 160 pp. (An informative book that, despite the writer's enthusiasm, presents a balanced and frequently cautionary view of the field. The basis for most of this chapter: his facts, my conclusions.)

Tenne-Sens, Andrej. "Telidon Graphics and Library Applications." *Information Technology and Libraries* 1, no. 2 (June 1982):98-110. (Examples of how one form of videotex could be used by libraries, with extensive discussion of Telidon graphics.)

18

Electronic Mail and Telefacsimile

Electronic mail services (e-mail) and telefacsimile (fax) both use telecommunications for person-to-person or person-to-group communications. Electronic mail is nothing more than a set of software, protocols, and connections. Telefacsimile combines special protocols with a set of technologies also used for other purposes.

Electronic mail and fax represent alternatives to the post office and the telephone. Both offer real advantages and pose real problems. Both have wide acceptance and appear headed for much wider acceptance and use--and both have, at times, been oversold. The two may even overlap in the future.

Electronic mail and fax serve the same basic function. In both cases one person sends a message to another person or to a group of people using telecommunications techniques. E-mail and fax offer one-way communication with the possibility of direct response. In both cases, the fields are more interesting for how they work, why they don't work as well as they could, and their potential, than for the technical details.

ELECTRONIC MAIL

Electronic mail or e-mail is well-named: it offers a way to send a message from one person to another, with the message sent at the convenience of the sender and dealt with at the convenience of the receiver. Electronic mail requires a computer at some point in the communications chain, although neither the sender nor the receiver necessarily needs to own a computer.

Electronic mail works something like this:

1. A person with a message to send creates the message, using either a word processing program or a text editor supplied as part of an e-mail system. In some cases, the person may be able to attach other files (spreadsheets, database samples, graphics) to the message.

2. The message sender initiates an e-mail function (sometimes this happens before creating the message) telling the e-mail system who the message is going to. Different mail systems handle this in different ways, but typically the sender gives the first command, then responds to prompts for the addressee's mailbox identification (electronic mail "address"), possibly a title or subject, and possibly other options. Good mail systems include options such as open copies ("cc:") and blind copies ("xc:"), mailing lists (so that a message can be sent to a pre-established group of interested parties), notification when the message has been received, and possibly a special "reply requested" message to the addressee.

3. Once the message is established and the e-mail system knows what to do with it, the program (which must be running on some computer) will acknowledge that a message has been sent. The sender can then move to other tasks.

4. In some systems, the message now goes into a "mailbox" file for the addressee on the same central computer. In others, the message may be forwarded to other computers until it reaches the appropriate mailbox file. Such indirect delivery may go through a dozen different computers and tens of thousands of miles, depending on the e-mail system and networks to which it is attached. Eventually, it should end up in a file that is available to the addressee (and, in a good system, *only* to the addressee).

5. When the addressee next uses the computer or calls the electronic mail service, he receives a message saying that mail is waiting. Good e-mail systems offer the addressee the option of scanning titles and sender's names before dealing with messages, reading messages with specific keywords and defer-

ring or ignoring others, or reading messages in the order they were sent.

6. The mail system should offer a number of options for dealing with each message once it is read. Typical options include responding immediately, forwarding the message to a third party, deleting the message immediately, printing it, marking it for automatic deletion at some later date, marking it for attention at some later date, or filing it (possibly with new keywords attached to retrieve it later).

That's all there is to electronic mail. Electronic mail combines text editing, disk storage, telecommunications (sometimes but not always), and a program to offer a useful form of person-to-person or person-to-group communication.

Advantages

Electronic mail has real advantages over the two major alternatives, the telephone and the U.S. Postal Service, at least for some situations. The advantages differ for each alternative.

Electronic Mail and the Telephone

Anyone who uses the telephone for business purposes knows about telephone tag, the "game" played when two busy people try to get in touch. It is not uncommon to lose the heart of a message in the struggle to get the other party on the phone. Electronic mail avoids that problem, just as standard mail does: once the message is edited and mailed, the sender can go on to something else.

The telephone can be an interruption and an annoyance. One or two one-minute telephone calls each hour can easily turn a two-hour job into an all-day job, and may make it impossible to complete the job. Electronic mail reduces the number of telephone calls, letting recipients deal with groups of messages all at once and when it is convenient to do so.

Electronic mail also eliminates the problems in pronunciation, hearing, and transcription that sometimes cause messages taken over the telephone to be incorrect or incomplete. While the information and spelling in a message appearing on the screen may be wrong, at least it will be exactly what the sender keyed in. The act of keying in the message may also cause the sender to take the time to be sure the message is complete and exact.

The final major advantage of electronic mail compared to the telephone is the ease of "narrowcasting," sending a message to a group of people at once. Conference calls can achieve the same effect, but only at some expense and with the considerable difficulty of getting everybody at the same time. Any good electronic mail system supports mailing lists, and the right mailing lists can be enormously useful. Using my own organization as an example, we have mailing lists for those who attend ALA conferences, those who review MARC materials, those who are concerned with technical standards, those working on (or interested in) nonroman cataloging support, the Board of Governors, members of specific committees, and so on. When I have a message to send to "ALA conference people," I address it to the name of the mailing list (ALACONF, in this case). I don't need to know who has joined the list or left it, although the mail system tells me in the course of sending the copies.

Electronic mail may also be cheaper than the telephone. A well-designed e-mail system should certainly be cheaper than the telephone when the effects of telephone tag (and the man-hours lost to the game) are included.

Electronic Mail and Paper Mail

The main advantage of electronic mail over paper mail is speed. When electronic mail uses a single central computer, delivery is virtually instantaneous. Even when mail must go over a complex network, delivery usually takes a few minutes (sometimes a few hours). Even the slowest electronic mail should be faster than the best first-class mail service.

Electronic mail can also be easier than paper mail. The software provides the "envelope"; all the sender needs to do is provide an address that is always much shorter than a mailing address. Responding to electronic mail is almost always easier than responding to paper mail: it usually requires only two commands (as brief as one or two characters) and time enough to key in a quick response.

Since electronic mail is usually less formal than paper mail, the cost and complexity of preparing a message is usually lower.

Electronic mail can be archived and retrieved much more easily than paper mail. Some systems even support full-text searching in order to find relevant mail by any word or words in the text. It is also much easier to send a group mailing by e-mail than through the mail, at least for a small group.

Disadvantages and Problems

Electronic mail is not without disadvantages. The technology itself causes certain problems and others come about because there are so many different e-mail options. The inherent disadvantages of electronic mail are those of mail as opposed to face-to-face or telephonic communication. Mail communications lose tone of voice and other clues to underlying meaning. Mail communications do not allow for instantaneous response: that is both an advantage and a disadvantage of mail.

With one interesting exception (covered in the next section), the problems of electronic mail have to do with multiplicity and integration. Simply speaking, electronic mail requires that the sender is able to send e-mail to the recipient and that the recipient checks for e-mail fairly frequently.

Consider the Postal Service and the telephone system. We all have postal addresses, and anybody can send mail from any address to any other address. Very nearly all of us have telephone numbers, and you can call any number from any other number. Most of us check our mail once a day; people who expect to get many important telephone calls have answering machines or services, and check for messages fairly frequently.

It's not that simple with electronic mail. There is not one Electronic Mail Service in the United States. Rather, there are probably thousands of e-mail systems in use. Many organizations and corporations have internal e-mail systems, which can be extremely productive but really replace interoffice memos, not the Postal Service. Going beyond internal e-mail, there are several competing commercial e-mail systems and a number of noncommercial networks through which electronic mail can be sent. If you want to send a message to someone who has an MCI Mail address, you need to be on MCI; Dialcom addresses require a different network, as do On-Tyme II, EasyLink, and so on. Within the noncommercial field, the picture is a bit brighter. While there are many different networks (Bitnet, Usenet, Uucs, Arpanet, and others), most of them interconnect at various levels.

The first problem, then, is that you can only send mail to people whose addresses you know. Some services go a bit further: it is possible to have the service print and deliver mail (through the Postal Service), either because the addressee is unknown or because he doesn't pick up his mail in some set amount of time. That raises the second problem: electronic mail only works if people use it. If a person checks a particular e-mail system only once a week, his electronic mail is almost certainly slower than paper mail. If he doesn't check e-mail at all, it is useless.

People will check e-mail frequently only if it is a normal part of their own work or if it is extremely convenient. Internal mail systems work as long as everybody uses terminals as part of daily work. They will be logged on fairly frequently and people will get their mail rapidly. At RLG, internal e-mail works extremely well because we all depend (to some extent) on the central computer to get our work done.

External mail systems present more of a problem. The non-commercial networks serve their own addressees well, because the mail becomes part of the "internal" system. For example, I am notified of mail from the University of Texas or Apple Computer just as rapidly as I am notified of mail from the next office. On the other hand, because it requires extra work to do so, I only check ALA's e-mail service (which uses a commercial system, ITT Dialcom) every two or three days. It really isn't much faster (for me) than paper mail because it requires extra effort. For that matter, I may still have another mail account on another network. If so, there may be "undelivered mail" that has been purged by the system or is more than one year old: because I wasn't getting or sending much mail on the system and had no other uses for it, I haven't checked it in more than a year.

That's an extreme case, but the problem is a real one. If people don't think of electronic mail as a regular part of work activity, it will be slower than paper mail in many cases.

It should also be noted that electronic mail works only for material in electronic form. There is no good way to send someone a color snapshot of your vacation over an electronic mail link.

Etiquette

The most surprising problem with electronic mail is one of etiquette. Experience in many institutions has shown that electronic mail can cause problems because people reply so freely and rapidly. For some reason, our internal censors that work during face-to-face, telephonic, and paper mail communication do not work as well for electronic replies.

There's a term for it: "flaming." It's a rare e-mail user who hasn't "flamed" at least once--sent a heated, abrupt reply to a message. Of course, flaming happens on the phone as well. The phone has two advantages. First, you can frequently tell by the tone of voice that what appears to be an outrageous question or comment is simply an innocent misunderstanding. Second, your heated reply is not in writing. With electronic mail, your off-the-cuff response to a question becomes a matter of record.

Many institutions that use electronic mail issue booklets or memos suggesting e-mail etiquette because so many problems arise. An optimist would say that it is refreshing to see what people actually think. A realist would note that we all think things on the spur of the moment that we would not wish to say, given an hour's reflection. With experience, you learn to tag certain messages for later consideration: if a message makes you angry, you should *never* answer it immediately.

Electronic Mail and the Library

If a library or any other organization is big enough and modern enough to have a terminal on almost every desk, a central computer, and physical distances of any magnitude, it should support an electronic mail system on the computer. The advantages outweigh the minor disadvantages. Once it becomes part of everyday life, electronic mail can be nearly indispensable.

Like other organizations, libraries also use electronic mail for external purposes. Some interlibrary lending systems are little more than controlled electronic mail, and ALANET mail offers advantages, particularly for groups of libraries that use it. Electronic mail should grow between libraries as telecommunications becomes more common. ILL (interlibrary loan) gains speed and other advantages through e-mail; other e-mail uses may be less obviously beneficial, but can be helpful to libraries.

Interlibrary loan systems also use telex, a slow but reliable method of transmitting text from one place to another. The only real advantage of telex is the tremendous number of telex addresses around the world; in most other respects, it is slower, less flexible, and less powerful than electronic mail or telefacsimile.

TELEFACSIMILE: JUST THE FAX

If electronic mail has much in common with paper mail, telefacsimile has much in common with the telephone. Most telefacsimile uses the telephone system to transmit images. The basic aspects of telefacsimile are older than many other current technologies and better established:

1. The sending and receiving unit must be "on the phone" at the same time, although the receiving unit may be a storage device.

2. The sending unit scans one or more pages to prepare a highly compressed digital image of the light and dark areas on the page.

3. The sending unit sends that digital image to the receiving telefax unit.

4. The receiving unit prints out the image immediately, or stores it for later printing.

Telefax deals with images, even though in some modern systems those images may be generated "images" based on computer-stored text. Telefax uses the phone to send paper mail: it regenerates pages at a distance. It has been around for a long time, always with some use but never a major success. That may be changing today.

Until recently all telefacsimile units were special devices incorporating scanners, printers, electronics, and telephone connections. The scanners would accept only cut sheets (i.e., unbound pages), and the printers usually produced mediocre images on unusual paper, using thermal printing or other techniques. Image density was barely acceptable and fax transmission rates were slow. More to the point, there weren't that many people that you could send faxes to.

Improved electronics have changed that, and so have personal computers. Some current fax units are circuit boards in personal computers that create fax images from stored text (or from input scanners) and generate pages on laser or dot-matrix printers using plain paper. If text has already been created on the computer, it need not be printed out but can be sent directly as fax copy.

Improved electronics have also resulted in improved standards. Traditional facsimile--"Group I" and "Group II" machines, using the standard classification for fax--reproduced pages at a resolution of 88 to 100 lines per inch. Current "Group III" scanners use 200 lines per inch, still cruder than laser printers but good enough for many functions. Group I units needed six minutes to transmit a low quality page; Group II, three minutes. Contemporary Group III units require less than one minute to transmit a fairly high-quality page. Group IV, expensive to produce and rarely used, is even faster. Most modern equipment is Group III, including nearly all PC-based equipment.

The group names identify a key advantage of telefax compared to most telecommunications: standards. Any Group III fax can communicate with any other Group III fax at 9,600 bps, with no special effort, and can receive lower-resolution facsimile at lower speeds from Group II machines. The standards (including data compression algorithms) are fully defined. Those standards have also helped fax to grow in recent years.

Advantages and Disadvantages

Telefacsimile can handle any printed page, although the results may not be perfect. Transmission is reasonably rapid, and involves very little "fiddling." There are already about one-half million Group III-compatible telefacsimile units so there are many opportunities for transmission. Fax is faster than overnight courier services and *potentially* cheaper, at least for a small number of pages.

On the other hand, fax is of no use unless both parties have machines and both parties have them available at the same time. Fax resolution is not good enough for some pictorial material, and many fax machines still use special papers that look and feel somewhat odd. Some experiments show fax to be as expensive as, or more expensive than, overnight courier services--and it is almost always more expensive than first class mail.

Telefacsimile may make more sense now than at any time in its long history, and its use is growing fairly rapidly. On the other hand, it will certainly not supplant any other technology, and seems unlikely to become a "hot item." For example, LITA does not have a Telefacsimile Interest Group and there are few books on the subject except for reports on library experiments.

If optical character recognition techniques improve, fax could have interesting new roles. When a fax board captures a transmission, that transmission could be treated as though it came from a scanner. Good software may, in the future, be able to convert the faxed page to machine-readable text.

Fax and the Library

Libraries have engaged in telefax experiments for at least two decades. Twelve libraries in New York State took part in the "FACTS" project in 1967 and 1968, using slow Group I machines to handle ILL requests. The machines were inadequate, the patrons were unwilling to accept faster but less legible copies, and there were other problems as well. Other early experiments also tended to be expensive and unsuccessful.

Experiments in the late 1970s were not terribly successful either. Transactions were expensive, as much as $12 to $24. Librarians discovered (as might have been expected) that most people didn't really need information as rapidly as they claimed. In some cases requested material arrived within hours--but the requesters did not pick it up for days. Experiments and ongoing projects continue, and more recent experience with Group III systems seems to be more positive. Telefacsimile certainly has some role in some libraries, although the size and nature of that role is still uncertain.

SUMMARY

Electronic mail and telefacsimile both offer high-speed alternatives for transmitting specific messages from one person or location to another person or location. Both have uses in libraries as in business, and neither presents a general solution to any problem. Electronic mail makes sense only in combination with other technologies--unless people use computers every day, they won't check electronic mail every day.

SELECTED READING

Boss, Richard W., and Hal Espo. "The Use of Telefacsimile in Libraries." *Library Hi Tech* 5, no. 1 (Spring 1987):33-42. (Little technical detail, but good examples of actual use.)

Mortensen, E. "Trends in electronic mail and its role in office automation." *Electronic Publishing Review* 5, no. 4 (December 1985):257-68. (Organizational and operational concepts to be considered in business use of electronic mail. Avoids nonsensical cost claims.)

Porter, Peggy. "'Dear PPO5': Interpersonal Communication and the Computer: Entering a Brave New World." *Library Hi Tech* 2, no. 1 (Spring 1984):23-27. (Practical considerations for electronic mail.)

Tracy, Janet, and William DeJohn. "Digital Facsimile: Columbia Law Library and Pacific Northwest Library Facsimile Network." *Library Hi Tech* 1, no. 3 (Winter 1983):9-14. Followed by literature review. (Relatively early report on library use of contemporary fax.)

19

Local Area Networks

Local Area Networks (LANs) make it possible to share files among several computers and send information from one computer to another. Local area networks or LANs serve thousands of organizations well, but seem to cause more confusion than most other aspects of computer technology. Part of that difficulty may be the multiplicity of LAN designs and the overlap between LANs and other sorts of networks. Another difficulty arises because LANs require different ways of thinking about computer programs and files. LANs cause difficulty because they require special expertise to design and install, and require ongoing supervision for successful operation.

Local area networks have been around for more than a decade, often without being called LANs. Since 1984 microcomputer analysts have labeled each new year the "Year of the LAN": the year in which businesses with many personal computers would link them together, resulting in vastly increased LAN installations. By 1988 the "Year of the LAN" has become a standing joke in the personal computer industry, while the installed base of LANs grows steadily but not spectacularly.

THE BASICS

A local area network is a combination of cables, computer processors, and software that connects computers and related devices and regulates the flow of information traffic among the devices. A company called Datapoint began introducing small computers into offices in the early 1970s. The computers either sat on people's desks or occupied their own desks. They did not require air conditioning or special power lines, and they were not particularly threatening to office workers. They were not particularly powerful, but the Datapoint operating system was excellent and thousands of companies used the computers for hundreds of purposes such as inventory, order entry and fulfillment, and word processing.

As usage grew, companies needed to add hard disks and faster printers and needed more computing power. They also needed to let more people use the same files. Some Datapoint computers supported multiple terminals, but not very many terminals on a single computer. Datapoint could have introduced massively more powerful models and told people to replace their existing equipment, but the more powerful models would probably require computer rooms and large capital investments. Instead, along with introducing somewhat more powerful models, it introduced the concept of increasing power by attaching computers together through the Attached Resource Computer (ARC) system.

ARC involved attaching a little box to each computer and running cables from box to box. With that cabling and some new software, an office could share a single disk drive among many computers, send information from one computer to another, and generally treat a group of small computers as a single, large multi-user system. Thousands of ARC systems were installed beginning in the mid-1970s. Datapoint didn't call it that at the time, but it was busily installing local area networks.

In 1977 Datapoint introduced ARCnet, using lower transmission rates and less expensive boxes, providing the ability to include non-Datapoint computers in the group of computers and explicitly recognizing that ARC was a local area network. By that time Xerox, Intel, and Digital Equipment Corporation had begun to promote Ethernet--another local area network--using technology that was very different from the technology used in ARCnet.

Since then both Ethernet and ARCnet have achieved broad acceptance and a number of other LAN designs have been introduced, including at least two from IBM. While LANs now number in the tens of thousands and connect more than one million devices, they have never been adopted on the massive scale predicted by industry analysts. For those businesses and institutions that have installed LANs and use them effectively, however, the systems make individual computers and computer users more effective in a number of ways.

Handling Multiple Computers

When many people in a company need personal computing power, it isn't the computers that cost so much. It is the software and peripherals, and making them all work coherently.

Assume for the moment that you are in charge of satisfying the staff computing needs in a fairly large library. You can make the case that there should be 50 personal computers. Fifty good-quality PCs represent a significant chunk of money, but not an enormous chunk: in 1987, $40,000 should suffice.

But that only buys 50 minimal personal computers with diskette drives and monitors and does not include mass storage, printers, or software. Of the 50 computer users, assume that 10 people will be creating or using large databases frequently and absolutely require hard disks, while the others need access to several megabytes of disk space once in a while. Everybody wants high-quality printing, but only five people need printers more than once or twice a day. Everybody needs software: all 50 need word processing; half need modems and telecommunications software; 20 will use spreadsheets at least once a week; and most users will need some form of database once in a while. Every user may have good reason to use each of the major varieties of software at least once in a while, as well as other important varieties such as outline processors and project managers.

Satisfying everybody's needs will cost much more than $40,000. If everybody gets what they could occasionally use, that means a large-capacity hard disk, laser printer, and modem for each computer, and four or five major software packages; it probably also means more powerful computers. Figure a startup cost of more than $5,000 per system or $250,000 overall--and that's without high-resolution color monitors, desktop publishing, scanners, facsimile, mice, and all the other wonders of "power computing."

It is much harder to justify $250,000 than $40,000, and you will still have the problem that everybody has separate files. This means the same data will be entered over and over and that people will be spending time carrying disks from one computer to another to share documents, small databases, and spreadsheet templates.

You probably can't justify $250,000. Instead, only 5 people will have laser printers, only 10 will have modems, only a handful will have hard disks, and only a few will have more powerful computers. Everybody may have word processing software, but other software will be doled out carefully. People will be expected to share the lasers and modems and even the hard disks. Other people may have low-cost ink-jet or dot-matrix printers, or they may not have printers at all. That can bring the total installed cost down to $100,000 or less.

That's one way of dealing with multiple computers, and for many organizations it is the most reasonable way. People share the laser printers, modems, and database software using "sneakernet"--hand-carrying diskettes from computer to computer as needed. If the users of the computers that have laser printers are willing to tolerate interruptions (or if the laser printers are on PCs reserved for such use), the arrangement may be perfectly comfortable.

Connectivity: Benefits of a LAN

Sneakernet may give all 50 users laser printing without buying 50 laser printers. It does not work as well when two people need to work on different parts of the same large database at the same time because it does nothing to connect the work of one person to the work of another. A working group with 50 computers can benefit from increased connections with one another's work and files.

The word *connectivity* dates back to 1893 as an aspect of geometry, and has more recently gained prominence as a computer buzz-word. Local area networks increase connectivity: they make it possible for information to flow directly from one computer or related device to another. Connectivity may also be used to refer to the ability to move data from a mainframe computer to a personal computer without difficulty; that is a different topic, one not explicitly covered in this book.

What does enhanced connectivity, in the form of a local area network, mean for the 50 computer users in your library? It can mean any or all of several things, among them the following:

1. Every computer user can print documents to a laser printer directly, with the document being printed as soon as any printer is available and without interrupting anyone else's work.

2. Several people can work on one database at the same time.

3. Two or more people can actually work on one spreadsheet simultaneously.

4. People can send questions or messages to other people by computer, and recipients can deal with the questions at their convenience (see the discussion of electronic mail in chapter 18).

It means that all 50 people can use more powerful computing equipment for a total of less than $250,000--but it does not mean that they can gain full power for as little as $100,000. A LAN system costs more than a collection of minimal individual systems, but can cost somewhat less than a similar collection of very powerful systems. On the other hand, a LAN with 50 attached computers may well require a full-time LAN administrator in addition to the computer specialist already needed to help 50 computer users work effectively.

A LAN may also mean that an organization can use several small computers to do the work of one large computer. A local library computer system could, at least conceivably, consist of one large microcomputer running circulation control (with its own database); another running catalog maintenance; and another running an online patron access catalog--or several running online patron access, all sharing a common database. With the proper LAN software, any terminal could use any computer as required; catalog maintenance could automatically update the online patron access catalog; and patrons could see circulation status as an integral part of catalog searches. A group of separate computers and databases can be an integrated system through use of a LAN.

That's the theory, and it sometimes works. Very few businesses buy LANs on a whim. While their benefits can be considerable, they are not as easily installed as a new personal computer or a new program. The difficulties in dealing with a LAN stem from its nature: cables connecting computers and devices, electronics to make use of the cables, software to make use of the electronics, and application software that can deal with multiple users of a single file or device.

TECHNICAL ASPECTS

Local area networks are characterized by five factors: the cabling used to connect stations; the topology of the connections; whether the cabling carries one signal or many signals; the speed of communication; and the protocols used to assure correct communications.

Many vendors offer local area networks, some for use with their own computers, some for use with many different computers. Typically, any LAN will be discussed in terms of cabling, topology, number of signals, speed, and protocol (e.g., "a baseband token-bus coaxial network running at five million bits per second"). In this case, *baseband* means that the cable is used to carry one signal at a time; *token-bus* refers to the protocol (token) and the topology (bus), *coaxial* refers to the cabling; and *five million bits per second* to the speed.

The first issue, however, is what constitutes a LAN and how it differs from some other network. A good definition incorporates three characteristics:

1. Any station in a LAN must be able to communicate directly with any other station.

2. A LAN must be under the direct control of a single agency (i.e., part of a single operation).

3. A LAN must use a single cable or set of cables.

Earlier definitions of LANs exclude campuswide networks, but current definitions include such large networks. More typically, a campuswide network is a hybrid: both a local area network in its own right and a network linking many smaller local area networks. A single local area network may also have smaller networks that are connected to the larger network only through a single "gateway" or common computer. Through complex webs such as these, every computer within an organization may have direct or indirect access to every other computer. For example, a college library's computer system may provide connections to administrative computing facilities and educational computing facilities in a way that provides for electronic mail throughout the campus, allows students to use the library's online catalog from their dorm rooms, and in other ways provides a richer information environment for every computer user on campus.

Cabling and Speed

Local area networks use twisted-pair wires, coaxial cables and fiber optic cables. The potential speed of a LAN depends heavily on the cabling. Twisted-pair wiring and similar copper wiring is relatively inexpensive and easy to run, but is limited to relatively low transmission rates. Coaxial cable is much more expensive than twisted-pair and far more difficult to install in an existing office (it is thicker and does not bend as readily), but can support much higher-speed transmission. Fiber optic cables provide the greatest capacity, are no more difficult to install than coaxial cable, and provide freedom from electrical interference and security problems; as costs come down, more LAN installations will use fiber optic cables.

Ultimately, the speed of a network is limited by the cable, but most networks run more slowly than their cabling will permit. Typical LAN speeds run from low hundreds of thousands of characters per second to millions of characters per second. Most sources cite LAN speeds in megaHertz or millions of bits per second. To convert bits to characters, divide by 8: a LAN that runs at 1.2 million bits per second transmits 150,000 characters per second under ideal conditions.

Topology

The definition of a local area network requires that each computer be able to send or receive messages to or from each other computer or device. With more than two or three computers in a system, direct links become hopelessly complex and expensive. The number of paths required is *N times N-1*, where *N* is the number of units. Since a two-way link offers two paths, a direct-connection network of 6 computers requires 15 links (30 paths); 10 computers require 45 links; 50 computers require 1,225 links; and 100 computers require 4,500 links. For this reason, every local area network provides indirect links. The topology of a network is the manner in which each computer or other unit is linked to each other unit--the shape of the set of indirect links. Networks can be configured as stars, rings, or buses, but almost all local area networks are either buses or rings.

A *star* network has a single central node to which all units are linked, like spokes from the hub of a wheel. All messages go through the central node, and the operation of the network depends entirely on that central node. A typical local library system can be considered a star network of terminals: the computer is the central node, and one terminal can talk to another terminal only through that computer. But a star network of terminals is not really a local area network; rather, it is a multi-user computer system.

A *ring* network has a single cable or set of cables connecting each unit to two adjacent units, with the overall cabling forming a closed loop--much as the outer rim connects the spokes of a wheel. In this case, however, the spokes are actually computers around the rim: there is no hub. Messages are passed around the ring, with the LAN connection at each unit monitoring messages and transmitting new messages as appropriate.

A *bus* network has a single cable or set of cables connecting adjacent units (or groups of units), but does not have a closed loop. Instead, electronic equipment at the open ends of the cable maintains continuous communications along the network, passing messages back down the cables as needed. If a star network is like the spokes of a wheel and a ring network is like the rim of a wheel, a bus network is like a railroad line, with computers at each stop: messages turn around at the end of the line if that turnaround is needed to reach their definition.

In practice, network topologies may be somewhat more complex. A bus network may actually be a series of small stars (with each station along the bus being the hub of its own set of spokes); a star network may be a "snowflake," with the central computer linking to smaller central nodes, each of which has its own star of units.

Networks vary as to the ease of connecting or disconnecting a single unit and the network's ability to keep operating with nonfunctioning units. Bus networks typically provide easy connection and disconnection: units can join the network while it is operating and a single unit failure will not bring down the network. Ring networks provide this level of durability only if they have automatic bypass mechanisms, so that signals can continue past a failed unit. Star networks are entirely dependent on the central computer, which is likely to be a larger and more stable computer than any node in a ring or bus network.

Number of Channels

Local area networks typically carry either a single high-speed channel of information--called *baseband*--or many channels of information--called *broadband*. Broadband systems require more electronics and typically better cabling, but permit the use of a single cabling system for several different purposes, including video in some cases. Campuswide networks (for example) tend to be broadband networks; small local area networks within offices tend to be baseband networks.

Protocol

When one cable links dozens of computers, a communications protocol must be established. When can a computer send a message? How does a computer know that a message is intended for it? How does the sending computer know that the message has been received? Two protocols dominate local area networks: token passing and CSMA/CD. Each has its proponents; both are widely used and perform well under most conditions. ARC and ARCnet use tokens and Ethernet uses CSMA/CD.

In the descriptions that follow, "computer" is used as shorthand for "computer or any other device on the network." Printers and other devices that are attached directly to the network will have special "intelligent" attachments so that they can function as computers for the purposes of receiving and identifying messages. A message may be a request for a record from a file, a line or set of lines to be printed, a command to be carried out on some other computer, or anything else that can be transmitted electronically.

Token Passing

A *token-passing* network establishes a special small message called a token. All other messages are attached to the token. When a token reaches a computer on the network, the computer can take several actions:

1. If the computer has a message to transmit, it adds that message to the string of other messages attached to the token.

2. If one or more messages have tags that identify the computer as the intended receiver, the computer accepts the messages and adds a tag to each message saying that it has been received.

3. If one or more messages originated from this computer and have already been marked as received, the computer deletes them.

After taking those actions, the computer passes the token and its messages to the next computer. (A simpler token-passing system may permit only one message to be attached to the token at any one time, but the principle is the same.) Since no computer attempts to transmit or receive unless it has possession of the token, it is not possible for two transmissions to interfere with each other.

Most early LANs used token passing because most early LANs were ARC networks. Token passing is deterministic: the network owner can predict the maximum delay for any message to be transmitted because tokens pass from station to station at a fixed (and very high) rate. Local area networks can be used to control manufacturing systems; in such cases, it is crucial that message delays be short and predictable, and such networks almost always use token-passing protocols.

CSMA/CD

CSMA/CD stands for *Carrier Sense Multiple Access/Collision Detection.* When a computer has something to send, it "listens" to the cable to see if transmission is currently taking place (as indicated by the carrier signal): this is carrier sensing. If nothing is being transmitted, it sends its message. But it is quite possible for more than one computer to start sending a message at the same time, which is collision. In a CSMA/CD network, the network electronics will sense collision; each computer will then wait a small period of time and try again.

CSMA/CD is not deterministic. If a network has many computers but relatively light traffic--each computer spends relatively little time sending and receiving messages--CSMA/CD will usually outperform token passing, given the same overall transmission speed. But as the load on a CSMA/CD network grows, transmission delays can get dramatically worse: the more collisions and more retries, the worse it will be. Conceivably, a CSMA/CD network could break down altogether, the electronic equivalent of traffic gridlock, with messages never being successfully transmitted. That can't happen with a token-passing network. On the other hand, CSMA/CD electronics should be simpler and cheaper than token-passing electronics, particularly the electronics for token buses.

The Real Issue: Performance

Discussions of LANs involve many more terms and trademarks, but the fundamental aspects of a LAN are the five just discussed. Unfortunately the five technical aspects of a LAN don't necessarily determine the answer to the most important issue: how well the LAN works in your environment, and what services it can perform. Services can be as simple as file sending and receiving, should generally include electronic mail, and can include file sharing, device sharing, and program sharing. Selection of a suitable LAN requires intimate knowledge of your computing environment, your current needs and future plans, LANs currently on the market and well supported in your area, and the level of ongoing support your organization can afford to provide.

Problems

Local area networks require new software, paths for cables, administration, and a different way of thinking about computing. The best time to install a local area network is before any individual computers have been installed--but that's not possible for most libraries or other organizations. The worst way to install a local area network is to bring in the cables and network software, install it, and hope for the best.

Connecting all the computers in an organization may be physically difficult; it may also be regarded as disruptive by computer users. Most people who make good use of personal computers regard them as personal tools, and if they are asked to give up their own disk space or software in favor of network file servers and network software, they may feel that they are losing control of their own work.

The primary problem with LANs is that they are networks of computers. The more capabilities provided over the network, the more care needs to be taken with the network itself. Some examples of the potential problems:

1. If a database can be updated from any computer on the network, the database software must provide locking mechanisms to prevent conflicting updates. Without such mechanisms, it is quite possible for two users to update the same record in an overlapping manner. Only the second update will actually have any effect, wiping out the first update. For example, a database record may contain a shop's inventory for an item. If the database shows 500 of a given item, a clerk may sell 200 and update the database. Without record locking, another clerk could simultaneously sell another 200 and update the database, working from the same 500-count record.

At the end of both transactions, the database will show that 300 items remain--but the shop will have only 100 items.

2. Every program running on the network itself must have file safety mechanisms. Without such mechanisms, two people editing manuscripts using the same word processing program may interfere with each other's work or, if both are working on the same manuscript, the work of one can be completely lost.

3. Network data access will almost always be slower than local data access. People need to adjust their expectations and be aware of the benefits of the network. For that and other reasons, electronic mail is a particularly good use of a new network because once people understand its uses, it is an enormous convenience and may help to make the network seem desirable.

4. File backup is even more important on network file servers. Fortunately it is easier to back up one big set of files than 20 small sets of files, as long as the backup is part of a network administrator's job.

5. If networks are not well configured, printers and other devices may be overloaded, leading to excessive delays and premature breakdowns. That may be particularly true with laser printers, since most inexpensive laser printers are not designed for continuous use eight hours a day. Networked printers require some supervision; since individual users can't predict when their listings are likely to be ready, they are less likely to attend to paper outages and other casual maintenance requirements.

6. Most networks require tuning: adjusting the network software and hardware configuration to provide the best performance. Tuning may mean adding more file servers, print servers, or modems, or modifying software parameters. Most networks other than the smallest require a part-time or full-time network administrator who may spend hours each day monitoring the performance of the network.

None of these problems are overwhelming, but they combine to make network installation a moderately expensive and intricate proposition.

Other Networks

Local area networks usually work within a single institution and rarely cover more than a mile or so between the most distant points. Computer-to-computer and terminal-to-computer networks can be much larger and more diverse. There are many such networks in the United States and abroad, and many networks connect to other networks.

The best-known networks in libraries are the shared technical processing networks and the online searching networks. OCLC, RLIN, WLN, and UTLAS operate star networks of leased lines, with the central computer or computers as the center of the star; increasingly, computers as opposed to terminals are at the other end of each line. Formal computer-to-computer communications will grow over these networks.

Most online searching networks and special networks such as ALANET use national packet-switching networks such as Telenet and Tymnet (as do, to some extent, OCLC, RLIN, and the others). From the perspective of the end-user and from the perspective of BRS or Dialog, the logical network is a star network, with the database at the center. From a communications perspective, the situation may be much more complex.

Besides the private leased-line networks such as OCLC and the public-switched networks, there are a number of computer-to-computer networks serving colleges and universities, the military, government systems, and many others. Some of the best known are Arpanet, Bitnet and Uucp (a network linking more than 1,000 computers running the Unix operating system). Such networks may combine leased lines, public networks, and even microwave, satellite, and radio links, and may link with other networks in intricate electronic webs.

SUMMARY

Local area networks can make more effective use of computing resources and allow people to work together on projects, but they require careful design and supervision to be worthwhile.

If your institution has a dozen personal computers, you probably have situations where files need to be shared and such devices as printers are underused. A local area network may improve your situation, but it may also impose a layer of complexity and expense that exceeds any benefits.

Special-purpose LANs, installed as part of a local library system, should not require the constant attention of general-purpose LANs. Libraries can benefit from both types of network, although perhaps not as dramatically as they benefit from the national networks.

SELECTED READING

Archer, Rowland. *The Practical Guide to Local Area Networks.* Berkeley: Osborne McGraw-Hill, 1986. 283 pp. Glossary; index. (Concentrates on personal computer networks, and most of the book takes detailed looks at five PC LAN systems. Down-to-earth, clear, good within its intended scope. Extensive glossary.)

Levert, Virginia M. "Applications of Local Area Networks of Microcomputers in Libraries." *Information Technology and Libraries* 4, no. 1 (March 1985):9-18. (Good introduction to LANs, still quite relevant.)

Persky, Gail et al. "A Geac Local Area Network for the Bobst Library." *Library Hi Tech* 2, no. 2 (Summer 1984):37-45.

There are many good current books on local area networks, particularly with regard to personal computers. *PC Magazine* has a long-running series of careful tests of local area networks and related options, including a growing decision flowchart for cases in which particular methodologies might be most suitable.

20

Conclusion

The only safe prediction about current technology is that new technologies will emerge, some (but not all) of which will be important. Almost as safe is the prediction that mature technologies will survive longer than might be expected. Librarians will be urged to adopt new technologies and media before they have become established, and will be accused of being technologically conservative; librarians and libraries will continue to make good use of new technologies, frequently in advance of most other fields.

This book discusses 20 current technologies of particular interest to libraries, as they appear to be in late 1987 and early 1988. I believe that almost every chapter will still be relevant in 1993, although some chapters may describe fading technologies by that point--and one or two sections may describe technologies that never became important. By 1998, on the other hand, I would expect some of the chapters to be of strictly historical and archival interest. Which ones? Not claiming to be a prophet, I won't attempt to make such predictions--except that I will flatly predict that print on paper will continue to thrive and that prophets will continue to announce the impending end of print-on-paper as a primary medium.

KEEPING UP WITH TECHNOLOGY

Don't expect an easy recommendation for keeping thoroughly informed on all new aspects of technology. If there is a way to do so without spending your entire life reading, I don't know what it is. Major developments usually become evident through the usual media--daily newspapers, news magazines, and periodicals specializing in science and technology.

In keeping up with contemporary technology, it is important to remember that some people equate possibility with feasibility and feasibility with desirability. New techniques can take years or decades to emerge from lab to market, and quite a few never make it. Even if a technology has been proven to be feasible, that does not automatically make it desirable or necessary, and certainly does not mean that older techniques for solving similar problems are automatically inferior.

Professional Associations

One good way to stay current with technology is to be part of the professional societies that deal with information technology. If you belong to the American Library Association and care about current technology, join LITA. Twenty-five dollars per year makes you part of the largest professional organization devoted solely to issues of information technology in libraries. It puts you in touch with thousands of library professionals, more than a dozen informal interest groups, conference programs, and other resources. With membership you also receive *Information Technology and Libraries*, a quarterly professional journal, and *LITA Newsletter*, a quarterly newsletter. The two quarterlies represent important continuing sources of information and opinion regarding technology in libraries. If you don't belong to ALA, consider joining it and LITA.

The American Society for Information Science also deals with technology issues, frequently from a somewhat more theoretical viewpoint than LITA. Most state library associations have sections, interest groups, or committees focusing on the impact of technology; similarly, library associations such as the Special Library Association should have subgroups that deal with technology. Every library deals with technology, both in the form of media and to support the work of the library; every library association will show some concern with current technology.

The Association for Computing Machinery (ACM) may be the largest professional association in the computer field, and includes many special interest groups and publications. Every field of technology has its own professional organizations and there are too many possibilities to include here.

Periodicals

For most of us, the best way to keep up with technology is to read about it. Better daily newspapers have their own science reporters and carry columns on current technology; the major news weeklies also maintain ongoing coverage of science and technology.

Within the library field, any number of publications focus on aspects of technology either as their primary focus or as a continuing topic. *Information Technology and Libraries* and *LITA Newsletter* were mentioned previously. *Library Hi Tech* and a number of other commercial publications focus on new technology; *American Libraries*, *Library Journal*, and other general library periodicals frequently include coverage of new technology in libraries.

The field of personal computing has many periodicals, none of which covers all of the field in a useful manner. *Byte Magazine* deals with many theoretical and practical issues in the field, frequently at a level that requires prior expertise on the part of the reader. *PC Magazine* offers unparalleled breadth and quality of reviewing in its own specialty, computers and peripherals following the various "PC standards" originated by IBM. Other magazines deal with other categories of computer, none quite as extensively. There are also specialized magazines for optical media, graphics processing, telecommunications, and almost every other aspect of technology. If you find yourself deeply interested in a particular area of technology, you will almost certainly find several periodicals wholly or partially devoted to it.

Maintaining Perspective

New technology can be fascinating, sometimes more fascinating than the technology that we actually live with. The announcement of a revolutionary new technology does not mean that it will succeed in the marketplace, or even that it will ever reach the marketplace. New technologies do emerge, but the patterns of emergence are not always predictable.

Once a technology becomes successful, it is likely to remain important for some time. New technology tends to complement existing technology rather than replace it, although there are exceptions to that rule.

If you care about new technology you should keep an eye on the latest announcements, but be careful to distinguish press releases from reality. You can usually ascertain the difference in discussions within LITA and elsewhere, but a touch of skepticism helps when reading "leading edge" articles from those with financial or other interest in the technology they discuss.

If you need to keep a library running and improve its services, you should pay more attention to current technology than to emerging technology and, just possibly, not worry too much about obsolescence. If it works effectively and efficiently, it's still current. If there are legitimate ways to make it work better, faster, and cheaper, those ways should become clear as you stay involved with the field.

Glossary

Acoustical In sound recordings, used to describe recordings made without the use of microphones or other electrical equipment as part of the recording chain. In acoustical recordings, the force of the voices and instruments that cause the recording stylus to vibrate directly. Also *acoustic*.

Analog Continuously varying in a form directly analogous to the original. Used to refer to recording and playback techniques, and in other fields. Television, radio, traditional sound recordings, audiocassettes, and videocassettes all use analog techniques, as do consumer videodiscs. Contrast to digital, where wave forms are translated into binary digits. Some analog computers have been made for special purposes, but there are no analog computers in general use.

Analytical Engine Programmable computing engine designed by Charles Babbage in 1836, widely considered to be the forerunner of computers.

ANSI American National Standards Institute, the accrediting agency, clearinghouse, and publisher for most voluntary technical standards in the United States. The United States member of ISO, the International Standards Organization.

Antiope Acquisition Numerique et Televisualisation d'Images Organisees en Pages d'Ecriture. French videotex and teletext system.

Aperture card A card, typically a Hollerith punched card, with a rectangular opening containing a small area of microfilm.

Archival Having the potential for retaining original characteristics for a very long period under suitable conditions.

ARCnet Local area network developed by Datapoint Corporation; the earlier form, ARC (Attached Resource Computer), was introduced in 1977 and was the first widely installed local area network. ARCnet uses a token bus protocol and is the basis for the IEEE (Institute of Electrical and Electronics Engineers) 802.4 token bus standard.

Arithmometer Mechanical calculator invented by Charles Xavier Thomas de Colmar in France around 1820. The first mass-produced calculator.

ASCII American Standard Code for Information Interchange. A standard (X3.4-1977) for representing characters as sets of binary digits (bits, stored as bytes). Virtually all personal computers use ASCII, as do CD-ROM and many other digital storage systems, including some (but not all) magnetic tape systems. The only competing American standard for character storage is EBCDIC (Extended Binary Coded Decimal Interchange Code), championed by IBM and thus very important in large computers. IBM's personal computers use ASCII.

Attenuation Reduction of strength. Usually refers to reduction of signal strength: either deliberate (a volume control is an attenuator) or because of physical limitations (all wires attenuate electrical energy; all optical fibers attenuate light).

Bandwidth The range of frequencies that can be handled by a circuit or system. Defined by the lowest and highest frequency that can be handled (e.g., the normal audio bandwidth is 20 Hertz to 20 kiloHertz). Also used in computing to refer to the bus width, the number of bits handled simultaneously.

Baseband Network cabling and communications system in which only one signal is communicated. Compare to *Broadband*.

Baud Number of state reversals (changes from one state to another) per second in telecommunications. Normally used to mean bits per second, which is not (strictly speaking) correct: 1,200 bps modems usually run at 600 baud, packing more information into each state reversal.

Bernoulli Variety of disk drive in which a flexible disk spins at high speed with the recording surface being deflected toward the recording head because of the curvature of the head. (Named for the Bernoulli Principle, the scientific principle that causes the deflection.) Any contamination of the disk (hair, dirt, etc.) will distort the aerodynamics and allow the surface to move back away from the head, making Bernoulli drives essentially crash-proof.

Beta The videocassette system developed and controlled by Sony. Also *Betamax.*

Binary Having only two states. Binary digits are either 0 or 1.

Bit Binary digit. A single unit of information in data processing with only two values: on or off, usually represented as "1" or "0." All digital computers and storage systems work entirely with data in the form of bits.

Bit-mapped Stored as an image made up of picture elements, rather than as text or as directions to create an image. Bit-mapped images require much more storage than characters or directions. For example, the bit-mapped representation of a single letter in this book could require 1,200 bits or more (or about 150 bytes), as opposed to the 8 bits or 1 byte required to store the character.

Broadband Network cabling and communication system carrying multiple signals simultaneously. A broadband LAN may carry voice, video, and computer information simultaneously.

Byte A group of bits that represents the next lowest unit of information, usually a character. A byte is usually made up of 8 bits and can have any of 256 different values. In some cases a byte may be encoded using fewer than eight or more than eight bits. For example, in some telecommunications, a byte requires from 9 to 11 bits for transmission; on a CD-ROM, a byte is encoded in 17 bits. In both these cases, however, the byte itself is made up of eight bits and the remainder is entirely overhead.

CAD Computer-assisted design (or, more generally, CADD: computer-assisted design and drafting).

Calculating clock Apparently the first mechanical calculator, built by Wilhelm Schickard in Tubingen, Germany in 1623.

Cartrivision American-designed videocassette system introduced in 1972 and abandoned in 1974. The system suffered from poor picture quality, insufficient backing, and other problems, notably a provision that made it impossible to rewind prerecorded motion-picture cassettes on home machines.

CAV Constant angular velocity. A rotating medium that turns at a constant rate of rotation. Analog discs (LPs, 78s) and magnetic disks use CAV, as do some videodiscs. On a CAV medium, the linear speed of the medium (the information area) changes continuously: at the inner edge of a disc, much less recording surface is available for each second. Compare to *CLV*.

CCITT International Telephone and Telegraph Consultative Committee (the acronym is from the original French name). European agency dealing with standards in these and related fields.

CD Compact disc. A 12-centimeter plastic-and-metal disc storing up to 75 minutes of sound in digital form or other digital information. The term is controlled and CD specifications are set by Philips and Sony.

CD-4 RCA Victor's methodology for carrying four discrete audio channels on a long-playing disc. The methodology used ultrasonic signals to carry the differences between front and rear channels; very few cartridges could play the recordings properly, and very few recordings ever yielded clear, undistorted four-channel sound. The system was a technological tour de force that exceeded real-world capabilities.

CDI Compact disc-interactive. A Philips-Sony specification for a computer-based player and CD format capable of combining text, software, audio, and video information and of playing audio and video simultaneously. The player and keyboard provide for interactive use of the medium.

CD-ROM Compact disc-read only memory. Physically identical to a CD, or compact disc, but used to store and retrieve information such as text, software, graphics, or sound.

CDV Compact disc-video, a special form of compact disc that combines 5 minutes of video with 20 minutes of CD-quality sound. Requires special players, such as the combined LaserVision/CDV/CD players available from Pioneer, Yamaha, and others.

CED Capacitance electronic data. Another name for the RCA SelectaVision VideoDisc system. A stylus rides in a grooved, partially conductive disc, translating differences in capacitance into information that becomes a television signal. No longer produced.

Ceefax Teletext system originated by the British Broadcasting Corporation (BBC) in Britain, with a pilot test beginning in 1974. The name comes from "see facts."

Cellulose acetate "Safety" film stock introduced around 1930. Does not burst into flame of its own accord, but does shrink and separate from the emulsion (image).

Cellulose nitrate Film stock used prior to the introduction of "safety" stock around 1930. Cellulose nitrate decomposes; in late stages and in sealed containers, it can spontaneously combust, starting a fire that cannot easily be controlled, since the film stock contains sufficient oxygen to feed the fire. The fire releases toxic gases that damage other materials.

CIRC Cross-interleaved Reed-Solomon code. An error detection and correction scheme that is part of the Philips-Sony CD and CD-ROM standard; it adds 8 bytes of data to each 24 bytes of user data.

Cladding In fiber optics, the sheathing portion of an optical fiber. It has a lower refractive index than the core--i.e., light travels faster through the cladding--which has the effect of insulating the core and causing light to reflect back into the core.

CLV Constant linear velocity. Any medium in which the recording or playback surface moves at a constant rate; if the medium uses a disc, the disc must change speed constantly to keep the surface movement constant. All "ribbon media" such as film, videotape, and audiocassette use CLV: the reels are always changing speed, but the tape or film moves at a constant speed. CD and CD-ROM use CLV, as do most videodiscs. CLV uses a medium much more efficiently than CAV, but is much less convenient for direct access to any particular point on the medium.

Coaxial cable Communications cable consisting of a copper wire or bundle of wires wrapped in insulation, with a copper tube around the insulation (and a protective wrapping for the copper tube). The tube and wire(s) share the same axis, thus the name *coaxial*. Coaxial cable can carry much higher frequencies than simple wire pairs.

COM Computer output microfilm. Microfilm generated directly from computer-stored information. Typically microfiche, but may be other microfilm media.

Compact disc *See CD.*

Compansion Short for compression-expansion, the technique used in the Dolby B noise reduction process: the dynamic range of high frequencies is compressed during recording and expanded during playback; the expansion reduces the level of background noise during quiet passages.

Core In fiber optics, the central material of an optical fiber, having a high refractive index (i.e., transmitting light at a relatively low speed). The core is surrounded by the cladding. Also core memory, the dominant form of direct-access computer memory until the last few years: wire grids with tiny magnetic rings (cores) at the intersections of the wires.

CPU Central processing unit, the heart of any computer.

CRT Cathode ray tube. Vacuum tube with a flat end on which light appears when phosphors are struck by an aimed cathode ray. Most television sets use CRTs as picture tubes (the exceptions are very small sets using LCD displays). CRTs are also widely used as computer displays. The combination of a CRT and keyboard is sometimes called a VDT, video display terminal.

CSMA/CD Carrier sense multiple access / collision detection. The protocol used in Ethernet and some other local area networks:

when a node on the network has a message to transmit, it "listens" until the network is clear. It then sends the message. If another node sends a message at the same time, the two collide and neither one is completed. Each node then waits a different amount of time before retransmitting. CSMA/CD offers better performance than token-passing (the other LAN protocol) on LANs with light traffic, but generally degrades more rapidly as traffic increases.

DAD Digital audio disc, the generic name for CD.

Daisywheel printer Printer that uses a flat circular plastic or metal printing element containing many spokes or "petals" with characters on them. Daisywheel printers are impact letter-quality printers; most modern electronic typewriters also use daisywheel printing elements.

DAT Digital audio tape. A form of digital audio using a very small cassette (smaller than an audiocassette) and helical scanning (similar to VCR).

DataROM Name used by Sony for a proposed read-only optical disc, somewhat larger than CD-ROM, with faster access.

dB *See Decibel.*

Deacidification Any of a number of processes for changing the chemical balance of paper from an acid balance to an alkaline balance; the alkaline (rather than neutral) balance provides a buffer against continued deterioration.

Decibel Standard unit for expressing change in acoustical or electrical energy. Almost always expressed with reference to a standard starting point, since it is actually a ratio rather than a quantity as such.

DEZ *See Diethyl zinc.*

Diazo Film using a coating that includes diazonium salts. The image is exposed by ultraviolet and developed using ammonia vapor; the ultraviolet decomposes the diazonium which would otherwise darken in the ammonia. Widely used for microfiche working copies, as it is much less expensive than silver halide film (but requires slow exposure, and is not suitable for direct photography). Not considered an archival product, but can be expected to last 100 years or more in archival conditions.

Diethyl zinc Agent used for mass deacidification in a process being tested by the Library of Congress. The process yields good results but the agent ignites in contact with air and explodes in contact with water. Handling problems have delayed large-scale deacidification.

Difference Engine The first of Charles Babbage's two computing engines, designed in 1823 but never completed. Pehr Scheutz of Stockholm produced a working Difference Engine in 1853.

Digital Consisting of numbers and numeric representations, typically binary numbers. Nearly all computers use digital techniques for storing and manipulating data, as do compact discs and CD-ROM (and the soundtracks of some videodiscs).

Digitize Convert to a digital form. Any image or sound can be digitized for computer storage and processing.

Direct capture In analog sound recording, a disc made without the use of tape recording during the recording process. Also called "direct to disc." The universal (and only) technique prior to the introduction of tape recorders, used more recently for some specialist recordings.

Diskette Any of several different magnetic recording media, all based on a flexible plastic disk, coated with magnetic material and encased in some sort of protective housing. More specifically, the eight-inch diskettes introduced by IBM. *See also Mini-diskette* and *Microdiskette.*

Dot matrix Used to refer to printers that form characters out of a grid (matrix) of dots. Most references to "dot-matrix printers" actually mean impact dot-matrix printers, as opposed to laser printers, ink-jet printers, and thermal printers (all of which are also dot-matrix printers).

dpi Dots per inch, a measure of image density or resolution. Equivalent to lpi, lines per inch. A 300-dpi printer can place dots at any or all of 300 dots vertically and horizontally in each inch, or 90,000 locations in a square inch.

DRAW Direct read after write. Synonymous with WORM, but sounds better and has only one spelled-out equivalent. Optical disc that can be written to but not erased.

DRCS Dynamically redefinable character sets. A method of transmitting and displaying graphics in videotex systems, in which revised character definitions (including graphic characters) may be sent to the terminal's RAM, allowing higher-quality graphics but requiring intelligent terminals. The French Antiope system and Japanese Captain system both use DRCS.

DVI Digital video interactive, GE/RCA's term for a proposed system able to store one hour of color video with stereo sound on a single CD. To date, DVI is nothing more than a preliminary demonstration of some advanced real-time data compression and decompression techniques.

DWIM Do what I mean. The computer instruction that every programmer needs but nobody has been able to make work.

ECC Error correction code. Any of various means of detecting and correcting errors in a stream of digital data by adding more data to the stream.

EDVAC Electronic discrete variable computer. A follow-on design to ENIAC; not the first true computer because its completion came after several British computers had been completed.

EIAJ Electronics Industry Association of Japan, an important standards-setting body.

ELD Electroluminescent display, a technology using thin coatings of phosphors and an electrical grid. The phosphor is excited directly by the grid (rather than indirectly by a cathode ray). ELDs can be flat and are used in some laptop and portable computers, and as backlighting in other laptop computers.

Electrical recording Recording in which microphones and other electrical equipment are part of the recording process. Virtually all sound recordings made since the late 1920s are electrical recordings.

Electronic mail Any system that allows one computer user to send a message to another user asynchronously (i.e., without the other user necessarily being online at the time).

Emissive Used to describe all display technologies that actually give off (emit) light, compared to non-emissive displays (which alter existing light but create no light). Emissive displays can be used in dark rooms; non-emissive displays cannot.

EMS Electronic mail service or system.

Emulsion A coating consisting of light-sensitive materials contained in a medium carried as one or more layers on a film base.

ENIAC Electronic numerator, integrator, analyzer, and computer. A programmable electronic calculator built at the University of Pennsylvania in 1945, designed by John W. Mauchly and J. Prosper Eckert.

EPROM Erasable programmable read only memory. Solid-state devices (chips) that can be programmed (have information written to them) using "PROM burners" that normally retain that information permanently, but that can be erased using high-intensity ultraviolet light or some other means and, later, reprogrammed. The term is itself an internal contradiction, but signifies that EPROMs are read-only under normal operating conditions.

Ethernet Local area network originally developed by Xerox, and introduced jointly by Digital Equipment Corporation (DEC), Xerox, and Intel. Ethernet is a baseband network system using CSMA/CD protocol.

EVR Electronic VideoRecorder. A playback-only video system using photographic images that was designed by CBS but never successfully marketed.

Fax Telefacsimile, a system for transmitting the images of pages and recreating the images at a receiver.

Fiche *See Microfiche.*

Fixed disk IBM's name for hard disks, specifically those used in IBM PC/XT, PC/AT, and PS/2 computers. One aspect of the term "fixed" is that these disks are not removable, although it is possible to buy removable hard disks.

Flong Material made up of alternate layers of blotting paper and tissue and used in stereotyping.

Floppy disk Familiar term to refer to diskettes, even though the complete diskette is never actually floppy.

Frame A single image on film, videodisc, or the equivalent. In video, the combination of two sets of horizontal scanning lines ("fields") that make up a single viewed image.

Free software Software that can legitimately be copied and handed out to others, sometimes called Freeware. Some free software is copyrighted but carries explicit notice that it may be freely copyrighted; other free software carries no copyright.

Galley A long steel tray on which lines of composed type are gathered. Galley proofs are made by spreading ink over the type and pressing paper over it. By analogy, the first proofs made from typesetting techniques that do not involve metal type (photocomposition, for example) are also considered "galley proofs." Essentially, any proofs made before type is made up into pages.

Gas plasma *See Plasma display.*

Geosynchronous Term used for satellites that stay over the same Earth location at all times because their orbital speed is identical to the rotational speed of Earth. Arthur C. Clarke established the basis for geosynchronous satellites in 1945; these satellites orbit over the equator at roughly 22,300 miles, and are used for most satellite communications links.

Gigabyte One billion bytes or characters (one thousand million). Sometimes abbreviated gig or Gb. A gigabyte may be either 1,000,000,000 bytes or the somewhat larger product of 1,024 times 1,024 times 1,024--1,073,741,824. There is rarely any way of knowing which is meant.

Gramophone Name used for Emile Berliner's original disc sound recording and playback system, and sometimes used as a synonym for phonograph since then.

Graphophone Name used for Alexander Graham Bell's recording and playback device, using wax-coated cardboard cylinders.

Hard disk Any magnetic storage device using rigid disks as bases for the recording material. Also called fixed disk or rigid disk.

Helical scan Method of recording in which a moving head (on a spinning drum) records diagonal strips along a moving tape. Used in all consumer videotape and in digital audio tape (DAT) recorders, it permits very high bandwidth recording on a slow-moving tape.

High Sierra Group A group of manufacturers and others interested in CD-ROM that first met in the High Sierra Hotel and Casino, Stateline, Nevada, in early 1985. The purpose of the group was to develop standards for the volume and file structures of CD-ROM. The group developed a standard that has become American National Standard Z39.60.

Hollerith card Eighty-column punched card or tab card, named for Herman Hollerith, who developed punched card sorting and counting for the 1890 census.

HoloTape RCA's first "SelectaVision" introduction in 1969. The system used lasers and holographic techniques to record pictures on plastic film. The system never made it out of the laboratory.

HSG *See High Sierra Group.*

Hz Abbreviation for Hertz, equivalent to one cycle per second.

Idiolect Each person's own particular dialect (pronunciation, vocabulary, and speech patterns).

Ink-jet printer Printer that creates images by applying dots of ink as needed. This may be done by forcing ink out of nozzles only when required ("drop on demand") or by deflecting an electrically charged continuous spray as required. It may also be done by heating a solid ink, using the term "jet" broadly.

Intaglio Printing technique in which the material to be printed is engraved into a printing plate. Ink is forced into the engraving, the surface of the plate is wiped clean, and a rolling press forces paper into the engraved lines to take the ink.

Integrated circuit Electronic device consisting of electrical elements created directly on a chip of silicon or other semiconductor that function as transistors, resistors, diodes, capacitors, and wiring for a circuit assembly.

Interface The connection between any two parts of a system. A keyboard and monitor serve as an interface between user and computer; other interfaces connect the computer and printer, computer and disk drive, and computer and mouse.

ISO International Standards Organization, the international body for technical standards.

K Normally 1,000 (kilo). When used to represent computer memory (RAM or other forms), K usually means 2^{10} or 1,024. When used by itself in connection with computers, K is usually short for kilobytes--1,024 bytes or characters.

KeyFax A teletext service attempted by a consortium of companies. KeyFax Interactive was a videotex service from the same companies.

LAN Local area network. A group of computers within a limited geographic area connected in order to share resources and information.

Land The area between two pits on a CD or CD-ROM.

Laser Light amplification by stimulated emission of radiation. A device that emits coherent (narrow-band) light, capable of being focused very sharply. Introduced in 1957, it is now used in all "optical media" such as videodiscs, compact discs, and CD-ROM, and in laser printers. Also used in some library systems as part of bar-code readers.

Laser printer Properly, a printer that uses a low-power laser to create charged areas on a photoconductive surface (drum or belt) as the first step in creating an image on plain paper. Broadly used for all desktop page printers including a few models that use other techniques to create the charges on the photoconductor.

LaserVision Trademark for the optical videodisc system originated by MCA and Philips and sustained by Pioneer during several lean years.

LCD Liquid crystal display. A solid-state device that can change from transparent to opaque (or vice-versa) when an electric current is applied. Commonly used in watches, electronic calculators, some portable computers, and some miniature television sets. LCDs use very little current (thus making them ideal for battery-operated devices).

LED Light-emitting diode. A solid-state device that can emit light when activated by electricity.

Line printer Any printer that deals with a complete line of characters at once, at least logically. Typically, a line printer receives a complete line of information and prints the actual characters in whatever order is fastest. Most contemporary line printers are large, fast, and relatively expensive, and are used in large computer shops.

Lithography Printing technique in which a flat surface is treated so that some areas will reject ink and others will attract it. The inked surface and paper are pressed together to transfer the ink.

Local area network *See LAN.*

LP Long-playing record. A trademark of Columbia, which introduced long-playing records in 1948.

lpi Lines per inch, a measure of resolution in phototypesetting and other graphic arts. Roughly equivalent to dpi, dots per inch, except when referring to halftones.

LSI Large-scale integrated circuit, containing thousands of circuit elements in a single chip.

LSP Linked Systems Project, a project begun in 1980 to establish computer-to-computer links within the library community. Funded by the Council on Library Resources (CLR), LSP initially involved the Library of Congress, Research Libraries Group, and Washington Library Network (now the Western Library Network). OCLC became active in LSP in 1984. The first production systems based on LSP are the authorities distribution systems between LC and RLG and, later, LC and OCLC and the authorities contribution system between RLG and LC.

LV *See LaserVision.*

MagTape RCA's term (actually SelectaVision MagTape) for its second attempt at a consumer video player. Using magnetic tape, the system was announced in 1972 and tested in 1974, but never went beyond test marketing.

Mat *See Matrix.*

Matrix Solid metal bar containing negative impressions of a character, from which type can be cast. Also used for other negative impressions from which positive versions are made in several media.

Meg Informal abbreviation for the prefix mega, or one million. When used in computing and related fields, meg usually means megabyte, a measure of memory that may be either around 1,000,000 characters or the somewhat larger product of 1K times 1K (i.e., 1,024 times 1,024), which is 1,048,576.

Microdiskette Three-and-a-half inch diskette encased in a rigid plastic shell, developed by Sony and used in the Macintosh, IBM PS/2 models, and many laptop and portable computers.

Microfiche Sheets of film used to store text and still pictures as small images, requiring a reader for intelligibility. Most contemporary microfiche are 4 by 6 inches or 105 millimeters by 148 millimeters. Photographic fiche contain 98 pages, in 14 columns of 7 rows. Each image is 10 millimeters by 12.5 millimeters, roughly one-twentyfourth the dimensions of an 8.5-by 11-inch-page. (This is known as "24x reduction.") Fiche generated from computer files (COM) usually contain 270 pages or frames recorded at "48x reduction," a misnomer since COM fiche represent originals, not copies. Microfiche may be photographic film or some other form capable of the high resolution required, such as diazo or vesicular film.

Microfilm Photographic film used to store text and still images in greatly reduced form, intended for use with a special viewer or reader. Microfilm is typically fine-grain (offering high resolution) and high-contrast (with few shades of gray) black-and-white film.

Microform General term for all media storing text (and other still visual images) in visible form but requiring some form of projection for intelligibility. Does not include "visual media" such as slides. The most common microform media are 35-millimeter roll microfilm and 105-millimeter by 150-millimeter microfiche.

Microgroove Columbia's term for the narrow groove (300 grooves per inch) that made long-playing records feasible.

Micron One one-millionth of a meter.

Micro-opaque Any microform medium consisting of small print on an opaque background. Frequently used without the hyphen as microopaque. Four forms of micro-opaque commercially produced at one time are Microcard, produced in 3-by-5-inch and 4-by-6-inch sizes; Microprint, 6-by-9-inch; Microlex, 6.5-by-8.5-inch; and Mini-Print, 6-by-9-inch.

Microprint Trademark of Readex Corporation for 6-by-9 inch opaque cards containing micro-images produced through offset lithography. A form of micro-opaque.

Micropublishing Publishing in microform media.

Mil One one-thousandth of an inch.

Minidiskette Five-and-a-quarter-inch diskette.

Modem Modulator/demodulator. A device used to shift between digital signals (as used in computers) and audio signals that can be transmitted over telephone circuits.

Monaural Commonly used synonym for the better monophonic. Properly, monaural would mean "one-ear" and be applicable only to telephones and other devices that convey sound only to one ear.

Monophonic Sound coming from a single source.

Morpholine An organic ammonia-based solvent used by the Barrow labs for mass deacidification. The solvent does not leave an alkaline residue and might pose health hazards; the process is no longer used.

Mosaic graphics Method for displaying graphics in videotex, in which a special set of characters consists of grids used for graphics. Prestel uses 3-by-2 grids, in other words, each "character" includes 6 rectangles, any or all of which may be black. Sixty-four different characters provide the full set of possibilities.

Mylar DuPont trademark for polyethylene terephthalate, the plastic used as the base material for most tape and diskettes.

Negative polarity Properly, having light and dark reversed from the original. By convention, light characters or other information on a dark background. Thus, most COM fiche are negative polarity even though they may be originals.

NISO National Information Standards Organization, the accredited standards organization directly concerned with standards in libraries, publishing, and information science. Formerly ANSI Committee Z39.

Node Used in local area networks to refer to any station on the network.

Non-emissive Used to refer to display technologies that alter or block existing light but create no light of their own. The most common non-emissive display technology is LCD.

NTSC National Television Systems Committee. "NTSC color" is the color television transmission technique used in the United States. According to some observers, the initials should stand for "never the same color."

OCR Optical character recognition. Generally, the process of turning scanned character images into machine-readable text. Also used for the two typefaces designed specifically for such recognition, OCR-A and OCR-B.

OROM Optical read only memory. Name used by 3M for a read-only optical disc somewhat larger than CD-ROM, with similar capacity but much faster access.

OSI Open Systems Interconnection Reference Model, ISO 7498: a standard that specifies a model for computer-to-computer connections.

Packet switching Telecommunications technique in which messages are broken down into uniquely identified packets. Different packets making up a message may take different routes through a network, and error detection may be applied at various steps. The packet identifications permit reassembly of the message at the receiving end.

Page printer Any printer that creates a page at a time, including, most prominently, laser printers.

Parity In computing (storage and memory), simple error-detection technique in which an extra bit is added to each character. The extra bit is set to either 1 or 0 so that the total number of 1 bits will either be even (for even parity) or odd (for odd parity). Computer magnetic tape recording always includes parity bits; telecommunications and RAM sometimes include parity bits. A parity check will reveal any single-bit error (in which one and only one bit is in error), by far the most probable error.

Pascaline Early calculator built by Blaise Pascal.

PCM Pulse code modulation, one form of digital encoding used to transform sound into a digital stream.

Phonograph Term used to describe the first sound recording device (Thomas Alva Edison's brass cylinder wrapped in tinfoil) and the most popular playback devices used from about 1906 onward, playing analog discs.

Phosphor Any substance that emits light when struck by radiation. In all CRTs, phosphors are chemical substances coating the inside face of the tube that emit light when struck by the cathode ray. A "slow" phosphor keeps glowing for an appreciable fraction of a second, whereas a "fast" phosphor will stop glowing if it is not re-excited ("refreshed") 30 times a second or more.

Photocomposition Preparing type through photographic methods, not involving the use of metal type.

Pit Raised point in a compact disc or CD-ROM that, taken in conjunction with the lands adjacent, conveys information. When the laser in a player is aimed at a pit, its light is diffracted; when it is aimed at a land, it reflects properly. The transition from pit to land or from land to pit can be detected readily; this transition, and the length of a pit or land, carry the information on a disc.

Pixel Abbreviation for picture element, the smallest addressable element in a display. For example, a fairly high-resolution display for personal computers may address 640 by 400 pixels: 400 rows, with 640 dots on each row, or a total of 256,000 pixels in all. The customary dividing line for very-high-resolution displays is a megapixel: one million or more pixels. (For example, the Wyse 700/Amdek 1280 displays 800 rows with 1,280 dots per row, or 1,024,000 pixels.) Also *pel*.

Plasma display Flat display consisting of cells of gases that glow when charged with electricity. Some Compaq portable computers use plasma displays, as do some other computers. Most plasma displays have a distinct dark-orange color.

Plotter Printing device that draws lines on paper using pens, moving the pens and (sometimes) the paper.

Polarity The relationship of dark and light on a film or other image.

Polycarbonate Any of a number of tough, heat-resistant plastics. Compact discs and CD-ROM discs use polycarbonate as a base material.

Positive polarity Properly, having the same relationship of light to dark as an original. By convention, dark text or other information against a light background.

Prestel British videotex system introduced in 1978 and commercially available in 1979. Originated by the British Post Office, Prestel uses mosaic characters for coarse graphics: each of 24-by-40 character positions on the TV screen becomes a 3-by-2 grid for graphics, for a total resolution of 72-by-80 picture elements.

PROM Programmable read only memory. Solid-state circuits that can be written to (programmed) by users once, using special "PROM burners." Once programmed, the circuits cannot be changed and retain information even when no power is applied.

Public-domain software Programs in which no copyright is claimed by the author. Some such programs carry an explicit disavowal of copyright. Public domain programs can legitimately be copied and handed out to others. The code can also be incorporated in other programs, including commercial programs.

QS Quadraphonic-stereo. System designed by Japanese electronic firms to carry four recording channels in the two channels of a long playing record through algebraic matrixing. As with SQ, the results were never wholly satisfactory.

Quad *See Quadraphonic.*

Quadraphonic Having sound originating from four sources. Quadraphonic records and tapes were introduced in the late 1960s and, with some exceptions, abandoned in the 1970s.

RAM Random access memory. Theoretically, any directly addressable memory (including disk). In practice the term is reserved for solid-state memory or "chips." It is always possible to write new information to RAM and to read it directly: this distinguishes it from ROM.

RAMAC Random access method of accounting and control, IBM's name for the first hard disk drive (the IBM 305), introduced in 1955.

Raster The area of a CRT on which the image is formed, and more importantly the scanning lines that form the image. Used in the combination "raster scanned" to refer to any display or printing method that works on a one-pixel-high line-by-line basis. All desktop laser printers and most CRT displays are raster scanned.

Reduction ratio The relationship between the dimensions of an original and the dimensions of the image in microform. A popular reduction ratio for microfilming text is 24x: this means that the original is 24 times as wide and 24 times as high as the image. By extension, "reduction" ratios used for COM are those that would yield a typical printed image. (A 48x COM fiche needs to be expanded 42 to 48 times for good legibility.)

Resolution The measure of the sharpness of an image. For film, this is expressed in discernible lines per millimeter. For printing, computer displays, and other applications, it is frequently expressed in lines per inch, pixels per inch, or dots per inch. The three measures are effectively equivalent in most (but not all) cases.

ROM Read-only memory. Direct-access memory that can't be changed. Used by itself, ROM usually means solid-state memory (chips). Some variants of ROM can be changed, but only under special conditions. *See also PROM* and *EPROM.*

RS-232 Standard for pin definitions and voltages to allow serial communications between any pair of devices. More precisely, EIA RS-232C, a standard of the Electronics Industry Association. RS-232 allows a very large number of implementations, causing considerable confusion in the marketplace.

Scanner Any device used in computing to convert lines or pages of text and graphics into machine-readable information. Also "optical scanner."

SelectaVision RCA's umbrella term for its many attempts at video playback systems.

Shareware *See User-supported software.*

Shrink-wrap license Software licensing agreement that asserts that a customer's removal of the plastic outer wrapping from the software package (the shrink-wrap) constitutes assent to the terms of the license. Most shrink-wrap licenses are extremely restrictive: eliminating any warranty that the software will actually do anything, but preventing the customer from using it on more than one machine or, in some cases, even selling it without permission.

Silver halide film Photographic film coated with light-sensitive silver compound.

SNI Standard network interconnection protocols, a definition of the protocols to be used in the Linked Systems Project.

SQ Stereo-quadraphonic, CBS's methodology for carrying four channels of sound in the two channels of a long-playing record, using algebraic matrixing. The matrix could not be completely reconstructed into four totally separate channels, but electronic devices could achieve a semblance of true four-channel sound. Some European classical recording companies continue to release SQ recordings.

Stepped Reckoner Mechanical calculator built by Gottfried Wilhelm von Liebniz in the early 1670s, establishing the principals that would lead to successful mechanical calculators.

Stereo *See Stereophonic.*

Stereophonic Sound originating from two sources. A good stereophonic system will produce sound apparently originating from an infinite number of points between the two speakers (and sometimes beyond their outer boundaries).

Stereotype Metal printing plate made by first pressing a sheet of damp absorbent material over a form of type, letting the material harden, then casting metal from the material.

Stick Printer's device used to hold a line of type in hand-set typography.

Teldec Joint venture of Telefunken and Decca Records to create a videodisc system. The system was marketed in Europe but was not successful: among other problems, the discs played for only 15 minutes each.

Telecommunications Any communication over a distance and the technology to support that communication. The term includes telephony, telegraphy, and broadcasting, as well as computer-based telecommunications.

Telefacsimile System for transmitting images of pages (or other images) and recreating those images at a remote site. Also *telefax* or *fax*.

Telematique French national program to spread computer communications throughout France, including videotex and other systems.

Teletel French name for videotex.

Teletext Generic name for information systems in which text and/or graphics pages are transmitted over broadcast television. A series of pages is transmitted in a continuous cycle; the receiver (either an addition to a television set or part of the television) waits for the requested page, stores transmitted information until the page is complete, then displays the page. Teletext systems are one-way: the person receiving the information cannot communicate with the sender.

Telidon Canadian videotex and teletext system, developed by Canada's Department of Communications.

Thermal printer Any printer that uses heat (rather than force or light) to create an image. Thermal printers may darken special paper by heating it, burn off the top layer of special coated paper, or form an image on normal paper by heating a wax-impregnated ribbon (usually called "thermal transfer" printing).

Thimble printer Similar to daisywheel, but the printing element resembles an oversized thimble. Nippon Electric (NEC) makes thimble printers.

Token passing A protocol for local area networks in which a specific piece of information (the token) passes from station to station in the network. A station can transmit a message only when it holds the token. Token-passing networks have predictable delays more-or-less regardless of the level of message traffic; they are particularly suitable for LANs with heavy traffic. Compare to *CSMA/CD*.

Trintex Potential videotex system undertaken by IBM and Sears Roebuck, with CBS an earlier partner in the development.

U-Matic Three-quarter-inch VCR system developed by Sony and widely used in business, industry, and education.

Ultrafiche Extremely high-reduction microfiche, containing hundreds or thousands of pages on a single fiche.

UNIVAC The Universal Automatic Computer, a commercial computer first installed in March 1951, designed by Mauchly and Eckert. *See also ENIAC.*

User-supported software Software that may be freely copied and handed out, but which is copyrighted and carries a notice requesting a specified donation from those who find the software useful.

Vapor phase deacidification One early method for deacidifying books. Pellets placed in boxes of books or envelopes interleaved in books released alkaline gases. Unfortunately the gas posed a health hazard and did not create an alkaline reserve in the paper.

VBI Vertical blanking interval. The portion of television transmission during which no picture is being transmitted: between the end of one frame and the beginning of the next. Teletext may be transmitted during this frame, as are closed captions.

VCR Videocassette recorder. Any unit that records and plays back video using a cassette (i.e., enclosed reel-to-reel mechanism).

Used primarily for Betamax, VHS, and 8-millimeter systems, but also refers to U-Matic recorders.

VDT Video display terminal. Frequently and incorrectly used as a name for CRT-based displays. Properly, a VDT is a terminal--a keyboard and display connected to a remote computing device.

Vector Broadly, any quantity that has magnitude and direction. In computer graphics, a line (i.e., a direction and length).

Vesicular Film composed of diazonium salts within a plastic. When exposed to ultraviolet, the diazonium decomposes and gives off nitrogen gas. Heat developing softens the plastic (polymer) and causes the gas to expand, forming bubbles or vesicles. Heat fixes the image. Vesicular copies are inexpensive but not archival.

VHD Video high density, JVC's name for a videodisc design using grooveless capacitance technology. VHD has been marketed in Japan but not in America.

VHS Video home system. Videocassette system developed by JVC (Japanese Victor, a subsidiary of Matsushita).

Videocassette A closed container holding a reel of videotape and an empty reel, with an opening through which the tape can be extracted.

Videodisc Generic term for disc systems that play full video signals. The surviving videodisc system is LaserVision, developed by Philips but kept alive by Pioneer. Capitalized VideoDisc, the term refers to SelectaVision VideoDisc, RCA's capacitance player that was first announced in 1975, actually marketed in 1981 and abandoned in 1984.

Videotex Generic term for systems that display information on television screens based on explicit requests, with the requests and information going over telephone lines. Videotex systems normally include some form of graphics as well as text.

Viewdata Original British name for videotex.

Viewtron Home videotex service attempted by Knight-Ridder. The first trial took place in 1980; the system was abandoned in 1986.

VLSI Very large scale integrated circuit, combining tens or hundreds of thousands of circuit elements in a single chip. Contemporary microcomputing depends on VLSI circuitry.

Voice recognition Any system that attempts to create machine-readable information based on input from the human voice.

Voice synthesis Any process for creating speech mechanically or electronically. In the case of most computerized voice synthesis systems, the synthesized speech is based on information formed from actual human speech.

VPD *See Vapor phase deacidification.*

VTR Videotape recorder. Any system that records video on tape. All VCRs are VTRs, but not all VTRs are VCRs: professional VTRs use open reels, usually with one-inch or two-inch tape.

WAN *See Wide area network.*

Wei T'o A mass deacidification process using methyl magnesium carbonate to soak books previously vacuum-dried. The process damages some inks and bindings but is not apparently hazardous.

Wide area network Computers connected together over extended distances compared to LAN, local area network. While LANs are usually called LANs, wide-area networks are frequently simply called networks. Many nationwide and worldwide computer networks exist, particularly in academia, such as BITNET, ARPANET, and USENET.

Winchester Usually used in a phrase, such as Winchester disk or Winchester technology. Winchester was the code name for IBM's high-density sealed hard disk project, and is used to refer to most sealed hard disks (those where the read/write heads and the disks are part of a single mechanism, whether the entire mechanism is replaceable or not).

WORM Writable but not erasable optical disc. The acronym comes either from write-once read mostly (most common attribution) or write-once read many times--or possibly even some other phrase.

Write-once Capable of being written to by the user, but not changed. Ink on paper is usually write-once, but the term is most often used for optical storage products, usually called WORM or DRAW.

XMODEM A protocol for transmitting data and detecting errors in the transmission. Entered into the public domain in the early years of microcomputing and used in almost every personal computer telecommunications program.

Index